Jiffy Phrasebook

FRENCH

Langenscheidt
NEW YORK

Phonetic Transcriptions: Walter Glanze Word Books
(The Glanze Intersound System)

Jiffy Phrasebooks are also available for many other languages.

Jiffy Travel Packs combine the Jiffy Phrasebooks with a travel-oriented 60-minute cassette. Each can be used independently of the other.
(Jiffy Travel Pack French ISBN 0-88729-976-8)

For detailed information please contact
Langenscheidt Publishers, Inc.
46-35 54th Road, Maspeth, NY 11 378
(718) 784-0055

Printed in Germany

INFORMATION

GUIDE TO THE USE OF THE PHRASEBOOK

This French phrasebook offers you all the important words and phrases you may need on a visit to France. The phonetic transcriptions which follow the French expressions are designed as an aid to correct pronunciation, and the systematic arrangement of the phrasebook will help you to find what you are looking for in the shortest possible time.

Structure of the phrasebook

The phrasebook is divided into 20 chapters. It begins with general words and phrases, followed by sections on transportation, accommodations, food and drink, and many other important aspects of travel abroad. There are chapters on shopping, health, cultural activities, and entertainment; the appendix gives you lists of common signs and abbreviations, weights and measures, and colors. For easy reference, English words and phrases are printed in heavy black type, while the French translations are in blue. Following these are the phonetic transcriptions of the French phrases in normal black type.
Occasionally two or more phrases have been combined and the interchangeable elements given in italics. For example, the sentence "Is it going to *rain (snow)?*" corresponds to the "Va-t-il *pleuvoir (neiger)*?" Thus "Is it going to rain?" is translated "Va-t-il pleuvoir?" and "Is it going to snow?" becomes "Va-t-il neiger?"
In the boxes you will find help on certain language difficulties, tips on general etiquette, and information on travel, eating out, using the telephone, etc., which will help you get by in everyday situations you may encounter while traveling abroad.
An asterisk at the beginning of a sentence indicates that this is something someone else might say to you.

French pronunciation

On pp. 8–11 you will find a detailed guide to French pronunciation. Most of the symbols used in the phonetic system are taken from the Latin alphabet, so you should have no difficulty getting accustomed to the transcriptions.

French grammar

If you would like to get to know some important aspects of French grammar, the brief survey on pp. 195–202 will give you a basic grounding. Apart from offering you an insight into the structure of the French language and helping you to understand the expressions in the phrasebook, this grammatical survey will also enable you to form simple sentences of your own.

Traveler's Dictionary and Index

The glossary at the end of the book is 53 pages long and is for quick reference to words and phrases. The translations are followed by phonetic transcriptions and page references, so that this glossary serves as an index as well.

Carry this phrasebook with you all the time to make the most of your stay.

CONTENTS

FRENCH PRONUNCIATION

The sounds of a foreign language have to be learned by hearing and imitating a native or near-native speaker of that language. No amount of written information will teach you the true pronunciation of a foreign word or phrase. Many transcription systems have been devised toward this purpose; but all of them use either unfamiliar combinations of letters or odd-looking new characters-combinations or characters that have to be learned in addition to learning the foreign language.

The pronunciation system that was developed for the Langenscheidt Language Guides*) is entirely different: The symbols you find here are the ones you are likely to be familiar with from your use of high-school, college, or desk dictionaries of the **English** language. (That is, the symbols are the same ordinary letters of the alphabet with the same markings, such as [ē] for the vowel sound in he.)

This new pronunciation system is meant to be **an approximation, serving practical needs**, as encountered by the traveler. But, then, even those complicated systems remain an approximation. The true sounds, as we have said, must be learned by listening.

The basic symbols you see in the table are the same that you will find in other Langenscheidt Language Guides for speakers of English. Therefore, when using these Guides in traveling from country to country, you don't have to shift from one set of symbols to another.

For French, the basic symbols of the table are supplemented by two symbols for sounds that have no equivalent in English. These two symbols are set in italic type – with the understanding that you may use the sound of the regular (the preceding nonitalicized) symbol until you have learned the special sound (using [ā] for [*ā*] and [ē] for *ē*]). This is one of the **backup** features that are unique to this system.

The syllables of a French word are usually stressed evenly, with perhaps a slightly greater emphasis on the last syllable. Therefore, no accent marks are shown (except for the two combinations mentioned beneath the table).

To avoid ambiguity, two neighboring vowel symbols (and occasionally two consonant symbols) are separated by a raised dot [·]. This separation is meant to be a convenience to the eye and usually does not mean a break in pronunciation: *réalité* [rā·älētā].

The transcription is that of individual words, even in a sentence (except for some "liaisons"; see also the comment beneath the table). The rhythm of a sentence or phrase has to be learned by ear.

---

*) The Glanze Intersound System

Vowels

Symbol	Approximate Sound	Examples
[ä]	The a of father; the o of mother.	*madame* [mädäm] *garage* [gäräzh] *gâteau* [gätō] *tasse* [täs]
[ā]	The a of fate (but without the "upglide").	*été* [ātā]
[*ā*]	A French sound that has to be learned by listening. (Round the lips for the o of nose; then, without moving the lips, try to pronounce the a of fate.) Until you have learned this sound, use the a of fate,, which will be understood.	*deux* [d*ā*] *chanteuse* [shäNt*ā*z] *oeuf* [*ā*f] *fleur* [fl*ā*r]
[e]	The e of met.	*adresse* [ädres]
[ē]	The e of he.	*midi* [mēdē] *dire* [dēr]
[*ē*]	A French sound that has to be learned by listening. (Round the lips for the o of nose; then, without the lips, try ro pronounce the e of he.) Until you have learned this sound, use the e of he, which will be understood.	*fumer* [f*ē*mā] *déjà vu* [dāzhä v*ē*]
[ō]	The o of nose (but without the "upglide").	*rideau* [rēdō] *rôle* [rōl]
[ô]	The o of often. (In French, sometimes shorter, as in *moment*; sometimes longer, as in *sport*.)	*moment* [mômäN] *sport* [spôr]
[o͞o]	The u of rule.	*trou* [tro͞o] *rouge* [ro͞ozh]
[ə]	The neutral vowel sound (like e in listen), always unstressed, such as the a in ago or the u in focus.	*je* [zhə] *demi* [dəmē]

[N]	This symbol does not stand for a sound but shows that the preceding vowel is nasal – is pronounced through nose and mouth at the same time. It has to be learned by listening. (Do not use [äng], [ông], or [eng] instead of nasals.)	*temps* [täN] *nom* [nôN] *matin* [mäteN] *parfum* [pärfeN]

Note also these combinations:

[ô·ä] as in *roi* [rô·ä], *voyage* [vô·äyäzh]
[ô·eN] as in *loin* [lô·eN]
[yeN] as in *bien* [byeN]
[*ē*·ē] as in *nuit* [n*ē*·ē]
[o͞o·ē] as in *weekend* [o͞o·ēkend], *oui* [o͞o·ē]
[o͞o·e] as in *souhaiter* [so͞o·etā]
(Each of these combinations should be pronounced as almost one "gliding" sound – also [ē′ē] and [o͞o′ē] below.)

Consonants

Here are the most important pronunciation rules: Although the pronunciation of most consonants in French is usually quite similar to English, French consonants are lighter and clearer. The initial *t* and *d* are subtler and pronounced next to the teeth. The initial *p* is softer. The final *s* is never pronounced except when in *liaison* (i.e. when preceding a word beginning with a vowel or a mute h, *pas à pas* [päzäpä]).

Vowel combinations with the letters *c* and *g* deserve special attention. You must distinguish between those which are followed by a, o, u, and consonants and those which are followed by e and i. The pronunciation of *c* and *g* depends on the letters which follow them:

c before a, o, u and consonants is like k [k]: *carte*.

c before e, i and y is an unvoiced s [s]: *cent*.

When a *c* followed by a, o or u is pronounced like [s] rather than [k], then a cedilla (*cédille*) indicates this: *garçon*.

g before a, o, u and consonants is like the g [g] in good: *gare*.

g before e, i and y is an unvoiced fricative [zh], e.g. the sound of the s in pleasure: *Gérard*.

When a *g* followed by a, o, or u takes the [zh] pronunciation rather than the [g] pronunciation, an e is added: *Georges*.

When a *g* followed by e, i or y takes the [g] pronunciation rather than the [zh] pronunciation, a u is added: *guichet*.

ch before vowels is usually pronounced like the sh [sh] in ship: *chapeau*; before consonants and at the end of the word like k [k]: *chronique*.

h is silent.

j is soft, pronounced like the s in pleasure [zh], never like the j in judge: *journal* [zhōōrnäl].

l combined with i is soft: *soleil* [sôlā·ē]

qu is pronounced like k [k], the u is silent: *quarante* [käräNt].

r is a "fricative" r, resembling the j of Spanish Juan: *rire* [rēr].

s at the beginning of a word and after consonants is unvoiced [s], pronounced like the s in safe: *salle* [säl].

s between vowels is voiced s, pronounced like the s in rose: *rosé* [rōzā].

y as a consonant is pronounced [y], like the y in yes: *payer* [pāyā]. A frequent combination ist [ny] as in *agneau* [änyō].

z is always a soft, voiced s [z] as in rose: *douze* [dōōz].

There are four exceptional cases in which the last syllable of a combination has no stress. This absence of stress is shown through a **preceding accent mark**:

[ē'ē] and [ōō'ē] as in *fille* [fē'ē] and *bouteille* [bōōtā'ē]
[b'əl] *as in table* [täb'əl]

or through **parentheses:**

[(ər)] as in *libre* [lēb(ər)]
[n(yə)] as in *ligne* [lēn(yə)]
(The [ə] in the last three examples should be pronounced as faintly as possible.)

French accent marks do not indicate stress but pronunciation. The *accent aigu* ´ (acute accent) over e indicates a closed sound: *é* = [ā]. The *accent grave* ` (grave accent) indicates an open sound: *è* = [ā], and is also used to differentiate between words which sound the same: *ou* = or, *où* = where. The *accent circonflexe* ˆ (circumflex accent) can be placed over all vowels [â, ê, î, ô, û] and indicates a drawing-out of the sound. The *cédille* (cedilla) is placed under the letter c to indicate the pronunciation [s]: *français* [fräNsā].

Among other aspects of French that may be learned through listening is "liaison", namely, the linking of the final sound of a word with the initial sound of the next (e.g. *à* [ä] *quelle* [kel] *heure* [ār] = [ä ke lār]) – and silent letters often becoming pronounced (e.g. *ils* [ēl] + *ont* [ôN] = [ēl zôN]) – or pronounced letters sometimes becoming changed (e.g. *en* [äN] + *avion* [ävyôN] = [änävyôN]).

GENERAL WORDS AND PHRASES

Greetings

Good morning!
Bonjour!
bôNzho͞or

Good afternoon!
Bonjour!
bôNzho͞or

Good evening!
Bonsoir!
bôNsô·är

Hello!
Salut!
sälē̆

Hello! ***(on answering phone)***
Allô
älō

Hi!
Salut!
sälē̆

> *In French it is considered impolite if you don't address someone with* monsieur, madame *or* mademoiselle *at the end of a greeting, when addressing someone, or after a short answer (like* oui, non, si *etc).*

Welcome! (Glad to see you!)
Soyez *le bienvenu (la bienvenue, les bienvenus).*
sô·äyā lə byeNvenē̆ (lä byeNvenē̆, lā byeNvenē̆)

How are you?
Ça va?
sä vä

***Did you have a good trip?**
Avez- vous fait bon voyage?
ävā-vo͞o fā bôN vô·äyäzh

I'm delighted to see *you*.
Très heureux de *vous (te)* voir!
trāzā̆rā̆ də vo͞o (tə) vô·är

How're *you doing*?
Comment *allez-vous (vas-tu)?*
kômäNtälā-vo͞o (vä-tē̆)

How's the family?
Comment va votre famille?
kômäN vä vôt(ər) fämē′ē

My **. . . is sick.**
Mon (Ma) . . . est malade.
môN (mä) . . . ā mäläd

Did you sleep well?
Avez-vous bien dormi?
ävā-vo͞o byeN dôrmē

And you?
Et vous?
ā vo͞o

Thanks, *just fine*.
Bien (Assez bien), merci!
byeN (äsā byeN), mersē

We're feeling *fine*.
Nous nous sentons *bien (très bien).*
no͞o no͞o säNtôN byeN (trā byeN)

***Thanks* for your cordial welcome.**
Je vous remercie (Nous vous remercions) de l'accueil cordial.
zhə vo͞o remersē (no͞o vo͞o remersē·ôN) də läkā̆′ē kôrdyäl

Forms of Address

Mr. *(name)*	Monsieur *(nom)*	məsyā
Mrs. *(name)*	Madame *(nom)*	mädäm
Sir, Madam	Monsieur, Madame	məsyā, mädäm
Miss	Mademoiselle	mädəmô·äzel
Ladies and Gentlemen!	Mesdames et Messieurs	mādämzā mesyā
Your wife/husband	Votre femme/mari	vôt(ər) fäm/märē
Doctor/Professor *(when addressing him)*	Monsieur le Docteur, Monsieur le Professeur	məsyā lə dôktār məsyā lə prôfesār

When using the "Monsieur le Docteur" *or* "Monsieur le Professeur" *form of address, the proper name is usually omitted.*

Letters

Mr. Jean Duval	Monsieur Jean Duval	məsyā zhäN dēväl
Mrs. Marie Duval	Madame Marie Duval	mädäm märē dēväl

In France, a married woman does not take her husband's first name.

Dear Mr. Duval	Cher Monsieur,	shār məsyā
Dear Mrs. Duval	Chère Madame,	shār mädäm
Dear Miss Duval	Chère Mademoiselle,	shār mädəmô·äzel
Dear Peter	Cher Pierre,	shār pyār
Dear Michèle,	Chère Michèle,	shār mēshel
Gentlemen	Messieurs,	mesyā
Dear Mr. Martin, *(to a respected friend)*	Monsieur,	məsyā
Dear Mrs. Martin,	Madame,	mädäm
Yours respectfully, *(old-fashioned form)*	Veuillez agréer, *Monsieur (Madame, Mademoiselle)*, l'expression de mes sentiments distingués.	vāyā ägrā·ā, məsyā (mädäm, mädəmô·äzel), lekspresyôN də mā säNtēmäN dēsteNgā
Yours sincerely, Cordially yours, Kindest regards,	Amitiés,	ämētyā
All the best, (Love,)	affectueusement,	äfektē·āzəmäN

Introductions

My name is . . .
Je m'appelle . . .
zhə mäpel

my son	mon fils	môN fēs
my daughter	ma fille	mä fē'ē
my friend *(male)*	mon ami	mônämē
my friend *(female)*	mon amie	mônämē
my friends	mes amis	māzämē

> *In French, a man speaking of his girlfriend will say* ma petite amie *and a woman speaking of her boyfriend will say* mon petit ami. *Other friends are referred to as* mon ami(e) *or* un(e) ami(e) à moi.

my fiancé	mon fiançe	môN fē·äNsā
my fiancée	ma fiançée	mä fē·äNsā

Glad to meet you. (How do you do?)
Très heureux de faire votre connaissance.
trāsārā də fār vôt(ər) kônesäNs

Haven't we seen one another before?
Ne nous connaissons-nous pas déjà de vue?
nə noo kônesôN-noo pä dāzhä də vē

Do you live here?
Vous habitez ici?
voozäbētā ēsē

Are you *Mr. (Mrs.)* Duval?
Êtes-vous *Monsieur (Madame)* Duval?
āt-voo məsyā (mädäm) dēväl

What is your name, please?
Quel est votre nom, s'il vous plaît?
kel ā vôt(ər) nôN, sēl voo plā

Where are you from?
D'où venez-vous?
doo venā-voo

We've been here for a week.
Nous sommes ici depuis une semaine.
noo sômzēsē depē·ē ēn smen

Do you like it here?
Ça vous plaît ici?
sä voo plā ēsē

***Are you* here alone?**
Êtes-vous seul(e)s (*Es-tu* seul[e]) ici?
āt-voo sāl (ā-tē sāl) ēsē

Where *do you work?*
Où est-ce que *vous travaillez (tu travailles)?*
o͞o eske vo͞o träväyā (tē trävä'ē)

What do you do for a living?
Quelle est votre profession?
kel ā vôt(ər) prôfesyôN

What are you studying? (What's your major?)
Qu'est-ce que *vous étudiez?*
keske vo͞ozātēdyā

> *The word* élève *is a general term for pupils up to the age of 18, whereas* lycéen *denotes those in a* lycée *(beginning at age 11), and* étudiant *generally means students at an institute of higher learning. A* professeur *is a teacher in a lycée or at an institute of higher learning.*

Got some time?
Avez-vous un peu de temps?
ävā-vo͞ozeN pā də täN

Shall we go *to the* . . .?
On va *au (à la)* . . .?
ôN vä ō (älä) . . .

What time shall we meet?
Quand nous retrouvons-nous?
käN no͞o rətro͞ovôN-no͞o

Please leave me alone!
Laissez-moi tranquille, s'il vous plaît.
lāsā-mô·ä träNkēl, sēl vo͞o plā

A Visit

Is *Mr. (Mrs., Miss)* . . . at home?
Monsieur (Madame, Mademoiselle) . . . est-il chez lui (est-elle chez elle)?
məsyā (mädäm, mädəmô·äzel) . . . etēl shā lē·ē (etel shāzel)

Could I speak to *Mr. (Mrs., Miss)* . . .?
Je peux parler à *Monsieur (Madame, Mademoiselle)* . . .?
zhə pā pärlā ä məsyā (mädäm, mädəmô·äzel) . . .

Does *Mr. (Mrs., Miss)* live here?
Est-ce que *Monsieur (Madame, Mademoiselle)* . . . habite ici?
eske məsyā (mädäm, mädəmô·äzel) . . . äbēt ēsē

I'm looking for . . .
Je cherche . . .
zhə shārsh . . .

When will *he (she)* be home?
Quand rentre-t-*il (elle)?*
käN räNtrətēl (-el)

I'll drop by again later.
Je reviendrai plus tard.
zhə revyeNdrā plē tär

When *can I (shall we)* come?
Quand est-ce *que je peux (qu'il nous faut)* venir?
käNdeske zhə pā (kēl no͞o fō) venēr

***I'd (We'd)* love to come.**
Je viendrai (Nous viendrons) très volontiers.
zhə vyeNdrā (nōō vyeNdrôN) trā vōlôNtyā

***Come in!**
Entrez!
äNtrā

***Please have a seat!**
Prenez place, s'il vous plaît!
prenā pläs, sēl vōō plā

***Come right in.**
Entrez!
äNtrā

***Just a minute, please.**
Une minute, s'il vous plaît!
ēn mēnēt, sēl vōō plā

Thanks so much for the invitation.
Merci beaucoup pour votre invitation!
mersē bōkōō pōōr vôtreNvētäsyôN

Am I bothering you?
Je vous dérange?
zhə vōō däräNzh

Please don't go to a lot of trouble.
Ne vous dérangez pas!
nə vōō däräNzhā pä

****What'll you have? (What may I offer you?)*/*Would you like . . .?**
Qu'est-ce que je peux vous offrir?/Est-ce que vous voulez . . .?
keske zhə pā vōōzôfrēr/eske vōō vōōlā . . .

Mr. (Mrs.)* Duval sends you *his (her) regards (love).
Monsieur (Madame) Duval vous transmet son bon souvenir.
məsyā (mädäm) dēväl vōō träNsmā sôN bôN sōōvnēr

I'm afraid I've got to go now.
Je regrette, mais il faut que je m'en aille maintenant.
zhə regret, mā ēl fō ke zhə mäNä'ē meNt·näN

Thanks so much for *a lovely evening (coming).*
Merci infiniment pour *cette charmante soirée (votre visite).*
mersē eNfēnēmäN pōōr set shärmäNt sô·ärā (vôt[ər] vēzēt)

Please give *Mr. (Mrs.)* . . . my best regards.
Saluez *Monsieur (Madame)* . . . de ma part, s'il vous plaît!
sälē·ā məsyā (mädäm) . . . də mä pär, sēl vōō plā

I hope we'll meet again soon!
J'espère que nous nous reverrons bientôt!
zhespār ke nōō nōō reverôN byeNtō

> *Your French may not be perfect, but the French, like anyone, are more receptive to foreigners who at least make the effort to speak their language. Try to use polite expressions such as* s'il vous plaît, merci beaucoup, pardon *etc. wherever appropriate.*

Farewells

> *The French say* À bientôt! *when they mean that they will be seeing you soon (but not necessarily). It's a more casual way of saying goodbye than* au revoir. *The greeting* Salut! *is a familiar term and depending on when it is said, it means Hi! or Bye!*

Good-bye!
Au revoir!
ō revô·är

See you soon!
À bientôt!
ä byeNtō

Good night!
Bonne nuit!
bônē·ē

See you tomorrow!
À demain!
ä demeN

All the best!
Bonne chance!
bôn shäNs

***Have a good trip!**
Bon voyage!
bôN vô·äyäzh

I'd like to say good-bye!
Je vais *vous (tè)* dire au revoir.
zhə vā vo͞o (tə) dēr ō-revô·är

I'm afraid we have to go.
Malheureusement nous devons partir.
mälārāz·mäN no͞o devôN pärtēr

Thanks so much for coming.
Je vous remercie de votre visite.
zhə vo͞o remersē də vôt(ər) vēzēt

Come again soon!
Au plaisir de vous revoir!
ō plāzēr də vo͞o revô·är

When can we get together again?
Quand nous reverrons-nous?
käN no͞o reverôN-no͞o

I'll give you a call tomorrow.
Je téléphonerai demain.
zhə tālāfōnərā dəmeN

Can I give you a lift home?
Vous permettez que je vous raccompagne chez vous?
vo͞o permetā ke zhə vo͞o räkôNpän(yə) shā vo͞o

It's pretty late.
Il est déjà tard.
ēl ā dāzhä tär

Give . . . my best!
Saluez . . .!
sälē·ā

Thanks very much.
Merci beaucoup!
mersē bōko͞o

I enjoyed myself very much.
Ça m' a beaucoup plu.
sä mä bōko͞o plē

I'll *take you to (give you a lift to)* the . . .
Je *vous accompagne (t'accompagne)* encore *jusqu'au (jusqu'à la)* . . .
zhə vo͞ozäkôNpän(yə) (täkôNpän[yə]) äNkôr zhēskō (zhēskä lä)

General Questions

When?
Quand?
käN

Why?
Pourquoi!
po͞orkô·ä

What?
Quoi?
kô·ä

Which? What kind of . . .?
Quel (Quelle?) . . .
kel (kel)

> *If you don't understand what someone has just said, you can say* Comment? *or* Pardon? *Using* Quoi? *in this situation is not appropriate.*

Who?
Qui?
kē

To whom?
À qui?
ä kē

With whom?
Avec qui?
ävekē

Whom?
Qui?
kē

How?
Comment?
kômäN

How long?
Combien de temps?
kôNbyeN də täN

How *much (many)*?
Combien de . . .?
kôNbyeN də

Where?
Où?
o͞o

Where from?
D'où?
do͞o

Where to?
Où?
o͞o

What for?
Pourquoi?
po͞orkô·ä

Is . . . allowed here?
Peut-on . . . ici?
pə̄tôN . . . ēsē

Can I . . .?
Est-ce que je peux?
eske zhə pə̄

Do you need . . .?
Avez-vous besoin de . . .
ävā-vo͞o bezô·eN də

Have you (got) . . .?
Avez-vous . . .?
ävā-vo͞o

What's that?
Qu'est-ce que c'est?
keske sā

When can I get . . .?
Je peux avoir . . . quand?
zhə pə̄ ävô·är . . . käN

What time do you *open (close)*?
À quelle heure vous *ouvrez (fermez)*?
äkelār vo͞ozo͞ovrā (fermā)

What would you like? (What can I do for you? / May I help you?)
Que désirez-vous?
ke dāzērā-vo͞o

What happened?
Qu'est-ce qui s'est passé?
keskē sā päsā

What does that mean?
Qu'est-ce que cela veut dire?
keske səlä və̄ dēr

***Whom do you wish to see?**
Qui cherchez-vous?
kē sharshā-vo͞o

How much does that cost?
Combien ça coûte?
kôNbyeN sä ko͞ot

What are you looking for?
Que *cherchez-vous (cherches-tu)*?
ke shārshā-vo͞o (shārsh-tē)

Who's there?
Qui est là?
kē ā lä

Who can (Could you) . . .?)
Qui peut (Vous pourriez) . . .?
kē p*ā* (vo͞o po͞orē·ā)

Whose is that?
À qui est-ce?
ä kē es

What's *your* name?
Quel est *votre (ton)* nom?
kel ā vôt(ər) (tôN) nôN

What do you call . . .?
Comment s'appelle . . .?
kômäN säpel . . .

How do I get *to* . . .?
Pour aller *à (au)* . . ., s'il vous plaît?
po͞or älā ä (ō) . . ., sēl vo͞o plā

How does that work?
Comment est-ce que cela marche?
kômäN eske səlä märsh

How long does it take?
Combien de temps faut-il?
kôNbyeN də täN fōtēl

How much do I get?
Je touche combien?
zhə to͞osh kôNbyeN

How much is it?
Ça fait combien?
sä fā kôNbyeN

Where *can I find* . . . *(is . . . located)*?
Où se trouve . . .?
o͞o sə tro͞ov . . .

Where *is (are)* . . .?
Où *est (sont)* . . .?
o͞o ā (sôN) . . .

Where's *the nearest* . . .?
Où est *le prochain (la prochaine)* . . .?
o͞o ā lə prôsheN (lä prôshen) . . .

Where can I . . .?
Je peux . . . où?
zhə p*ā* . . . o͞o

Where can I *get (find)* . . .?
Je peux *avoir (trouver)* . . . où?
zhə p*ā*zävô·är (tro͞ovā) . . . o͞o

Where *is (are)* there . . .?
Où y a-t-il . . .?
o͞o yätēl . . .

Where *do you live?*
Où *habitez-vous (habites-tu)?*
o͞o äbētā-vo͞o (äbēt-t*ē*)

Where are we?
Où sommes-nous?
o͞o sôm-no͞o

Where do you come from?
D'où *venez-vous (viens-tu)?*
do͞o venā-vo͞o (vyeN-t*ē*)

Where are you going?
Où *allez-vous (vas-tu)?*
o͞o älā-vo͞o (vä-t*ē*)

Where does this *road (path)* lead?
Où va *ce chemin (cette route)?*
o͞o vä se shmeN (set ro͞ot)

Wishes, Requests

Would you please *bring (give, show)* me . . . .?
Apportez (donnez, montrez) -moi . . ., s'il vous plaît.
äpôrtā (dônā, môNtrā) -mô·ä . . . sēl vo͞o plā

Would you please tell me . . .?
Dites-moi . . ., s'il vous plaît.
dēt-mô·ä . . ., sēl vo͞o plā

Would you please *get (fetch)* . . .?
Allez me *chercher* . . ., s'il vous plaît.
älā mə shārshā . . ., sēl vo͞o plā

Beg your pardon? (Say again?)
Pardon?
pärdôN

What can I do for you? (May I help you?)
Que désirez-vous?
ke dāzērā-vo͞o

***I'd (We'd)* like . . .**
J'aimerais (Nous aimerions) . . .
zhāmerā (no͞ozāmeryôN) . . .

I need . . .
J'ai besoin de . . .
zhā bezô·eN də . . .

I'd rather have . . .
J'aimerais mieux . . .
zhāmerā myā̈ . . .

Could I *have (get)* . . .?
Je peux *avoir* . . .?
zhə pā̈zävô·är . . .

Please help me!
Aidez-moi, s'il vous plaît.
ādā-mô·ä, sēl vo͞o plā

Certainly!
Bien entendu.
byeNäNtäNdē̈

Allow me? (Excuse me?)
Vous permettez?
vo͞o permetā

Get well soon!
Bon rétablissement!
bôN rātäblēs·mäN

All the best!
Bonne chance!
bôn shäNs

Have *a good time (fun)!*
Amusez-vous bien!
ämē̈zā-vo͞o byeN

I wish *you* . . .
Je *vous (te)* souhaite . . .
zhə vo͞o (tə) so͞o·et . . .

Thanks

Thanks (Thank you) very much!
Merci (Merci bien)!
mersē (byeN)

Thanks a lot!
Merci beaucoup!
mersē bōkōō

No, thanks.
Non, merci.
nôN, mersē

Thank you too!
Merci à _vous (toi)_ aussi!
mersē ä vōō (tô·ä) ôsē

I'm very grateful to you.
Je _vous (te)_ suis très reconnaissant.
zhə vōō (tə) sē·ē trā rekônāsäN

Thanks very much for _your help (all your trouble)!_
Merci beaucoup pour _votre aide (vos efforts)!_
mersē bōkōō pōōr vôtrād (vōzefôr)

You're welcome.
Je vous en prie.
zhə vōōzäN prē

_I (We)_ thank you so much for . . .
Je vous remercie (Nous vous remercions) infiniment pour . . .
zhə vōō remersē (nōō vōō remersyôN) eNfēnēmäN pōōr . . .

Thanks a million!
Mille mercis!
mēl mersē

Don't mention it.
Il n' y a pas de quoi.
ēlnyä pä də kô·ä

Glad to do it.
À votre service.
ä vôt(ər) servēs

Yes and no

Yes.
Oui.
ōō·ē

Certainly.
Certainement.
sārten·mäN

Of course.
Cela va sans dire.
səlä vä säN dēr

I'd be glad to.
Très volontiers.
trā vôlôNtyā

Good! (Fine!)
Bien! (Très bien!)
byeN (trā byeN)

Right!
C'est ça!
sā sä

Terrific!
Extra!
eksträ

With pleasure!
Avec plaisir!
ävek plāzēr

No.
Non.
nôN

Never.
Jamais.
zhämā

Nothing.
Rien.
rē·eN

Certainly not! (No way!)
En aucun cas!
äNōkeN kä

Out of the question!
Pas question!
pä kestyôN

I'd rather not!
Il vaut mieux pas.
ēl vō my*ā* pä

I _don't want to (can't)._
Je ne _veux (peux)_ pas.
zhə nə v*ā* (p*ā*) pä

Perhaps (Maybe).
Peut-être.
p*ā*tāt(ər)

Probably.
Probablement.
prôbäbləmäN

Pardon

Excuse me!
Excusez-moi!
ekskēzā-mô·ä

I beg your pardon!
Pardon!
pärdôN

Please excuse me!
Excusez-moi, s'il vous plaît.
ekskēzā-mô·ä, sēl voo plā

I'm very sorry.
Je suis désolé.
zhə sē·ē dāzōlā

Please forgive me!
Pardonnez-moi!
pärdônā-mô·ä

I'm extremely sorry.
Je regrette infiniment.
zhə rəgret eNfēnēmäN

I must apologize to *you*.
Je *vous (te)* prie de m'excuser.
zhə voo (tə) prē də mekskēzā

Please don't be angry!
Ne m'en veuillez pas!
nə mäN vāyā pä

> Excusez-moi *and* Pardon *are ways of excusing yourself, but they are also used to catch someone's attention. For example:* "Pardon, monsieur. Où se trouve le Grand Hôtel?" *(Excuse me, sir. Where is the Grand Hotel?)*

Regrets

What a pity! (Too bad!)
(Quel) dommage!
(kel) dômäzh

To my (great) regret ...
À mon (grand) regret ...
ä môN (gräN) rəgrā

What a shame that ...
Quel dommage, que
kel dômäzh ke

I'm so very sorry about that.
J'en suis désolé.
zhäN sē·ē dāzōlā

I'm afraid that isn't possible.
Malheureusement c'est impossible.
mälārāzəmäN seteNpôsēb'əl

I'm afraid that can't be done.
Je crois bien que ce n'est pas possible.
zhə krô·ä byeN ke sə nā pä pôsēb'əl

Congratulations and Condolences

Congratulations!

I congratulate you ...	Mes félicitations!	mā fālēsētäsyôN
on *your* birthday	Bon anniversaire!	bônänēversār
on *your* engagement .	pour *vos (tes)* fiançailles	poor vō (tā) fē·äN-sä'ē
on *your* marriage	pour *votre (ton)* mariage	poor vôt(ər) (tôN) märē·äzh

All the best! (Best wishes!)
Toutes mes félicitations!
to͞ot mā fālēsētäsyôN

Happy birthday!
Bon anniversaire!
bônänēversār

Merry Christmas!
Joyeux Noël!
zhô·äyā nō·el

Happy New Year!
Bonne année!
bônänā

***I (We)* wish you ...**
Je vous *souhaite (Nôus* vous *souhaitons)* ...
zhə vo͞o so͞o·et (no͞o vo͞o so͞o·etôN) ...

All the best!
Bonne chance!
bôn shäNs

Good luck!
Bonne chance!
bôn shäNs

Our warmest sympathy.
Nous vous assurons de notre sympathie.
no͞o vo͞ozäsērôN də nôt(ər) seNpätē

My sincerest condolences.
Mes sincères condoléances.
mā seNsār kôNdōlā·äNs

Complaints

I'd like to register a complaint.
Je désire faire une réclamation.
zhə dāzēr fār *e*n rākläməsyôN

I'd like to speak to the manager.
Je voudrais parler au gérant.
zhə vo͞odrā pärlā ō zhāräN

I'm afraid I'll have to make a complaint about ...
Il faut que je fasse une réclamation au sujet de ...
ēl fō ke zhə fäs *ē*n rākläməsyôN ō s*ē*zhā də ...

That's very annoying.
C'est très fâcheux.
sā trā fäsh*ā*

... *is (are)* missing.
Il n'y a pas de ...
ēlnyä pä də ...

I haven't got any ...
Je n'ai pas de ...
zhə nā pä də ...

... doesn't work.
... ne marche pas.
... nə märsh pä

... is not in order.
... ne marche pas.
... nə märsh pä

... is out of order.
... ne fonctionne pas.
... nə fôNksyôn pä

... *is (are)* broken.
... *est cassé (sont cassés).*
... ā käsā (sôN käsā)

... *is (are)* torn.
... *s'est déchiré (se sont déchirés).*
... sā dāshērā (sə sôN dāshērā)

Communication

Do you speak English?
Parlez-vous anglais?
pärlā-vōōzäNglā

German?
allemand?
älmäN

French?
français?
fräNsā

Can you understand me?
Vous comprenez?
vōō kôNprenā

I understand.
Je comprends.
zhə kôNpräN

I can't understand a thing.
Je ne comprends rien.
zhə nə kôNpräN rē·eN

Would you please speak a little slower?
Parlez un peu plus lentement, s'il vous plaît!
pärlā eN p*ā* pl*ē* läNtəmäN, sēl vōō plā

What do you call . . . in French?
Comment dit-on en français . . .?
kômäN dētôN äN fräNsā

How do you say that in French?
Comment dit-on ça en français?
kômäN dēt-ôN sä äN fräNsā

What does that mean?
Qu'est-ce que ça veut dire?
keske sä v*ā* dēr

I beg your pardon? (Say again?)
Pardon?
pärdôN

How do you pronounce this word?
Comment prononce-t-on ce mot?
kômäN prônôNstôN sə mō

Would you please translate this for me?
Pourriez-vous le traduire pour moi, s'il vous plaît.
pōōrē·ā-vōō lə träd*ē*·ēr pōōr mô·ä, sēl vōō plā

Would you please write that down for me?
Écrivez(-le), s'il vous plaît.
ākrēvā(-lə), sēl vōō plā

Would you spell that please?
Épelez, s'il vous plaît.
āpəlā, sēl vōō plā

Weather

How's the weather going to be?
Quel temps fera-t-il?
kel täN ferätēl

What's the weather report?
Qu'annonce la météo?
känôNs lä mātā·ō

The barometer's *rising (falling)*.
Le baromètre *monte (descend)*.
lə bärōmāt(ər) môNt (desäN)

We're going to have . . .
Nous aurons . . .
nōōzôrôN

fine weather	du beau temps	dē bō täN
bad weather	du mauvais temps	dē mōvā täN
changeable weather	un temps instable	eN täN eNstäb'əl

It's going to stay nice.
Il continue à faire beau.
ēl kôNtēnē ä fär bō

It looks like rain.
On dirait qu'il va pleuvoir.
ôN dērā kēl vä plāvô·är

Is it going to *rain (snow)*?
Va-t-il *pleuvoir (neiger)*?
vätēl plāvô·är (nāzhā)

Is the weather going to stay nice?
Continuera-t-il à faire beau?
kôNtēnē·ərätēl ä fär bō

How are the road conditions between here and . . .?
Quel est l'état des routes pour . . .?
kel ā lātä dā rōōt pōōr

It's very slippery.
Il y a du verglas.
ēlyä dē verglä

– very hot.
Il fait très chaud.
ēl fā trā shō

– *foggy (misty)*.
Il y a du brouillard.
ēlyä dē brōōyär

– very muggy.
Il fait très lourd.
ēl fā trā lōōr

– very windy.
– du vent.
– dē väN

– stormy.
– une tempête.
– ēn täNpāt

It's *cold (hot)*.
Il fait *froid (chaud)*.
ēl fā frô·ä (shō)

I'm *cold (hot)*.
J'ai *froid (chaud)*.
zhā frô·ä (shō)

What's the temperature?
Quelle température fait-il?
kel täNpārätēr fātēl

It's . . . *above (below)* zero.
Le thermomètre marque . . . *au-dessus (au-dessous)* de zéro.
lə termōmāt(ər) märk . . . ōdəsē (ōdəsōō) də zārō

The weather's going to change.
Le temps va changer.
lə täN vä shäNzhā

It'll be nice again.
Le temps se remet au beau.
lə täN sə remetō bō

The wind has dropped.
Le vent est tombé.
lə väN ā tôNbā

The wind has changed.
Le vent a tourné.
lə väN ä to͞ornā

We're going to have a thunderstorm.
Nous aurons un orage.
no͞ozôrôN eNôräzh

There's going to be a storm.
Il y aura de la tempête.
ēlyôrä dəlä täNpāt

Is the fog going to lift?
Est-ce que le brouillard se dissipera?
eske lə bro͞oyär sə dēsēperä

It's stopped raining.
Il a cessé de pleuvoir.
ēl ä sesā də plāvô·är

It's clearing up.
Le temps s'éclaircit.
lə täN sāklārsē

The sun is shining.
Il fait du soleil.
ēl fā dē sôlā'ē

The sun is burning hot.
Le soleil est brûlant.
lə sôlā'ē ā brēläN

The sky is clear.
Le ciel est dégagé.
lə syel ā dāgäzhā

> *European temperatures are always measured in degrees Celsius. Here's a handy conversion table:*
> *Fahrenheit to Celsius = (x—32) 5/9 = °C*
> *Celsius to Fahrenheit = 32 + 9/5x = °F*

air	air *m*	ār
atmospheric pressure	pression *f* atmosphérique	presyôN ätmôsfārēk
barometer	baromètre *m*	bärōmāt(ər)
climate	climat *m*	klēmä
cloud	nuage *m*	nē·äzh
cloudburst	pluie *f* torrentielle	plē·ē tôräNsyel
cloud cover, cloudy skies	nuages *m/pl.*	nē·äzh
cloudy	couvert	ko͞ovār
dawn	aube *f*	ôb
dew	rosée *f*	rōzā
draft	courant *m* d'air	ko͞oräN dār

dusk	crépuscule *m*	krāpēskēl
fog	brouillard *m*	brōōyär
frost	gelée *f*	zhelā
hail	grêle *f*	grāl
heat	canicule *f*	känēkēl
high pressure (system)	anticyclone *m*	äNtēsēklôn
ice	glace *f*	gläs
icy road	verglas *m*	verglä
it's freezing	il gèle	ēl zhāl
it's hailing	il grêle	ēl grāl
it's raining	il pleut	ēl plā
it's snowing	il neige	ēl nāzh
it's thawing	il dégèle	ēl dāzhāl
it's windy	il fait du vent	ēl fā dē väN
lightning	éclair *m*	āklār
low pressure (system)	basses pressions *f/pl.*	bäs presyôN
mist	brouillard *m*	brōōyär
moon	lune *f*	lēn
***north (east)* wind**	vent *m du nord (d'est)*	väN dē nôr (dest)
precipitation	chute *f* de pluie	shēt də plē·ē
road conditions	état *m* des routes	ātä dā rōōt
shower	averse *f*	ävers
snow	neige *f*	nāzh
snow flurries	tourbillons *m/pl.* de neige	tōōrbēyôN də nāzh
***south (west)* wind**	vent *m du sud (d'ouest)*	väN dē sēd (dōō·est)
star	étoile *f*	ātô·äl
storm	tempête *f*	täNpāt
sun	soleil *m*	sôlā'ē
sunrise	lever *m* du soleil	levā dē sôlā'ē
sunset	coucher *m* du soleil	kōōshā dē sôlā'ē
temperature	température *f*	täNpārätēr
thaw	dégel *m*	dāzhāl
thunder	tonnerre *m*	tônār
thunderstorm	orage *m*	ôräzh
weather	temps *m*	täN
weather prediction	prévisions *f/pl.* météo-rologiques	prāvēzyôN mātā·ô-rōlōzhēk
weather report	météo(rologie) *f*	mātā·ō(rōlōzhē)
wind	vent *m*	väN

Numbers

CARDINAL NUMBERS

0	zéro	zārō
1	un	eN
2	deux	dā
3	trois	trô·ä
4	quatre	kät(ər)
5	cinq	seNk
6	six	sēs
7	sept	set
8	huit	ē·ēt
9	neuf	nāf

10	dix	dēs
11	onze	ôNz
12	douze	do͞oz
13	treize	trāz
14	quatorze	kätôrz
15	quinze	keNz
16	seize	sāz
17	dix-sept	dēset
18	dix-huit	dēzē·ēt
19	dix-neuf	dēznāf
20	vingt	veN
21	vingt et un	veNtā·eN
22	vingt-deux	veNdā
23	vingt-trois	veNtrô·ä
30	trente	träNt
40	quarante	käräNt
50	cinquante	seNkäNt
60	soixante	sô·äsäNt
70	soixante-dix	sô·äsäNdēs
80	quatre-vingts	kätrəveN
90	quatre-vingt-dix	kätrəveNdēs
100	cent	säN
200	deux cents	dāsäN
1.000	mille	mēl

When writing numbers in French, the function of periods and commas is reversed from the English function. Commas are used in decimals, and periods in numbers of four or more digits. Thus 1,000 – one thousand – becomes 1.000 – mille (mēl) *in French, and 1.5 – one point five – is translated as* 1,5 – un virgule cinq (eN vērgəl seNk).

2.000	deux mille	dā mēl
10.000	dix mille	dē mēl
1.000.000	un million	eN mēlyôN
1.000.000.000	un milliard	eN mēlyär

ORDINAL NUMBERS

When speaking about days of the month, the French do not use ordinal numbers. Thus the fourteenth of July is le quatorze juillet (lə kätôrz zhē·ēyā). *The same applies to Roman numerals: Louis XVI is spoken of as* Louis Seize (lo͞o'ē sāz). *(see page 34).*

1.	premier	prəmyā	**6.**	sixième	sēzyām
2.	deuxième; second	dāzyām; səgôN	**7.**	septième	setyām
			8.	huitième	ē·ētyām
3.	troisième	trô·äzyām	**9.**	neuvième	nāvyām
4.	quatrième	kätrēyām	**10.**	dixième	dēzyām
5.	cinquième	seNkyām	**11.**	onzième	ôNzyām

12.	douzième	do͞ozyām
13.	treizième	trāzyām
14.	quatorzième	kätôrzyām
15.	quinzième	keNzyām
16.	seizième	sāzyām
17.	dix-septième	dēsetyām
20.	vingtième	veNtyām
21.	vingt et unième	veNt-ā-ēnyām
22.	vingt-deuxième	veN-dāzyām
23.	vingt-troisième	veNtrô·äzyām
30.	trentième	träNtyām
40.	quarantième	käräNtyām
50.	cinquantième	seNkäNtyām
60.	soixantième	sô·äsäNtyām
70.	soixante-dixième	sô·äsäNt-dēzyām
80.	quatre-vingtième	kätrə-veNtyām
90.	quatre-vingt-dixième	kätrə-veN-dēzyām
100.	centième	säNtyām
200.	deux centième	dā säNtyām
1.000.	millième	mēlyām
10.000.	dix millième	dē(s) mēlyām
1.000.000.	millionième	mēlyônyām

Time

What time is it?
Quelle heure est-il?
kel*ā*r etēl

It's one o'clock.
Il est une heure.
ēl āt*ē*n*ā*r

It's exactly three o'clock.
Il est exactement trois heures.
ēl ātāgzäktəmäN trô·äz*ā*r

It's half past seven.
Il est sept heures et demie.
ēl ā set*ā*r ā dəmē

It's five (minutes) past four.
Il est quatre heures cinq.
ēl ā kätr*ā*r seNk

Have you got the exact time?
Avez-vous l'heure exacte?
ävā-vo͞o l*ā*r egzäkt

It's about two o'clock.
Il est environ deux heures.
ēl ātäNvērôN d*ā*z*ā*r

It's quarter past five.
Il est cinq heures et quart.
ēl ā seNk*ā*r ā kär

It's quarter to nine.
Il est neuf heures moins le quart.
ēl ā n*ā*v*ā*r mô·eN lə kär

It's ten (minutes) to eight.
Il est huit heures moins dix.
ēl ā *ē*·ēt*ā*r mô·eN dēs

> *The 24 hour clock is used on timetables, signs, announcements, TV schedules and in written French in general. In spoken French, however, you can use the 12 hour clock, adding* du matin, de l'après-midi *or* du soir *to the time if there is any doubt.*

When?
À quelle heure?
ä kel*ā*r

At ten o'clock (10:00).
À dix heures.
ä dēz*ā*r

At eleven sharp.
À onze heures précises.
ä ôNz*ā*r prāsēz

At *half-past nine (nine-thirty)*.
À neuf heures *et demie (trente)*.
ä n*ā*v*ā*r ā dəmē (träNt)

At eight-fifteen P.M.
À huit heures et quart du soir.
ä *ē*·ēt*ā*r ā kär d*ē* sô·är

From eight to nine A.M.
De huit à neuf du matin.
də *ē*·ēt ä n*ā*f d*ē* mäteN

Between ten and twelve A.M.
Entre dix et onze du matin.
äNt(ər) dēsā ôNz d*ē* mäteN

At five P.M.
À cinq heures de l'après-midi.
ä seNk*ā*r də läprā-mēdē

At seven P.M.
À sept heures du soir.
ä set*ā*r d*ē* sô·är

In half an hour.
Dans une demi-heure.
däNzēn dəmē-*ā*r

Not before seven.
Pas avant sept heures.
päzäväN set*ā*r

It's *(too)* late.
Il est *(trop)* tard.
ēl ā (trō) tär

Is this clock right?
Cette montre est à l'heure?
set môNtrātä l*ā*r

In two hours.
Dans deux heures.
däN d*ā*z*ā*r

Shortly after eight.
Peu après huit heures.
p*ā* äprā *ē*·ēt*ā*r

It's still too early.
Il est encore trop tôt.
ēl ātäNkôr trō tō

It's too *fast (slow)*.
Elle *avance (retarde)*.
el äväNs (retärd)

Times of the Day

During the day.
Pendant la journée.
päNdäN lä zhōōrnā

In the morning.
Le matin.
lə mäteN

During the morning.
Dans la matinée.
däN lä mätēnā

This *morning (afternoon, evening)*.
Ce matin (Cet après-midi. Ce soir).
sə mäteN (setäprā-mēdē, sə sô·är)

At noon.
À midi.
ä mēdē

Around noon.
Vers midi.
vār mēdē

In the afternoon.
L'après-midi.
läprā-mēdē

In the evening.
Le soir.
lə sô·är

At night.
La nuit.
lä n*ē*·ē

Tonight.
Cette nuit.
set n*ē*·ē

At midnight.
À minuit.
ä mēn*ē*·ē

Daily (Every day).
Tous les jours.
tōō lā zhōōr

Hourly (Every hour).
Toutes les heures.
tōōt lāz*ā*r

The day before yesterday.
Avant-hier.
äväNtē·ār

Yesterday.
Hier.
ē·ār

Today.
Aujourd'hui.
ōzhōōrd*ē*·ē

Tomorrow.
Demain.
dəmeN

Tomorrow morning.
Demain matin.
dəmeN mäteN

The day after tomorrow.
Après-demain.
äprā-dəmeN

A week from now.
Dans une semaine.
däNz*ē*n smen

A week from Wednesday.
Mercredi en huit.
mārkrədi äN *ē*·ēt

Two weeks from now.
Dans quinze jours.
däN keNz zhōōr

This noon.
Ce midi.
sə mēdē

A month ago.
Il y a un mois.
ēlyä eN mô·ä

At the moment.
Actuellement.
äktē·ēləmäN

For the last ten days.
Depuis dix jours.
depē·ē dē zhōōr

Within a week.
Dans les huit jours.
däN lā ē·ē zhōōr

This coming weekend.
Le week-end prochain.
lə ōō·ēkend prôsheN

***Last (Next)* year.**
L'année *dernière (prochaine)*.
länā dernyār (prôshen)

Every year (Annually).
Tous les ans.
tōō lāzäN

Every week (Weekly).
Toutes les semaines.
tōōt lā smen

From time to time.
De temps en temps.
də täNzäN täN

Now and then.
De temps à autre.
də täNzä ôt(ər)

About this time.
À cette *heure (date)*.
ä set ār (dät)

During this time (Meanwhile).
Pendant ce temps (Entre-temps).
päNdäN sə täN (äNtrətäN)

a little while ago	récemment	rāsämäN
any time	à tout moment	ä tōō mômäN
earlier	plus tôt	plē tō
later	plus tard	plē tär
now	maintenant	meNtənäN
on time	à temps	ä täN
previously (before)	avant	äväN
recently	l'autre jour	lōt(ər) zhōōr
since	depuis	depē·ē
sometimes	quelquefois	kelkefô·ä
soon	bientôt	byeNtō
temporarily (for the time being)	en ce moment	äN sə mômäN
until	jusqu'à	zhēskä
second	seconde *f*	səgôNd
minute	minute *f*	mēnēt
hour	heure *f*	ār
day	jour *m*	zhōōr
week	semaine *f*	smen
month	mois *m*	mô·ä
year	année *f*, an *m*	änā, äN
half year	six mois	sē mô·ä
quarter, three months	trois mois	trô·ä mô·ä

Days of the Week

Monday	lundi *m*	leNdē
Tuesday	mardi *m*	märdē
Wednesday	mercredi *m*	mārkrədē
Thursday	jeudi *m*	zhädē
Friday	vendredi *m*	väNdrədē
Saturday	samedi *m*	sämdē
Sunday	dimanche *m*	dēmäNsh

Months

January	janvier *m*	zhäNvyā
February	février *m*	fāvrē·ā
March	mars *m*	märs
April	avril *m*	ävrēl
May	mai *m*	mā
June	juin *m*	zhē·eN
July	juillet *m*	zhē·ēyā
August	août *m*	o͞o(t)
September	septembre *m*	septäNb(ər)
October	octobre *m*	ôktōb(ər)
November	novembre *m*	nôväNb(ər)
December	décembre *m*	dāsäNb(ər)

Seasons, Holidays

Spring	printemps *m*	preNtäN
Summer	été *m*	ātā
Fall/Autumn	automne *m*	ôtôn
Winter	hiver *m*	ēvār
New Year's Eve	(la) Saint-Sylvestre	(lä) seN sēlvest(ər)
New Year's Day	jour *m* de l'an	zho͞or də läN
Good Friday	vendredi *m* saint	väNdrədē seN
Easter; Christmas	Pâques *m*; Noël *m*	päk; nō·el

Public Holidays in France: New Year's Day, Easter Sunday and Monday, May Day (May 1), Ascension Day, Whitsunday and Whitmonday, France's National Day (July 14), The Assumption (August 15), All Saints' Day (November 1), Armistice Day (November 11), Christmas Day.
Recently, another holiday has been added: Armistice Day *(May 8 – commemorating the end of World War II).*

The Date

What's the date today?
Nous sommes le combien aujourd'hui?
no͞o sôm lə kôNbyeN ōzho͞ordē·ē

It's the second of July.
Aujourd'hui, c'est le deux juillet.
ōzho͞ordē·ē, se lə dā zhē·ēyā

On the *fifteenth of May (May fifteenth)*, 19 . . .
Le quinze mai dix-neuf cent . . .
lə keNz mā dēz-nāf säN . . .

On the fifth of *this (next)* month.
Le cinq *de ce mois (du mois prochain)*.
lə seNk də sə mô·ä (dē mô·ä prôsheN)

Until the 10th of March.
Jusqu'au dix mars.
zhēskō dē märs

On April first of *this (last)* year.
Le premier avril *de cette année (de l'année passée)*.
lə prəmyā ävrēl də cetänā (də länā päsā)

We leave on *the twentieth of September (September 20th)*.
Nous partirons le vingt septembre.
no͞o pärtērôN lə veN septäNb(ər)

We arrived on *the twelfth of August (August 12th)*.
Nous sommes arrivés le douze août.
no͞o sômzärēvā lə do͞oz o͞o

Thank you for your letter of February 2nd.
Je vous remercie (Nous vous remercions) de votre lettre du deux février.
zhə vo͞o remersē (no͞o vo͞o remersyôN) də vôt(ər) let(ər) dē dā fāvrē·ā

Age

I'm twenty years old.
J'ai vingt ans.
zhā veNtäN

I'm over 18.
J'ai plus de dix-huit ans.
zhā plē də dēzē·ēt äN

Children under 14.
Enfants au-dessous de quatorze ans.
äNfäN ō-dəso͞o də kätôrzäN

I was born on the . . .
Je suis né le . . .
zhə sē·ē nā lə . . .

He's *younger (older)*.
Il est *plus jeune (plus âgé)*.
ēl ā plē zhān (plēzäzhā)

– under age.
– mineur.
mēnār

– grown up.
– adulte.
ädēlt

At the age of . . .
À l'âge de . . . ans.
äläzh də . . . äN

At my age.
À mon âge.
ä môNäzh

Family

aunt	tante *f*	täNt
boy	garçon *m*	gärsôN
brother	frère *m*	frār
brother-in-law	beau-frère *m*	bō-frār
cousin *(female)*	cousine *f*	ko͞ozēn
cousin *(male)*	cousin *m*	ko͞ozeN
daughter; girl	fille *f*	fē'ē
daughter-in-law	belle-fille *f*	belfē'e
family	famille *f*	fämē'ē
father	père *m*	pār
father-in-law	beau-père *m*	bō-pār
grandchild	petit-fils *m*	pətē-fēs
granddaughter	petite-fille *f*	pətēt-fē'ē
grandfather	grand-père *m*	gräN-pār
grandmother	grand-mère *f*	gräN-mār
grandparents	grands-parents *m/pl.*	gräN-pärälN
grandson	petit-fils *m*	pətē-fēs
husband	mari *m*	märē
mother	mère *f*	mār
mother-in-law	belle-mère *f*	bel-mār
nephew	neveu *m*	nev*ā*
niece	nièce *f*	nē·ās
parents	parents *m/pl.*	päräN
sister	sœur *f*	s*ā*r
sister-in-law	belle-sœur *f*	bel-s*ā*r
son; son-in-law	fils *m*; gendre *m*	fēs; zhäNdrə
uncle	oncle *m*	ôNk'əl
wife	femme *f*; épouse *f*	fäm; āpo͞oz

The terms époux *and* épouse *(husband and wife) are more formal than the common reference to one's spouse as* mon mari *(my husband) and* ma femme *(my wife).*

Occupations

apprentice	apprenti *m*	äpräNtē
artist	artiste *m*	ärtēst
auto mechanic	mécanicien *m*	mākänēsyeN
baker	boulanger *m*	bo͞oläNzhā
bank teller	employé *m* de banque	äNplô·äyā də bäNk
bookkeeper	comptable *m*	kôNtäb'əl
bookseller	libraire *m*	lēbrār
bricklayer	maçon *m*	mäsôN
butcher	boucher *m*	bo͞oshā
cabinetmaker	ébéniste *m*	ābānēst
carpenter	menuisier *m*	men*ē*·ēzyā
chef	chef cuisinier *m*	shef k*ē*·ēzēnyā
civil servant	fonctionnaire *m*	fôNksyônār
clergyman	prêtre *m*	prāt(ər)
cobbler	cordonnier *m*	kôrdônyā
computer programmer	programmeur *m*	prôgräm*ā*r
confectioner	pâtissier *m*	pätēsyā
cook	cuisinier *m*	k*ē*·ēzēnyā
dentist	dentiste *m, f*	däNtēst
doctor	médecin *m*	mādəseN
dressmaker	tailleur *m*	täy*ā*r
driver	chauffeur *m*	shôf*ā*r
driving instructor	moniteur *m* d'auto-école	mônēt*ā*r dôtō-ākôl
druggist *(pharmacist)*	pharmacien *m*	färmäsyeN
druggist *(drugstore owner)*	droguiste *m*	drôgēst
electrician	électricien *m*	ālektrēsyeN
engineer *(scientific)*	ingénieur *m*	eNzhāny*ā*r
engineer *(railroad)*	mécanicien *m* (de train)	mākänēsyeN (də treN)
farmer	agriculteur *m*	ägrēk*ə*lt*ā*r
fisherman	pêcheur *m*	pāsh*ā*r
forester	garde *m* forestier	gärd fôrestyā
gardener	jardinier *m*	zhärdēnyā

glazier	vitrier *m*	vētrēyā
interpreter	interprète *m*	eNterprāt
journalist	journaliste *m*	zho͞ornälēst
judge	juge *m*	zh*ē*zh
kindergarten teacher	jardinière *f* d'enfants	zhärdēnyār däNfäN
lawyer	avocat *m*	ävōkä
librarian	bibliothécaire *m*	bēblē·ōtākār
locksmith	serrurier *m*	ser*ē*ryā
mailman	facteur *m*	fäkt*ā*r
mechanic	mécanicien *m*	mākänēsyeN
metalworker	métallurgiste *m*	mātäl*ē*rzhēst
midwife	sage-femme *f*	säzh-fäm
miner	mineur *m*	mēn*ā*r
musician	musicien *m*	m*ē*zēsyeN
notary	notaire *m*	nôtār
nurse *(female)*	infirmière *f*	eNfērmyār
nurse *(male)*	infirmier *m*	eNfērmyā
optician	opticien *m*	ôptēsyeN
painter	peintre *m*	peNt(ər)
pastry chef	pâtissier *m*	pätēsyā
pharmacist	pharmacien *m*	färmäsyeN
plumber	plombier *m*	plôNbyā
postal clerk	employé *m* de postes	äNplô·äyā də pôst
pupil	élève *m, f*; lycéen *m*	ālāv; lēsā·eN
railroad man	cheminot *m*	shəmēnō
retailer	commerçant *m*	kômersäN
retiree	retraité *m*	retrātā
salesperson	vendeur *m*	väNd*ā*r
scholar	savant *m*	säväN
scientist	scientifique *m*	syäNtēfēk
sculptor	sculpteur *m*	sk*ē*lpt*ā*r
secretary	secrétaire *m, f*	sekrātār
shoemaker	cordonnier *m*	kôrdônyā
storekeeper	propriétaire *m* d'un magasin	prôprē·ātār deN mägäzeN
student	étudiant *m*	ēt*ē*dyäN
tailor	tailleur *m*	täy*ā*r
teacher	instituteur *m*, professeur *m*	eNstēt*ē*t*ā*r, prôfes*ā*r

technician	technicien *m*	teknēsyeN
trainee	apprenti *m*	äpräNtē
translator	traducteur *m*	trädəktār
truck driver	camionneur *m*	kämyônār
veterinarian	vétérinaire *m*	vātārēnār
waiter	serveur *m*	servār
waitress	serveuse *f*	servāz
watchmaker	horloger *m*	ôrlōzhā
wholesaler	grossiste *m*	grōsēst
worker	ouvrier *m*	o͞ovrēyā
writer	écrivain *m*	ākrēveN

There is no simple rule for forming the feminine of occupations (and other nouns). There is un artiste *and* une artiste *for example, as well as* tailleur *and* tailleuse. *Nouns ending in* -er *and* -ier *change the ending to* -ère *and* ière *respectively:* boucher *and* bouchère, ouvrier *and* ouvrière. *Nouns ending in* -teur *usually change the ending to* -teuse *and* -trice: facteur *and* factrice. *But there is no feminine form for* auteur, docteur, médecin *and* professeur. *The word* femme *generally precedes these nouns:* une femme médecin.

Education

Where are you studying?
Où étudiez-vous?
o͞o ātədyā-vo͞o

What college or university do you attend?
À quelle université étudiez-vous?
ä kel ənēversētā ātədyā-vo͞o

I'm at ... *college (university).*
Je vais à l'université *de (des)* ...
zhə vāzä lənēverzētā də [dā]

I'm *studying (majoring in)* ...
J'étudie ... (comme matière principale).
zhātədē ... [kôm mätyār preNsēpäl]

lecture	cours *m*	ko͞or
major	matière *f* principale	mätyār preNsēpäl
school	école *f*	ākôl
– boarding school	internat *m*	eNternä
– business school	école *f* de commerce	ākôl də kômers
– grammar school	école *f* primaire	ākôl prēmār
– high school *(acad.)*	académie *f*	äkädāmē
– *(general)*	lycée *m*; collège *m*	lēsā; kôlāzh

– vocational school	centre *m* de formation professionnelle	säNt(ər) də fôrmäsyôn prôfesyônel
subject	matière *f*	mätyār
– American studies	langue *f* et littérature *f* américaines	läNgā lētārātēr ämārēken
– archaeology	archéologie *f*	ärkā·ōlōzhē
– architecture	architecture *f*	ärkētektēr
– art history	histoire *f* de l'art	ēstô·är də lär
– biology	biologie *f*	bē·ōlōzhē
– business admin.	gestion *f*	zhestyôN
– chemistry	chimie *f*	shēmē
– computer science	informatique *f*	eNfôrmätēk
– dentistry	études *f/pl.* dentaires	ātēd däNtār
– economics	économie *f*	ākônōmē
– education	pédagogie *f*	pādägōzhē
– English	langue *f* et littérature *f* anglaises	läNgā lētārätēr äNglāz
– geology	géologie *f*	zhā·ōlōzhē
– history	histoire *f*	ēstô·är
– journalism	journalisme *m*	zhōōrnälēsm
– law	droit *m*	drô·ä
– mathematics	mathématiques *f/pl.*	mätāmätēk
– mechanical engineering	construction *f* mécanique	kôNstrēksyôN mākänēk
– medicine	médecine *f*	mādəsēn
– painting	peinture *f*	peNtēr
– pharmacy	pharmacie *f*	färmäsē
– physics	physique *f*	fēzēk
– political science	sciences *f/pl.* politiques	sē·äNs pôlētēk
– psychology	psychologie *f*	sēkōlōzhē
– Romance languages	langues *f/pl.* romanes	länNg rômän
– sociology	sociologie *f*	sōsē·ōlōzhē
– veterinary medicine	médecine *f* vétérinaire	mādəsēn vātārēnār
– zoology	zoologie *f*	zō·ōlōzhē
technical college	école *f* supérieure technique	ākôl sēpāryār teknēk
university	université *f*	ēnēversētā

La Sorbonne *is the familiar name for one of the many branches of the Université de Paris.*

ON THE ROAD

Asking the Way

Where *is (are)* . . .?
Où *est (sont)* . . .?
o͞o·ā (sôN) . . .

How do I get to . . .?
Pour aller à . . .?
po͞or älā ä . . .

Is this the road to . . .?
Est-ce la route de . . .?
es lä ro͞ot də . . .

How many kilometers is it to the next town?
Combien de kilomètres y a-t-il jusqu'à la prochaine ville?
köNbyeN də kēlōmāt(ər) yätēl zhēskä lä prōshen vēl

8 kilomètres = *5 miles*

Is this the right way to . . .?
Est-ce la bonne direction pour . . .?
es lä bôn dēreksyôN po͞or . . .

Do I have to go . . .?
Dois-je aller . . .?
dô·äzhälā . . .

Right.
À droite.
ä drô·ät

Left.
À gauche.
ä gōsh

Straight ahead.
Tout droit.
to͞o drô·ä

Back.
En arrière.
äNäryār

Here.
Ici.
ēsē

There.
Là.
lä

This way.
Dans cette direction.
däN set dēreksyôN

As far as . . .
Jusqu'à . . .
zhēskä . . .

How long?
Combien de temps?
kôNbyeN də täN

Where (to)?
Où?
o͞o

How far is it to . . .?
C'est loin d'ici (à) . . .?
se lô·eN dēsē (ä) . . .

Would you please show me that on the map?
Indiquez-le-moi sur la carte, s'il vous plaît.
eNdēkā-lə mô·ä sēr lä kärt, sēl vo͞o plā

Vehicles

camping trailer	caravane *f*	käräväṅ
car	voiture *f*	vô·ätēr
– **delivery truck**	camionnette *f*	kämyōnet
– **passenger car**	voiture *f* particulière	vô·ätēr pärtēkēlyār

***– ranch (station)* wagon**	voiture *f* familiale	vô·ätēr fämēlyäl
– truck	camion *m*	kämyôN
bicycle	bicyclette *f*	bēsēklet
horse cart	roulotte *f*	ro͞olôt
moped	cyclomoteur *m*	sēklōmôtär
motorcycle	moto *f*	môtō
motor scooter	scooter *m*	sko͞otär
trailer	remorque *f*	remôrk
vehicle	véhicule *m*	vā·ēkēl

Renting a Car

Where can I rent a car?
Je peux louer une voiture où?
zhə pā lo͞o·ā ēn vô·ätēr o͞o

I'd like to rent a car.
J'aimerais louer une voiture.
zhāmerā lo͞o·ā ēn vô·ätēr

... with chauffeur.
... avec chauffeur.
... ävek shōfär

... for *2 (6)* people.
... pour *deux (six)* personnes.
... po͞or dā (sē) persôn

... for *one day (one week, two weeks).*
... pour *un jour (une semaine, deux semaines).*
... po͞or eN zho͞or (ēn smen, dā smen)

How much will it cost?
Ça coûte combien?
sä ko͞ot kôNbyeN

... including full coverage insurance?
... l'assurance tous risques inclus?
... läsēräNs to͞o rēsk eNklē

Will I have to pay for the gasoline myself?
Dois-je payer l'essence moi-même?
dô·äzh pāyā lesäNs mô·ä mām

How much will I have to deposit?
Je dois vous verser une caution de combien?
zhə dô·ä vo͞o versā ēn kôsyôN də kôNbyeN

***When (Where)* can I pick up the car?**
Quand (Où) puis-je venir chercher la voiture?
käN (o͞o) pē·ēzh vənēr shershā lä vô·ätēr

Will somebody be there when I bring the car back?
Est-ce qu'il y aura quelqu'un quand je ramènerai la voiture?
es kēlyôrä kelkeN käN zhə rämānərā lä vô·ätēr

On a Drive

I'm *going (driving)* to ...	**Are you going to ...?**
Je vais à ...	Allez-vous à ...?
zhə vāzä ...	älāvōōzä ...

To go by *car (motorcycle, bicycle)*.	**Fast.**	**Slow.**
Aller *en voiture (en moto, à bicyclette).*	Vite.	Lentement.
älā äN vô·ätēr (äN môtō, ä bēsēklet)	vēt	läNtmäN

access road	route *f* d'accès	rōōt däksā
automobile club	automobile club *m*	ôtōmōbēl klēb
bike lane	piste *f* cyclable	pēst sēkläb'əl
bridge	pont *m*	pôN
center strip	bande *f* médiane	bäNd mādē·än
city limits sign	panneau *m* de localité	pänō də lōkälētā
curve	virage *m*	vēräzh
detour	déviation *f*	dāvē·äsyôN
direction sign	panneau *m* indicateur	pänō eNdēkätār
driver's license	permis *m* de conduire	permē də kôNdē·ēr
driveway	entrée *f*	äNtrā
exit	sortie *f*	sôrtē
falling rocks	chute *f* de pierres	shēt də pyār
highway	auto-route *f*	ôtōrōōt
highway patrol	police *f* routière	pôlēs rōōtyār
intersection	croisement *m*	krô·äzmäN
lane	chaussée *f*	shôsā
limited parking zone	zone bleue *f*	zōn blā
maximum speed	vitesse *f* maximum	vētes mäksēmôm
(mountain) pass	col *m*	kôl
no parking	stationnement *m* interdit	stäsyônmäN eNterdē
no passing	interdiction *f* de dépasser	eNterdēksyôN də dāpäsā
no stopping	arrêt *m* interdit	ärā eNterdē
parking disc	disque *m* bleu	dēsk blā
parking lot	parking *m*	pärkēng
parking meter	parcomètre *m*	pärkōmāt(ər)
path	chemin *m*	shəmeN
– footpath	trottoir *m*	trôtô·är
railroad crossing	passage *m* à niveau	päsäzh ä nēvō

registration	immatriculation *f*	ēmätrēkeläsyôN
right of way	priorité *f*	prē·ôrētā
road	route *f*	ro͞ot
– coastal road	route *f* côtière	ro͞ot kôtyār
– country road	route *f* de campagne	ro͞ot də käNpän(yə)
– cross road	route *f* secondaire	ro͞ot səgôNdār
– main ***road (street)***	route *f* (rue *f*) principale	ro͞ot (rē) preNsēpäl
road sign	panneau *m* de signalisation	pänō də sēnyälēzäsyôN
road under construction	route en travaux	ro͞ot äN trävō
route	route *f*	ro͞ot
sidewalk	trottoir *m*	trôtô·är
side wind	vent *m* latéral	väN lätäräl
slippery road ***(literally: danger of sliding)***	(attention) route glissante	(ätäNsyôN) ro͞ot glēsäNt
speed limit	limitation *f* de vitesse	lēmētäsyôN də vētes
steep downgrade	pente *f*	päNt
steep upgrade	côte *f*	kōt
traffic	circulation *f*	sērkeläsyôN
traffic circle	sens *m* giratoire	säNs zhērätô·är
traffic light	feux *m/pl.*	fā
traffic regulations	code *m* de la route	kôd də lä ro͞ot
trip (journey)	voyage *m* en voiture	vô·äyäzh äN vô·ätēr
– brake	freiner	frānā
– drive	conduire	kôNdē·ēr
– get in lane	se ranger	sə räNzhā
– get out ***(of the car)***	descendre	desäNd(ər)
– hitch-hike	faire de l'auto-stop	fār də lôtōstôp
– park	stationner	stäsyônā
– pass ***(on the road)***	dépasser; doubler	dāpäsā; do͞oblā
– stop	arrêter	ärātā
– turn ***(the car)***	faire demi-tour	fār dəmē-to͞or
– turn ***(into a road)***	tourner	to͞ornā
– turn off ***(a road)***	bifurquer	bēfērkā
winding road	route *f* en lacets	ro͞ot äN läsā
zebra crossing	passage *m* clouté	päsäzh klo͞otā

Garage, Parking Lot

Where can I leave my car *(for safekeeping)*?
Je peux garer ma voiture où?
zhə pā̆ gärā mä vô·ätēr o͞o

Is there a garage near here?
Il y a un garage dans le coin?
ēlyä eN gäräzh däN lə kô·eN

Have you still got a vacant *garage (parking space)*?
Avez-vous encore *un garage (un box)* de libre?
ävävo͞ozäNkôr eN gäräzh (eN bôks) də lēb(ər)

Where can I leave the car?
Je peux laisser la voiture où?
zhə pā̆ lāsā lä vô·ätēr o͞o

Can I leave it here?
Je peux la laisser ici?
zhə pā̆ lä lāsā ēsē

Can I park here?
Je peux me garer ici?
zhə pā̆ mə gärā ēsē

Is this parking lot guarded?
Le parking est gardé?
lə pärkēng ā gärdā

Is there a space free?
Y a-t-il encore une place libre?
ēyätēl äNkôr ē̆n pläs lēb(ər)

How long can I park here?
Combien de temps je peux stationner ici?
kôNbyeN də täN zhə pā̆ stäsyônā ēsē

How much does it cost to park here *overnight (until . . .)*?
Combien coûte le garage *une nuit (jusqu'à . . .)*?
kôNbyeN ko͞ot lə gäräzh ē̆n nē̆·ē (zhē̆skä . . .)

Is the garage open all night?
Le garage est-t-il ouvert toute la nuit?
lə gäräzh etēl o͞ovār to͞ot lä nē̆·ē

When do you close?
Quand fermez-vous?
käN fermā vo͞o

I'll be leaving *this evening (tomorrow morning at eight)*.
Je partirai *ce soir (demain à huit heures)*.
zhə pärtērā sə sô·är (dəmeN ä ē̆·ētā̆r)

I'd like to take my car out of the garage.
Je voudrais sortir ma voiture du garage.
zhə vo͞odrā sôrtēr mä vô·ätēr dē̆ gäräzh

Gas Station, Car Repair

Where's the nearest gas station?
Où est la station d'essence la plus proche?
o͞o ā lä stäsyôN desäNs lä plē prôsh

How far is it?
C'est à quelle distance?
sātä kel dēstäNs

Fifteen liters of *regular (high test)*, please.
Donnez-moi quinze litres *d'essence ordinaire (de super)*, s'il vous plaît.
dônā mô·ä keNz lēt(ər) desäNs ôrdēnār (də sēpār), sēl vo͞o plā

1 gallon = approx. 4 litres

I'd like 20 liters of diesel, please.
Je voudrais vingt litres de diesel.
zhə vo͞odrā veN lēt(ər) də dyezel

Fill her up, please.
Faites le plein, s'il vous plaît.
fāt lə pleN, sēl vo͞o plā

I need *water (coolant)*.
J'ai besoin d'eau (du radiateur).
zhā bəzô·eN dō (dē rädē·ätār)

A road map, please.
Une carte routière, s'il vous plaît.
ēn kärt ro͞otyār, sēl vo͞o plā

Would you please fill up the radiator?
Faites le plein d'eau du radiateur, s'il vous plaît.
fāt lə pleN dō dē rädē·ätār, sēl vo͞o plā

Would you please check the brake fluid?
Vérifiez le liquide de freins, s'il vous plaît.
vārēfē·ā lə lēkēd də freN, sēl vo͞o plā

anti-freeze	antigel *m*	äNtēzhel
attendant	pompiste *m*	pôNpēst
brake fluid	liquide *m* de freins	lēkēd də freN
car repair service	service-entretien *m*	servēs äNtrətyeN
coolant	fluide *m* réfrigérant	flē·ēd rāfrēzhāräN
(cooling) water	eau *f* du radiateur	ō dē rädē·ätār
gasoline	essence *f*	esäNs
gasoline can	jerrycan *m*	zherēkän
gas station	station *f* d'essence	stäsyôN desäNs
gas tank	réservoir *m* d'essence	rāzervō·är desäNs
oil	huile *f*	ē·ēl
reserve tank	bidon *m* de réserve	bēdôN də rāzārv
spark plug	bougie *f* d'allumage	bo͞ozhē dälēmäzh
water	eau *f*	ō
– distilled water	eau *f* distillée	ō dēstēlā

Oil

Please check the oil.
Vérifiez le niveau d'huile, s'il vous plaît.
vārēfē·ā lə nēvō dē·ēl, sēl vo͞o plā

I need *motor oil (gear oil).*
Il me faut d'huile *de moteur (de graissage)*.
ēl mə fō dē·ēl də môtār (də gresäzh)

Have I got enough oil?
Y a-t-il encore assez d'huile?
ēyätēl äNkôr äsā dē·ēl

. . . liters of oil please.
. . . litres d'huile, s'il vous plaît.
. . . lēt(ər) dē·ēl, sēl vo͞o plā

1 liter = approx. 2 pints

Please fill up the oil tank.
Faites le plein d'huile, s'il vous plaît.
fāt lə pleN dē·ēl, sēl vo͞o plā

Please change the oil.
Changez l'huile, s'il vous plaît.
shäNzhā lē·ēl, sēl vo͞o plā

gear oil	huile *f* de graissage	ē·ēl də gresäzh
lubrication	lubrification *f*	lēbrēfēkäsyôN
motor oil	huile *f* de moteur	ē·ēl də môtār
oil	l'huile *f*	lē·ēl
– special/standard	spéciale/normale	spesyäl/nôrmäl
oil can	burette *f*	bēret
oil change	vidange *f* d'huile	vēdäNzh dē·ēl
oil level	niveau *m* d'huile	nēvō dē·ēl

Tires

Can you *repair (retread)* this tire?
Pouvez-vous *réparer (rechaper)* ce pneu?
po͞ovā-vo͞o rāpärā (reshäpā) sə pnā

One of the tires had a blow-out.
Un pneu a crevé.
eN pnā ä krəvā

Please change this tire.
Changez ce pneu, s. v. p.
shäNzhā sə pnā, sēl vo͞o plā

A new inner tube, please.
Une nouvelle chambre à air, s'il vous plaît.
ēn no͞ovel shäNb(ər) ä ār, sēl vo͞o plā

Would you please pump up the spare tire?
Gonflez le pneu de rechange, s'il vous plaît.
gôNflā lə pnā də rəshäNzh, sēl vo͞o plā

Would you please check the tire pressure?
Vérifiez la pression des pneus, s'il vous plaît.
vārēfē·ā lä presyôN dā pnā, sēl vo͞o plā

The front tires are 22.7, and the rear ones are 28.4.
À l'avant 1,6, à l'arrière 2,0 kg.
äläväN eN vērgel sēs, äläryār dā kēlōgräm

> *Since tire pressure varies from car to car, it's a good idea to write down the pressure needed for your car and keep it handy for reference.*

blow-up	crevaison *f*	krevāzôN
inner tube	chambre *f* à air	shäNb(ər) ä ār
jack	cric *m*	krēk
puncture	trou *m*	tro͞o
tires *(in general)*	pneus *m/pl.*	pnā
– tubeless tire	pneu *m* plein	pnā pleN
tire change	changement *m* de pneu	shäNzh·mäN də pnā
tire pressure	pression *f* des pneus	presyôN dā pnā
valve	soupape *f*	so͞opäp
wheel	roue *f*	ro͞o
– back wheel	roue *f* arrière	ro͞o äryār
– front wheel	roue *f* avant	ro͞o äväN
– reserve wheel	roue *f* de secours	ro͞o də səko͞or
– wheels	roues *f/pl.*	ro͞o

Car Wash

Please wash the *windshield (the windows)*.
Nettoyez *le pare-brise (les vitres)*, s'il vous plaît.
netô·äyā lə pärbrēz/lā vēt(ər), sēl vo͞o plā

I'd like my car washed, please.
Lavez la voiture, s'il vous plaît.
lävā lä vô·ätēr, sēl vo͞o plā

Please clean out the inside too.
Nettoyez aussi l'intérieur de la voiture, s'il vous plaît.
netô·äyā ôsē leNtārē·ār dəlä vô·ätēr, sēl vo͞o plā

Breakdown, Accident

***I've (We've)* had a breakdown.**
Je suis (Nous sommes) en panne.
zhə sē·ē (no͞o sôm) äN pän

. . . is *busted (not working)*.
. . . ne marche pas.
. . . nə märsh pä

I've had an accident.
J'ai eu un accident.
zhā *ē* eNäksēdäN

May I use your phone?
Je peux téléphoner de chez vous?
zhə p*ā* tālāfônā də shā vo͞o

Would you please call the police?
Appelez la police, s'il vous plaît.
äplā lä pôlēs, sēl vo͞o plā

Get a doctor!
Faites venir un médecin!
fāt vənēr eN mādəseN

Call an ambulance quickly.
Faites venir une ambulance immédiatement!
fāt vənēr *ē*n äNb*ē*läNs ēmādē·ätmäN

Please help me!
Aidez-moi, s'il vous plaît.
ādā-mô·ä, sēl vo͞o plā

I need bandages.
J'ai besoin de pansement.
zhā bezô·eN də päNs·mäN

Could you lend me . . .?
Pouvez-vous me prêter . . .?
po͞ovā-vo͞o mə prātā . . .

Could you . . .?
Pourriez-vous . . .?
po͞orē·ā vo͞o . . .

– give me a ride?
– m'emmener un bout de chemin?
– mämnā eN bo͞o də shəmeN

– tow my car?
– remorquer ma voiture?
– remôrkā mä vô·ät*ē*r

– get me a *mechanic (a tow truck)*?
– m'envoyer *un mécanicien (une dépanneuse)*?
– mäNvô·äyā eN mākänēsyeN (*ē*n dāpän*ā*z)

– look after the injured?
– prendre soin des blessés?
– präNd(ər) sô·eN dā blesā

Where is there a *service station (repair shop)*?
Où y a-t-il *une station-service (un garage)*?
o͞o yätēl *ē*n stäsyôN servēs (eN gärāzh)

Would you please give me your name and address?
Donnez-moi vos nom et adresse, s'il vous plaît.
dônā-mô·ä vō nôN ā ädres, sēl vo͞o plā

It's your fault.
C'est de votre faute.
sā də vôt(ər) fōt

I had the right of way.
J'avais la priorité.
zhävā lä prē·ôrētā

Nobody's hurt.
Personne n'est blessé.
persôn nā blesā

Will you be my witness?
Pouvez-vous être mon témoin?
po͞ovā-vo͞o āt(ər) môN tāmô·eN

You've damaged . . .
Vous avez abîmé . . .
vo͞ozävā äbēmā . . .

. . . is (badly) injured.
. . . est (grièvement) blessé.
. . . ā grē·äv·mäN blesā

Thanks very much for your help.
Merci beaucoup pour votre aide!
mersē bōko͞o po͞or vôtrād

Where is your car insured?
Où est assurée votre voiture?
o͞o ātäsərā vôt(ər) vô·ätər

accident	accident *m*	äksēdäN
bandages	pansement *m*	päNs·mäN
body and fender damage	dégâts *m/pl.* matériels	dāgä mätārē·el
breakdown	panne *f*	pän
careful!	Attention!	ätäNsyôN
collision	collision *f*	kôlēzyôN
damage	dommages *m/pl.*	dômäzh
dealership garage	garage *m* concessionnaire	gäräzh kôNsesyônār
emergency ward	poste *m* de secours	pôst də səko͞or
fire department	pompiers *m/pl.*	pôNpyā
first aid station	poste *m* de secours	pôst də səko͞or
head-on collision	collision *f* de face	kôlēzyôN də fäs
help	aide *f*, secours *m*	ād, səko͞or
injury	blessure *f*	blesər
insurance	assurance *f*	äsəräNs
mechanic	mécanicien *m*	mākänēsyeN
rear-end collision	télescopage *m*	tāläskôpäzh
repair shop	atelier *m* de réparation	ätelyā də rāpäräsyôN
service station	station-service *f*	stäsyôN servēs
towing service	service *m* de dépannage	servēs də dāpänäzh
tow line	câble *m* de remorquage	käb'əl də remôrkäzh
tow truck	dépanneuse *f*	dāpänəz

Repair Workshop

Where's the nearest *garage (Volkswagen garage)*?
Où est *le garage* (i.e. *Volkswagen*) le plus proche?
o͞o ā lə gäräzh (fōlksvägān . . .) lə plē̆ prôsh

. . . isn't working right.
. . . n'est pas en bon état.
. . . nāpä äN bônātä

. . . is out of order (isn't working).
. . . ne marche pas.
. . . nə märsh pä

Can you fix it?
Pouvez-vous faire cela?
po͞ovā-vo͞o fār səlä

Where can I have this fixed?
Qui peut faire cela?
kē pā̆ fār səlä

Would you please check the . . .
Vérifiez . . ., s'il vous plaît.
vārēfē·ā . . ., sēl vo͞o plā

Would you please give me . . .
Donnez-moi, s'il vous plaît . . .
dônā-mô·ä, sēl vo͞o plā . . .

Would you please fix this.
Réparez cela, s'il vous plaît.
rāpärā səlä, sēl vo͞o plā

Have you got manufacturer's spare parts for . . .?
Avez-vous des pièces de rechange d'origine pour . . .?
ävā-vo͞o dā pyās də reshäNzh dôrēzhēn po͞or . . .

How soon can you get the spare parts?
Quand aurez-vous les pièces de rechange?
käNdôrā-vo͞o lā pyās də reshäNzh

I need a new . . .
J'ai besoin *d'une nouvelle (d'un nouveau)* . . .
zhā bezô·eN dē̆n no͞ovel (deN no͞ovō) . . .

Can I still drive it?
Puis-je encore rouler ainsi?
pē̆·ēzhäNkôr ro͞olā eNsē

Just do the essentials, please.
Ne faites que les réparations strictement nécessaires.
nə fāt ke lā rāpäräsyôN strēkt·mäN nāsesār

When will it be ready?
Quand la voiture sera-t-elle prête?
käN lä vô·ätē̆r serätel prāt

How much *does (will)* it cost?
Ça *coûte (coûtera)* combien?
sä ko͞ot (ko͞oterä) kôNbyeN

Car Parts, Repairs

accelerator	accélérateur *m*	äkselārätār
– accelerate	accélérer	äkselārā
– slow down	ralentir	räläNtēr
air filter	filtre *m* d'air	fēlt(ər) dār
air pump	pompe *f* à air	pôNp ä ār
anti-freeze	antigel *m*	äNtēzhāl
automatic transmission	changement *m* de vitesse automatique	shäNzh·mäN də vētes ôtōmätēk
axle	essieu *m*	esyā
backfire	raté *m*	rätā
ball bearings	roulement *m* à billes	ro͞olmäN ä bē'ē
battery	batterie *f*	bätərē
bearing	coussinet *m*	ko͞osēnā
blinker	clignotant *m*	klēnyôtäN
body	carrosserie *f*	kärôsrē
bolt; nut	vis *f*; écrou *m*	vēs; äkro͞o
brake drum	tambour *m* de frein	täNbo͞or də freN
brake fluid	liquide *m* de freinage	lēkēd də frenäzh
brake lights	feux *m/pl.* de stop	fā də stôp
brake lining	garniture *f* de frein	gärnētēr də freN
brakes	freins *m/pl.*	freN
– disc brake	frein *m* à disques	freN ä dēsk
– foot brake	frein *m* à pied	freN ä pyā
– hand brake	frein *m* à main	freN ä meN
bulb	ampoule *f*	äNpo͞ol
– change the bulb	changer l'ampoule	shäNzhā läNpo͞ol
bumper	pare-chocs *m*	pär-shôk
cable	câble *m*	käb'əl
camshaft	arbre *m* à cames	ärbrä käm

The battery *has run down (needs charging).*
La batterie *est vide (Il faut recharger la batterie).*
lä bätərē ā vēd (ēl fō reshärzhā lä bätərē)

The brakes aren't working right.
Les freins ne sont pas en bon état.
lā freN nə sôN päzäN bônātä

They're *slack (too tight).*
Ils sont *peu (trop)* serrés.
ēl sôN pā (trō) serā

The brake drums are getting too hot.
Les tambours de frein chauffent.
lā täNbo͞or də freN shōf

carburetor	carburateur *m*	kärbərätär
carburetor jet	gicleur *m*	zhēklär
car door	portière *f*	pôrtyār
car keys	clé *f* de la voiture	klā də lä vô·ätər
chain	chaîne *f*	shān
– snow chains	chaînes *f/pl.* antidérapantes	shān äNtēdāräpäNt
chassis	chassis *m* de la voiture	shäsē də lä vô·ätər
clutch	embrayage *m*	äNbrāyäzh
– clutch pedal	pédale *f* d'embrayage	pādäl däNbrāyäzh
compression	compression *f*	kôNpresyôN
condenser	condensateur *m*	kôNdäNsätär
connecting rod	bielle *f*	byel
– connecting rod bearing	coussinet *m* de tête de bielle	ko͞osēnā də tāt də byel
contact	contact *m*	kôNtäkt
crankshaft	vilebrequin *m*	vēlbrekeN
cylinder	cylindre *m*	sēleNd(ər)
– cylinder head	culasse *f*	kəläs
– cylinder head gasket	joint *m* de culasse	zhô·eN də kəläs
diesel nozzle	gicleur *m* diesel	zhēklär dyezel
differential	différentiel *m*	dēfäräNsyel
dip stick	réglette-jauge *f*	rāglet-zhôzh
distributor	distributeur *m*	dēstrēbətär
door lock	serrure *f* de la portière	serər də lä pôrtyār
drive shaft	arbre *m moteur (de couche)*	ärb(ər) môtär (də ko͞osh)

The dynamo isn't charging.
La dynamo ne fonctionne pas.
lä dēnämō nə fôNksyôn pä

It won't stay in ... gear.
La ... vitesse est mal enclenchée.
lä ... vētes ā mäl äNkläNshā

The gearshift needs to be checked over.
Il faut contrôler la boîte à vitesses.
ēl fō kôNtrôlā lä bô·ät ä vētes

There's oil leaking out of the gear-box.
Il y a de l'huile qui goutte de la boîte à vitesses.
ēlyä də lē·ēl kē go͞ot də lä bô·ät ä vētes

dynamo	dynamo *f*	dēnämō
exhaust	échappement *m*	āshäp·mäN
fan	ventilateur *m*	väNtēlätār
fan belt	courroie *f* trapézoidale	kōōrô·ä träpāzō·ēdäl
fender	garde-boue *m*	gärd-bōō
fire extinguisher	extincteur *m*	ekstεNktār
float	flotteur *m*	flôtār
free wheel (hub)	moyeu *m* à roue libre	mô·äyā ä rōō lēb(ər)
fuel injector	pompe *f* à injection	pôNp ä eNyeksyôN
fuel lines	conduite *f* d'essence	kôNdē·ēt desäNs
fuel pump	pompe *f* à essence	pôNp ä esäNs
fuse	fusible *m*	fēsēb'əl
gas	accélérateur *m*	äkselārätār
gasket	joint *m*	zhô·eN
gear	vitesse *f*	vētes
– neutral	point *m* mort	pô·eN môr
– reverse	marche *f* arrière	märsh äryār
– to put it in gear	passer en ... vitesse	päsā äN ... vētes
gear box	boîte *f* de vitesses	bô·ät də vētes
gear lever	levier *m* de changement de vitesse	levyā də shäNzh-mäN də vētes
gearshift	changement *m* de vitesse	shäNzh·mäN də vētes
grease	graisse *f*	gres
handle	poignée *f*	pô·änyā
headlight	phare *m*	fär
– dimmed headlights	feux *m/pl.* de croisement	fā də crô·äz·mäN

The heating doesn't work.
Le chauffage ne fonctionne pas.
lə shôfäzh nə fôNksyôn pä

The radiator has sprung a leak.
Il y a de l'eau qui goutte du radiateur.
ēlyä də lō kē gōōt dē rädē·ätār

The clutch *slips (won't disengage)*.
L'embrayage *glisse (ne débraie pas)*.
läNbrāyäzh glēs (nə dābrā pä)

– high beam	feux *m/pl.* de route	fā də ro͞ot
– parking lights	feux *m/pl.* de position	fā də pôzēsyôN
– rear lights	feux *m/pl.* arrières	fā äryār
heating system	chauffage *m*	shôfäzh
hood	capot *m*	käpō
horn	avertisseur *m* sonore	ävertēsār sônôr
– flashing signal	avertisseur *m* lumineux	ävertēsār lēmēnā
hub	moyeu *m*	mô·äyā
hub cap	enjoliveur *m*	äNzhôlēvār
ignition	allumage *m*	älēmäzh
– ignition cable	fil *m* d'allumage	fēl dälēmäzh
– ignition key	clé *f* de contact	klā də kôNtäkt
– ignition lock	serrure *f* de contact	serēr də kôNtäkt
– ignition system	installation *f* de l'allumage	eNstäläsyôN də lälēmäzh
indicator light	lampe-témoin *f*	läNp-tāmô·eN
insulation	isolement *m*	ēzôlmäN
interrupter	interrupteur *m*	eNterēptār
lamp	lampe *f*	läNp
license plate	plaque *f* d'immatriculation	pläk dēmätrēkēläsyôN
lighting system	éclairage *m*	āklārāzh
lubricant	lubrifiant *m*; graisse *f*	lēbrēfē·äN; gres
mileage indicator	compteur *m* kilométrique	kôNtār kēlōmātrēk
motor	moteur *m*	môtār
– diesel motor	moteur *m* diésel	môtār dyezel
– rear motor	moteur *m* à l'arrière	môtār äläryār
– two-stroke motor	moteur *m* (à) deux temps	môtār (ä) dā täN

The motor lacks power.
Le moteur ne tire pas.
lə môtār nə tēr pä

– is overheating.
– chauffe.
– shôf

– knocks.
– cogne.
– kôn(yə)

– suddenly stalls.
– cale.
– käl

– misses.
– a des ratés.
– ä dā rätā

nationality plate	plaque *f* de nationalité	pläk də näsyônälētā
oil filter	filtre *m* à huile	fēlt(ər) ä *ē*·ēl
oil pump	pompe *f* à huile	pôNp ä *ē*·ēl
paint job	laque *m, f*	läk
pedal	pédale *f*	pādäl
piston	piston *m*	pēstôN
– piston ring	segment *m* de piston	segmäN də pēstôN
pipe	chambre *f* à air	shäNb(ər) ä är
radiator	radiateur *m*	rädē·ät*ār*
– radiator grill	volet *m* du radiateur	vôlā d*ē* rädē·ät*ār*
rear view mirror	rétroviseur *m*	rātrōvēz*ār*
repair	réparation *f*	rāpäräsyôN
reserve fuel can	bidon *m* de réserve	bēdôN də rāzärv
roof	capote *f*	käpôt
screw	vis *f*	vēs
seat belt	ceinture *f* de sécurité	seNt*ēr* də sāk*ē*rētā
shock absorber	amortisseur *m*	ämôrtēs*ār*
short circuit	court-circuit *m*	ko͞or-sērk*ē*·ē
***sliding (sun)* roof**	toit *m* ouvrant	tô·ä o͞ovräN
solder	souder	so͞odā
speedometer	tachymètre *m*	täkēmāt(ər)
spoke	rayon *m*	rāyôN
seat	siège *m*	syāzh
– back seat	siège *m* arrière	syāzh äryār
– driver's seat	siège *m* du conducteur	syāzh d*ē* kôNd*ē*kt*ār*
– front seat	siège *m* avant	syāzh äväN
– front passenger seat	siège *m* avant droit	syāzh äväN drô·ä
spare part	pièce *f* de rechange	pyās də reshäNzh
spare wheel	roue *f* de secours	ro͞o də səko͞or

The windshield wiper *smears (is broken off)*.
L'essuie-glace *nettoie mal (est cassé)*.
les*ē*·ē-gläs netô·ä mäl (ā käsā)

This screw needs *tightening (loosening)*.
Cette vis doit être *serrée (desserrée)*.
set vēs dô·ätät(ər) serā (deserā)

The fuse has blown.
Le fusible est fondu.
lə f*ē*zēblā fôNd*ē*

spark	étincelle *f*	āteNsel
spark plug	bougie *f* d'allumage	bo͞ozhē däl*ē*mäzh
spring	ressort *m*	resôr
starter	démarreur *m*	dāmär*ā*r
steering	conduite *f*	kôNd*ē*·ēt
– steering wheel	volant *m*	vôläN
switch	commutateur *m*	kôm*ē*tät*ā*r
thermostat	thermostat *m*	termôstä
(screw) thread	filet *m*	fēlā
top	capote *f*	käpôt
transmission	boîte *f* de vitesses	bô·ät də vētes
trunk	coffre *m*	kôf(ər)
tube	chambre *f* à air	shäNbrä ār
valve	soupape *f*	so͞opäp
warning triangle	triangle *m* avertisseur	trē·äNgl ävertēs*ā*r
washer	produit *m* du lave-vitre	prôd*ē*·ē d*ē* läv-vēt(ər)
wheel	roue *f*	ro͞o
windshield	pare-brise *m*	pär-brēz
windshield washer	lave-vitre *m*	läv-vēt(ər)
windshield wiper	essuie-glace *m*	es*ē*·ē-gläs

Would you please straighten out my bumper?
Redressez le pare-chocs, s'il vous plaît.
redresā lə pär-shôk, sēl vo͞o plā

Would you please *check (clean)* the carburetor?
Voudriez-vous *vérifier (nettoyer)* le carburateur?
vo͞odrē·ā·-vo͞o vārēfē·ā (netô·äyā) lə kärb*ē*rät*ā*r

Would you please change the spark plugs?
Changez les bougies, s'il vous plaît.
shäNzhā lā bo͞ozhē, sēl vo͞o plā

Tools

Can you loan me . . .?
Pourriez-vous me prêter . . .?
poorē·ā-voo mə prātā

I need . . .
J'ai besoin de . . .
zhā bezô·eN də

air pump	pompe *f* à air	pôNpä ār
bolt	vis *f*	vēs
– nut	écrou *m*	ākroo
cable	câble *m*	käb'əl
chisel	ciseau *m*	sēzō
cloth	chiffon *m*	shēfôN
drill	foret *m*	fôrā
file	lime *f*	lēm
funnel	entonnoir *m*	äNtônô·är
hammer	marteau *m*	märtō
inspection light	lampe-témoin *f*	läNp-tāmô·eN
jack	cric *m*	krēk
pincers	tenailles *f/pl.*	tenä'ē
pliers	pinces *f/pl.*	peNs
rag	chiffon *m*	shēfôN
sandpaper	papier *m* verré	päpyā verā
screw	vis *f*	vēs
screwdriver	tournevis *m*	toorn·vēs
socket wrench	clé *f* à douille	klā ä doo'ē
string	ficelle *f*	fēsel
tool	outil *m*	ootē
– tool *box (kit)*	coffre *m* à outils	kôfrä ootē
wire	fil *m* métallique	fēl mātälēk
– a piece of wire	un bout de fil métallique	eN boo də fēl mātälēk
wrench	clé *f* anglaise	klā äNglāz

TRAFFIC SIGNS

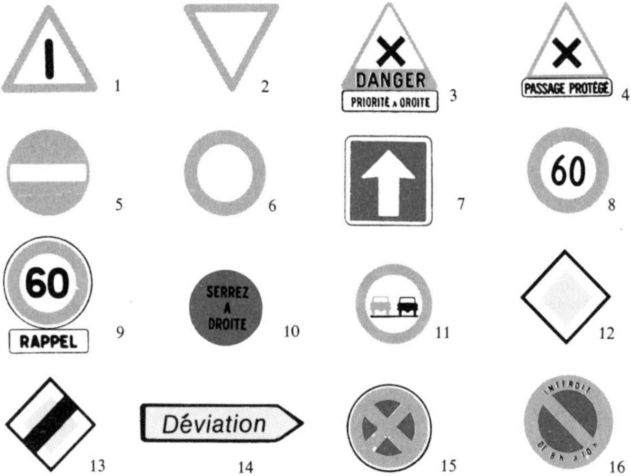

1 DANGER Danger · 2 YIELD RIGHT OF WAY Cédez le passage · 3 DANGER – GIVE WAY TO TRAFFIC FROM RIGHT Priorité à droite · 4 PRIORITY CROSSING *(for you)* Intersection de priorité · 5 DO NOT ENTER Sens interdit · 6 NO VEHICLES ALLOWED Circulation interdite à tout véhicule dans les deux sens · 7 ONE WAY STREET Sens unique · 8 SPEED LIMIT *(kilometers)* Limitation de vitesse · 9 SPEED LIMIT CONTINUED Rappel de vitesse limitée · 11 NO PASSING Interdiction de dépasser · 10 KEEP RIGHT Serrez à droite · 12 PRIORITY ROAD Route à priorité · 13 END OF PRIORITY ROAD Fin de route à priorité · 14 DETOUR Déviation · 15 NO STOPPING Arrêt interdit · 16 NO PARKING *between 8 and 10 a.m.* Stationnement interdit (entre 8 et 10h)

> Road signs are color and shape-coded. Triangular signs with a red rim are *warning signs*; round blue signs are *regulatory signs*; round signs with a red rim are *prohibit movement signs*; rectangular yellow signs with a black rim are *destination signs*; rectangular blue signs with white letters are *destination signs* on highways.

ON THE BUS

Where is the next bus stop?
Où est l'arrêt d'autobus le plus proche?
o͞o ā lärā dôtōbēs lə plē prôsh

Where do the buses to . . . stop?
Où s'arrêtent les autobus pour . . .?
o͞o särāt lāzôtōbēs po͞or . . .

Is that far?
Est-ce loin?
es lô•eN

When does *a (the first/last)* bus leave for . . .?
Quand part *un (le premier/dernier)* autobus pour . . .?
käN pär eNôtōbēs (lə prəmyā / dernyā ôtōbēs) po͞or

Which bus goes to . . .?
Quel autobus va à . . .?
kel ôtōbēs vä ä . . .

Where does the bus go?
Où va l'autobus?
o͞o vä lôtōbēs

***Is there a bus (Does this bus go)* to . . .?**
Y a-t-il un autobus pour . . . (Cet autobus va-t-il à . . .)?
ēyätēl eNôtōbēs po͞or . . . (set ôtōbēs vätēl ä . . . .)

When do we get to . . .?
Quand arrivons-nous à . . .?
käNdärēvôN-no͞o ä . . .

Do I have to change buses for . . .?
Faut-il changer d'autobus pour . . .?
fōt-ēl shäNzhā dôtōbēs po͞or . . .

Where do I have to change?
Où faut-il changer?
o͞o fōt-ēl shäNzhā

***One (Two)* round-trip ticket(s), please.**
Un ticket (Deux tickets) aller et retour pour . . .
eN tēkā (dā tēkā) älā ā reto͞or po͞or

One full-fare and one half-fare to . . . please.
Un ticket et une demi-place pour . . ., s'il vous plaît.
eN tēkā ā ēn dəmē-pläs po͞or . . ., sēl vo͞o plā

bus	autobus *m*	ôtōbes
bus terminal	terminus *m*	termēnēs
direction	direction *f*	dēreksyôN
driver	conducteur *m*	kôNdēktār
luggage	bagages *m/pl.*	bägäzh
route	ligne *f*	lēn(yə)
stop	arrêt *m*	ärā
ticket	ticket *m*, billet *m*	tēkā, bēyā
transfer	ticket *m* de correspondance	tēkā də kôrespôNdäNs

At the Station

BY TRAIN

Where is the *station (main station)?*
Où est la gare (centrale)?
o͞o ā lä gär (säNträl)

Where *is (are)* ...?
Où *est (sont)* ... ?
o͞o ā (sôN)

baggage check area	l'enregistrement *m* des bagages	läNrezhēstrəmäN dä bägäzh
baggage claim area	la consigne	lä kôNsēn(yə)
first aid station	l'infirmerie *f*	leNfērmərē
information office	le bureau de renseignements	lə bērō də räNsen(yə)mäN
Platform 2	le quai deux	lə kā dā
rest room	les toilettes *f/pl.*, les lavabos *m/pl.*	lā tô·älet, lā läväbō
room referral office	la réservation de chambres	lä rāzerväsyôN də shäNb(ər)
ticket window	le guichet	lə gēshā
a time table	l'horaire *m.*	lôrār
waiting room	la salle d'attente	lä säl dätäNt

Time Table

arrival/departure	arrivée *f*/départ *m*	ärēvā/dāpär
connection	correspondance *f*	kôrespôNdäNs
couchette sleeper	voiture-couchettes *f*	vô·ätēr-ko͞oshet
dining car	wagon-restaurant *m*	vägôN-restôräN
express train	train *m* direct; express *m*	treN dērekt; ekspres
fast train	rapide *m*	räpēd
motorail service	train *m* auto-couchettes	treN ôtō-ko͞oshet
platform	voie *f*; quai *m*	vô·ä; kā
rail car	automotrice *f*	ôtōmôtrēs
sleeper/sleeping car	wagon-lit *m*	vägôN-lē
suburban train	train *m* de banlieue	treN də bäNlēyā

A couchette *car provides overnight travelers with a simple bench and blanket to stretch out during the night. A sleeping car* (wagon-lit) *contains little bedrooms complete with private washing facilities.*

system time table ...	indicateur *m*, Chaix *m* .	eNdēkätär, shäks
through car	voiture *f* directe	vô·ätēr dērekt
track	voie *f*	vô·ä

Information

When is there a *local (express)* train to ...?
Quand part un *train omnibus (express)* pour ...?
käN pär eN treN ômnēbēs (ekspres) pōōr ...

Where is the train to ...?
Où est le train pour ...?
ōō ā lə treN pōōr ...

Is this the train to ...?
Est-ce le train pour ...?
es lə treN pōōr ...

Does this train go by way of ....?
Ce train passe par ...?
sə treN päs pär ...

Does this train stop in ...?
Ce train s'arrête à ...?
sə treN särāt ä ...

Is the train from ... late?
Le train de ... a du retard?
lə treN də ... ä dē retär

How late?
Combien?
kôNbyeN

When does it get to ...?
Quand arrive-t-il à ...?
käNdärēvtēl ä ...

Can we make a connection to...?
Avons-nous une correspondance pour ...?
ävôN-nōō ēn kôrespôNdäNs pōōr ...

Do we have to change trains?
Faut-il changer de train?
fōtēl shäNzhā də treN

Where?
Où?
ōō

***Is there a dining car (Are there sleepers)* on the train?**
Le train a un *wagon-restaurant (wagon-lit)?*
lə treN ä eN vägôN-restôräN (vägôN-lē)

Can I interrupt the trip in ...?
Je peux interrompre mon voyage à ...?
zhə päzeNterôNp(ər) môN vô·äyäzh ä ...

What platform does the train from ... come in on?
Sur quel quai arrive le train de ...?
sēr kel kā ärēv lə treN də ...

What platform does the train for ... leave from?
De quel quai part le train pour ...?
də kel kā pär lə treN pōōr ...

Tickets

– round trip.
– aller et retour.
– älā ā reto͞or

– one way.
– aller.
– älā

– first class.
– de première.
– də prəmyār

– second class.
– de seconde.
– də səgôNd

I'd like to reserve a seat on the twelve o'clock train to . . .
Je voudrais réserver une place pour le train de douze heures pour . . .
zhə vo͞odrā rāzervā ēn pläs po͞or lə treN də do͞ozär po͞or . . .

How long is the ticket valid?
Jusqu'à quand ce billet est-il valable?
zhēskä käN sə bēyā etēl väläb'əl

I'd like to interrupt the trip in . . .
J'aimerais interrompre le voyage à . . .
zhāmerā eNterôNp(ər) lə vô·äyäzh ä . . .

I'd like to reserve . . .
Je voudrais réserver . . .
zhə vo͞odrā rāzervā . . .

Please reserve two seats.
Réservez deux places, sil vous plaît.
rāzervā dā pläs, sēl vo͞o plā

How much is the fare to . . .?
Le billet pour . . . coûte combien?
lə bēyā po͞or . . . ko͞ot kôNbyeN

fare	prix *m* du billet	prē dē bēyā
group fare ticket	billet *m* de groupe	bēyā də gro͞op
half fare	demi-place *f*	dəmē-pläs
one-day round-trip	aller et retour valable vingt-quatre heures	älā ā reto͞or väläb'əl veN-käträr
round-trip ticket	billet *m* circulaire	bēyā sērkelār
seat reservation	réservation *f* de place assise	rāzerväsyôN də pläs äsēz
sleeper reservation	réservation *f* de wagon-lit	rāzerväsyôN də vägôN-lē
supplemental fare ticket	supplément *m*	sēplāmäN
ticket	ticket *m*; billet *m*	tēkā; bēyā
– one-way ticket	billet *m* aller	bēyā älā
– reduced fare ticket	billet *m* à tarif réduit	bēyā ä tärēf rādē·ē

Baggage

In European countries, you can check your bag with the railroad, just as you do with an airline, and then pick it up at your destination. If you are checking your baggage to be forwarded, you should go to the Enregistrement des bagages (äNrezhēstrəmäN dā bägäzh). *If you are simply checking your luggage within the station, go to the* Consigne (automatique), (kôNsēnyə ōtōmätēk).

I'd like to . . .
Je voudrais . . .
zhə vo͞odrā . . .

– send this luggage on to . . .
– faire enregistrer ces bagages pour . . .
– fãr äNrezhēstrā sā bägäzh po͞or . . .

– leave this luggage here.
– laisser ces bagages ici.
– lesā sā bägäzh ēsē

– *insure (claim)* my luggage.
– *faire assurer (retirer)* mes bagages.
– fãr äsərā (retērā) mā bägäzh

Here's my claim check.
Voici le bulletin d'enregistrement.
vô·äsē lə bəlteN däNrezhēstrəmäN

There are two suitcases and a traveling bag.
Il y a deux valises et un sac de voyage.
ēlyä dā välēz ā eN säk də vô·äyäzh

Will my baggage be on the same train?
Mes bagages partent par le même train?
mā bägäzh pärt pär lə mām treN

When does it get to . . .?
Quand arriveront-ils à . . .
käNdärēvərôNt-ēlzä . . .

These aren't mine.
Ce ne sont pas mes bagages.
se nə sôN pä mā bägäzh

One suitcase is missing.
Il manque une valise.
ēl mäNk ən välēz

baggage, luggage	bagages *m/pl.*	bägäzh
baggage check area/ forwarding office . .	enregistrement *m* des bagages	äNrezhēstrəmäN dā bägäzh
baggage claim/(deposit)area	consigne *f*	kôNsēn(yə)
claim check	bulletin *m* d'enregistrement	bəlteN däNrezhēstrəmäN
hand luggage	bagage *m* à main	bägäzh ä meN

luggage locker ...... consigne *f* automatique .... kôNsēn(yə) ôtōmätēk
suitcase .... valise *f* .... välēz
traveling bag .... sac *m* de voyage ...... säk də vô·äyäzh

Porter

porter .... porteur *m* .... pôrtär

Please bring this *luggage (suitcase)* ...
Ces bagages (Cette valise), s'il vous plaît,
sā bägäzh (set välēz), sēl vo͞o plā

– to the ... train.
– au train pour ...
– ō treN po͞or

– to the baggage check area.
– à la consigne (à l'enregistrement des bagages).
– älä kôNsēn(yə) (ä läNrezhēstrəmäN dā bägäzh)

– to the exit.
– à la sortie.
– älä sôrtē

– to a taxi.
– au taxi.
– ō täksē

– to the ... bus.
– à l'autobus pour ...
– ä lôtōbēs po͞or ...

How much does that cost?
Ça coûte combien?
sä ko͞ot kôNbyeN

On the Platform

Is this the train *to (from)* ...?
Est-ce le train *pour (venant de)* ...?
es lə treN po͞or (venäN də) ...

Where is ...?
Où est ...?
o͞o ā ...

– first class?
– la première classe?
– lä prəmyär kläs

– the through car to ...?
– la voiture directe pour ...?
– lä vô·ätēr dērekt po͞or ...

European express trains frequently get reassembled at major stations with different cars going to different destinations. Make sure before you get aboard that your car will take you where you want to go.

– the luggage car?
– le fourgon?
– lə fo͞orgôN

– car number ...?
– la voiture numéro ...?
– lä vô·ätēr nēmārō ...

– the couchette car?
– la voiture-couchettes?
– lä vô·ätēr-ko͞oshet

– the sleeping car?
– le wagon-lit?
– lə vägôN-lē

– the dining car?
– le wagon-restaurant?
– lə vägôN-restôräN

There.
Là (Là-bas).
lä (läbä)

Up front.
À l'avant.
äläväN

In the middle.
Au milieu.
ō mēlēy*ā*

At the rear.
À l'arrière (En queue).
äläryār (äN k*a*)

What time does the train arrive?
À quelle heure arrive le train?
ä kel*ā*r ärēv lə treN

CHEF DE GARE
shef də gär
Station Master

SORTIE
sôrtē
Exit

RENSEIGNEMENTS
räNsen(yə)mäN
Information

ACCÈS AU QUAIS
äksā ō kā
To Trains

ENREGISTREMENT DES BAGAGES
äNrezhēstrəmäN dā bägäzh
Luggage Checking

VOIE
vô•ä
Platform (Track)

POSTE DE SECOURS
pôst də səkōōr
First Aid

EAU POTABLE
ō pôtäb'əl
Drinking Water

LAVABOS
läväbō
Rest Rooms

MESSIEURS
mesy*ā*
Gentlemen

DAMES
däm
Ladies

PONT
pôN
Overpass

SALLE D'ATTENTE
säl dätäNt
Waiting Room

PASSAGE SOUTERRAIN
päsäzh sōōtereN
Underpass

On the Train

Is this seat taken?
Cette place est libre, s'il vous plaît?
set pläs ā lēb(ər), sēl vōō plā

That's my seat.
C'est ma place.
sā mä pläs

Mind if I *open (close)* the window?
Vous permettez que *j'ouvre (je ferme)* la fenêtre?
vōō permetā kə zhōōv(ər) (zhə fārm) lä fenāt(ər)

Could you please help me?
Pourriez-vous m'aider, s'il vous plaît?
po͞orē·ā-vo͞o mādā, sēl vo͞o plā

Would you mind changing places?
Pourrions-nous changer de place?
po͞orē·ôN-no͞o shäNzhā də pläs

I don't like riding backwards.
Je n'aime pas rouler dans le sens contraire de la marche.
zhə nām pä ro͞olā däN lə säNs kôNtrār dəlä märsh

***Tickets, please.**
Les billets, s'il vous plaît.
lā bēyā, sēl vo͞o plā

How many stations before . . .?
Combien d'arrêts y a-t-il encore jusqu'à . . .?
kôNbyeN därā yätēl äNkôr zhēskä . . .

Will we get to . . . on time?
Arrivons-nous à l'heure à . . .?
ärēvôN-no͞o älār ä . . .

Where are we now?
Où sommes-nous maintenant?
o͞o sôm-no͞o meNtənäN

How long do we stop here?
Combien de temps le train s'arrête ici?
kôNbyeN də täN lə treN säret ēsē

***All change, please!**
Tout le monde descend!
to͞o lə môNd·desäN

Will I make it on time to change trains for . . .?
Est-ce que j'aurai la correspondance pour . . .?
eske zhôrā lä kôrespôNdäNs po͞or . . .

***Passengers for . . . change at . . .**
Messieurs les voyageurs pour . . . changez à . . .
mesyā lā vô·äyäzhār po͞or . . . shäNzhā ä . . .

***Passengers for . . . get on the *front (rear)* of the train!**
Messieurs les voyageurs pour . . ., montez en voiture *à l'avant (à l'arrière)* du train!
mesyā lā vô·äyäzhār po͞or . . . môNtā äN vô·ätēr ä läväN (äläryār) dē treN

NON-FUMEURS	FUMEURS	LIBRE	OCCUPÉ
No smoking	**Smoking**	**Vacant**	**Occupied**

WAGON-RESTAURANT	WAGON-LIT
Dining Car	**Sleeping Car**

***all aboard!**	en voiture, s'il vous plaît!	äN vô·ätēr, sēl vo͞o plā
arrival	arrivée *f*	ärēvā
arrive	arriver	ärēvā
baggage, luggage	bagages *m/pl.*	bägäzh
baggage car	fourgon *m*	fo͞orgôN
barrier	barrière *f*	bäryār
car	voiture *f*	vô·ätēr
car door	portière *f*	pôrtyār
change trains	changer de train	shäNzhā də treN
compartment	compartiment *m*	kôNpärtēmäN
conductor	contrôleur *m*	kôNtrôlār
connection	correspondance *f*	kôrespôNdäNs
depart	partir	pärtēr
departure	départ *m*	dāpär
engine, locomotive	locomotive *f*	lōkōmōtēv
entrance	entrée *f*	äNtrā
exit	sortie *f*	sôrtē
fare	prix *m* du billet	prē dē bēyā
– discount	tarif *m* réduit	tärēf rādē·ē
get *in (aboard)*	monter (en voiture)	môNtā (äN vô-ätēr)
get off	descendre	desäNd(ər)
heating	chauffage *m*	shôfäzh
– cold	froid	frô·ä
– warm	chaud	shō
information	renseignement *m*	räNsen(yə)mäN
luggage rack	filet *m*	fēlā
passenger	voyageur *m*	vô·äyäzhār
platform	quai *m*	kā
railroad	chemin *m* de fer	shəmeN də fār
route	ligne *f*	lēn(yə)
station	gare *f*	gär
station master	chef *m* de gare	shef də gär
stop	arrêt *m*	ärā
system time table	indicateur *m*, Chaix *m*	eNdēkätār, shāks
ticket	billet *m*, ticket *m*	bēyā, tēkā
track	voie *f*	vô·ä
train	train *m*	treN
window seat	coin-fenêtre *m*	kô·eN-fnāt(ər)

BY AIR

Information and Reservations

Is there a (direct) flight to . . .?
Y a-t-il un vol (direct) pour . . .?
ēyätēl eN vôl (dērekt) po͞or

Is there a connection to . . .?
J'ai une correspondance pour . . .?
zhā ēn kôrespôNdäNs po͞or

When is there a plane *today (tomorrow)* to . . .?
À quelle heure part *aujourd'hui (demain)* un avion pour . . .?
äkelär pär ōzho͞ordē·ē (demeN) eNävyôN po͞or

When is the next plane to . . .?
Quand part le prochain appareil pour . . .?
käN pär lə prôshenäpärā'ē po͞or

Does the plane make a stopover in . . .?
L'appareil fait escale à . . .?
läpärā'ē fāteskäl ä

When do we get to . . .?
À quelle heure serons-nous à . . .?
äkelär serôN-no͞ozä

Are there still seats available?
Il y a encore des places libres?
ēlyä äNkôr dā pläs lēb(ər)

How much is a (round-trip) flight to . . .?
Combien coûte un vol (aller et retour) à . . .?
kôNbyeN ko͞ot eN vôl (älā ā reto͞or) ä

What's the luggage allowance?
À combien de bagages a-t-on droit?
ä kôNbyeN də bägäzh ätôN drô·ä

How much does excess baggage cost?
Les bagages en excédent, c'est combien?
lā bägäzh äNeksādäN, sā kôNbyeN

How much is the airport service charge?
La taxe d'aéroport, c'est combien?
lä täks dä·ārōpôr, sā kôNbyeN

How do I get to the airport?
Pour aller à l'aéroport?
po͞or älā älä·ārōpôr

When is check-in time?
Je dois me présenter au guichet à quelle heure?
zhə dô·ä mə prāzäNtā ō gēshā äkelär

I'd like to reserve a seat on the Friday flight to . . .
Je voudrais faire une réservation pour un vol pour . . ., vendredi, s. v. p.
zhə vo͞odrā fār ēn rāzerväsyôN po͞or eN vôl po͞or . . ., väNdrədē, sēl vo͞o plā

I'd like to reserve a round-trip ticket to . . . on the 8th of May.
Réservez un vol aller et retour pour le huit mai pour . . ., s'il vous plaît.
rāzervā eN vôl älā ā rəto͞or po͞or lə ē·ē mā po͞or . . ., sēl vo͞o plā

– First Class.
– première classe.
– prəmyār kläs

– Economy Class.
– classe économique.
– kläs ākônōmēk

How much does it cost?
Combien dois-je payer?
kôNbyeN dô·äzh pāyā

How long is the ticket valid?
Quelle est la durée de validité du billet d'avion?
kel ā lä dērā də välēdētā dē bēyā dävyôN

I have to *cancel (change)* my reservation.
Il me faut *annuler (changer)* la réservation.
ēl mə fōtänēlā (shäNzhā) lä rāzerväsyôN

What is the cancellation fee?
La taxe d'annulation, c'est combien?
lä täks dänēläsyôN, sā kôNbyeN

At the Airport

Can I take this along as hand luggage?
Puis-je prendre cela comme bagage à main?
pē·ēzh präNd(ər) səlä kôm bägäzh ä meN

Where is *the waiting room (Exit B, Gate B)*?
Où est *la salle d'attente (la sortie B)*?
o͞o ā lä säl dätäNt (lä sôrtē bā)

Where is the information counter?
Où sont les renseignements?
o͞o sôN lā räNsen(yə)mäN

Where's the duty-free shop?
Où peut-on acheter des marchandises hors-taxe?
o͞o pātôN äshtā dā märshäNdēz ôr-täks

Is the plane to . . . late?
L'appareil pour . . . a du retard?
läpärā·ē po͞or . . . ä dē retär

Has the plane from . . . already landed?
L'avion venant de . . . a-t-il déjà atterri?
lävyôN vənäN də . . . ätēl dāzhä äterē

On the Plane

***Kindly refrain from smoking.**
Éteignez vos cigarettes!
ātenyā vō sēgäret

***Please fasten your seat belts.**
Attachez vos ceintures!
ätäshā vō seNtẽr

How high are we flying?
À quelle altitude sommes-nous?
ä kel ältētẽd sôm-nōō

Where are we now?
Où sommes-nous maintenant?
ōō sôm-nōō meNt·näN

What *mountains are those (river is that)*?
Quelle montagne (Quel fleuve) est-ce?
kel môNtän(yə) (kel flãv) es

Can I have . . .?
Je peux avoir . . .?
zhə pãzävô·är

I feel sick.
J'ai mal au cœur.
zhā mäl ō kãr

Have you got an air-sickness remedy?
Avez-vous un remède contre le mal de l'air?
ävā-vōō eN rəmād kôNt(ər) lə mäl dəlār

When do we land?
Quand atterrissons-nous?
käNdäterēsôN-nōō

How's the weather in . . .?
Quel temps fait-il à . . .?
kel täN fātēl ä . . .

aircraft	avion *m*	ävyôN
air jet *(over the seat)*	buse *f* d'aération *f*	bẽz dä·äräsyôN
airline	compagnie *f* aérienne	kôNpänyē ä·ärē·en
air passenger	passager *m*	päsäzhā
airport	aéroport *m*	ä·ārōpôr
airport service charge	taxe *f* d'aéroport	täks dä·ārōpôr
air sickness	mal *m* de l'air	mäl də lār
approach	approche *f*	äprôsh
arrival	arrivée *f*	ärēvā
charter plane	charter *m*	shärtār
climb	s'élever	sāləvā
crew	équipage *m*	ākēpäzh
destination	destination *f*	destēnäsyôN
duty-free goods	marchandises *f/pl.* hors-taxe	märshäNdēz ôr-täks
emergency chute	glissoire *f* de secours	glēsô·är də səkōōr
emergency exit	sortie *f* de secours	sôrtē də səkōōr
emergency landing	atterrissage *m* forcé	äterēsäzh fôrsā

engine	réacteur *m*	rā·äktər̄
excess baggage	excédent *m* de bagages	eksādäN də bägäzh
exit	sortie *f*	sôrtē
flight	vol *m*	vôl
flight attendant	hôtesse *f* de l'air	ôtes də lār
fly	voler	vôlā
flying time	durée *f* de vol	dērā də vôl
fog	brouillard *m*	brooyär
fuselage	fuselage *m*	fēzəläzh
gate	pont *m* d'embarquement	pôN däNbärkmäN
hand luggage	bagage *m* à main	bägäzh ä meN
helicopter	hélicoptère *m*	ālēkôptār
information	information *f*	eNfôrmäsyôN
information counter	guichet *m* d'information	gēshā deNfôrmäsyôN
intermediate landing	escale *f*	eskäl
jet	turbo-réacteur *m*	tērbō-rā·äktər̄
jet plane	avion *m* à réaction	ävyôN ä rääksyôN
land	atterrir	äterēr
landing	atterrissage *m*	äterēsäzh
landing gear	train *m* d'atterrissage	treN däterēsäzh
life jacket	gilet *m* de sauvetage	zhēlā də sōvtäzh
pilot	commandant *m* de bord	kômäNdäN də bôr
plane	avion *m*	ävyôN
reservation	réservation *f*	rāzerväsyôN
return flight	vol *m* de retour	vôl də retoor
route	ligne *f* aérienne	lēn(yə) ä·ārē·en
scheduled flight	vol *m* régulier	vôl rāgēlyā
seat belt	ceinture *f*	seNtēr
– fasten seat belts	attachez vos ceintures	ätäshā vō seNtēr
stopover	escale *f*	eskäl
system timetable	indicateur *m* des liaisons aériennes	eNdēkätər̄ dā lē·äzôN ä·ārē·en
take-off	départ *m*	dāpär
thunderstorm	orage *m*	ôräzh
ticket	billet *m* d'avion	bēyā dävyôN
waiting room	salle *f* d'attente	säl dätäNt
weather	temps *m*	täN
wing	aile *f*	āl

ON BOARD SHIP

Information, Ship Tickets

When does *a ship (the ferry)* leave for . . .?
Quand part *un bateau (le ferry-boat)* pour . . .?
käN pär eN bätō (lə ferē-bōt) po͞or . . .

Where?
Où?
o͞o

How often does the car ferry go to . . .?
Combien de fois *(par jour/par semaine)* le ferry-boat va à . . .?
kôNbyeN də fô·ä (pär zho͞or/pär smen) lə ferē-bōt vä ä . . .
or: Est-ce que le ferry-boat va *souvent* à . . .?
eske lə ferē-bōt vä so͞oväNt ä . . .

How long does the crossing (from . . .) to . . . take?
Quelle est la durée de la traversée (de . . .) à . . .?
kel ā lä dērā də lä träversā (də . . .) ä . . .

How far is the railroad station from the harbour?
Quelle est la distance entre la gare et le port?
kel ā lä dēstäNs äNt(ər) lä gär ā lə pôr

What are the ports of call?
Dans quels ports fait-on escale?
däN kel pôr fātôN eskäl

When do we *dock (land)* at . . .?
Quand faisons-nous escale à . . .?
käN fāzôN-no͞o eskäl ä . . .

Can I get a connection to . . .?
J'ai une correspondance pour . . .?
zhä ēn kôrespôNdäNs po͞or . . .

Can we go ashore at . . .?
Peut-on descendre à terre à . . .?
pātôN desäNdrä tār ä . . .

For how long?
Combien de temps?
kôNbyeN də täN

Will there be any land excursions?
A-t-on organisé des excursions?
ätôN ôrgänēzā dāzekskērsyôN

Where can we get tickets?
On prend les billets où?
ôN präN lā bēyā o͞o

When do we have to be back on board?
À quelle heure faut-il être à bord?
äkelār fōtēl āträbôr

I'd like . . .
Je voudrais . . .
zhə vo͞odrā . . .

– to book passage to . . .
– un billet pour . . .
– eN bēyā po͞or . . .

– two tickets on the . . . to . . . tomorrow.
– deux billets sur le . . . qui part pour . . . demain.
– dā̆ bēyā sēr lə . . . kē pär po͞or . . . dəmeN

– a round-trip ticket from . . . to . . . and back.
– un billet circulaire de . . . à . . . et retour.
– eN bēyā sērkēlār də . . . ä . . . ā reto͞or

– a ticket for a *car (motorcycle, bicycle)*.
– un billet pour une *auto (motocyclette, bicyclette)*.
– eN bēyā po͞or ēn ôtō (môtōsēklet, bēsēklet)

– a single cabin.
– une cabine individuelle.
– ēn käbēn eNdēvēdē·el

– an *outside (inside)* cabin.
– une cabine *extérieure (intérieure)*.
– ēn käbēn ekstārē·ār (eNtārē·ār)

– a double cabin.
– une cabine à deux personnes.
– ēn käbēn ä dā persôn

First Class.
Première classe.
prəmyār kläs

Tourist Class.
Classe touriste.
kläs to͞orēst

In the Harbor

Where is the „. . ." lying?
Où a accosté le „. . ."?
o͞o ä äkôstā lə . . .

Where does the „. . ." dock?
Où accoste le „. . ."?
o͞o äkôst lə . . .

Does this ship sail to . . .?
Est-ce que ce bateau va à . . .?
eske se bätō vä ä . . .

When does she sail?
À quelle heure part-il?
äkelār pärtēl

Where is the *shipping company's office (harbor police station, customs office)*?
Où est *la compagnie de navigation (la police du port, l'administration des douanes)*?
o͞o ā lä kôNpänyē də nävēgäsyôN (lä pôlēs dē pôr, lädmēnēsträsyôN dā do͞o·än)

Where can I pick up my luggage?
Où est-ce que je reprends mes bagages?
o͞o eske zhə repräN mā bägäzh

I come from the „. . .".
Je viens du „. . .".
zhə vyeN dē . . .

On Board

I'm looking for cabin no. ...
Je cherche la cabine numéro ...
zhə shārsh lä käbēn nēmārō ...

Where's my baggage?
Où sont mes bagages?
o͞o sôN mā bägäzh

Have you got ... on board?
Avez-vous ... à bord?
ävā-vo͞o ... ä bôr

Please, where is ...?
Où est ..., s'il vous plaît?
o͞o ā ..., sēl vo͞o plā

the bar	le bar	lə bär
the ***barber shop (beauty parlor)***	*le salon de coiffure (le salon de beauté)*	lə sälôN də kô·äfēr (lə sälôN də bōtā)
the dining room	la salle à manger	lä säl ä mäNzhā
the lounge	la salle de séjour	lä säl də sāzho͞or
the purser's office	le bureau du commissaire	lə bērō dē kômēsār
the radio room	la cabine radio	lä käbēn rädē·ō
the reading room	la salle de lecture	lä säl də lektēr
the ship's photographer	le photographe de bord	lə fōtōgräf də bôr
the sick bay	l'hôpital	lôpētäl
the swimming pool	la piscine	lä pēsēn
the tour guide's office	le guide	lə gēd

I'd like to speak to the ...
J'aimerais parler au ...
zhāmrā pärlā ō

– captain	capitaine	käpēten
– chief steward	maître-d'hôtel	mātrə dôtel
– deck officer	premier officier	prəmyā ôfēsyā
– luggage master	responsable des bagages	respôNsäb'əl dā bägäzh
– purser	commissaire	kômēsār
– ship's doctor	médecin de bord	mādəseN də bôr
– tour guide	guide	gēd

Steward, please bring me ...
Garçon, apportez-moi ..., s'il vous plaît.
gärsôN, äpôrtā-mô·ä ..., sēl vo͞o plā

What is the voltage here?
Quel est le voltage?
kel ā lə vôltäzh

Please call the ship's doctor!
Appelez le médecin de bord, s'il vous plaît.
äplā lə mādəseN də bôr, sēl vo͞o plā

Have you got anything for seasickness?
Avez-vous un remède contre le mal de mer?
ävā-vo͞o eN remād kôNt(ər) lə mäl də mār

air conditioning	climatisation *f*	klēmätēzäsyôN
anchor	ancre *f*	äNk(ər)
bank	rivage *m*	rēväzh
barge	chaland *m*	shäläN
bay	baie *f*	bā
blanket	couverture *f*	ko͞overtēr
board	bord *m*	bôr
– on board	à bord	ä bôr
boat	bateau *m*	bätō
– fishing trawler	bateau *m* de pêche	bätō də pāsh
– launch	barcasse *f*	bärkäs
– lifeboat	canot *m* de sauvetage	känō də sōvtäzh
– motorboat	bateau *m* à moteur	bätō ä môtār
– sailboat	bateau *m* à voiles	bätō ä vô·äl
bow	proue *f*	pro͞o
breeze	brise *f*	brēz
bridge	passerelle *f* de manœuvre	päserel də mänāv(ər)
buoy	bouée *f*	bo͞o·ā
cabin	cabine *f*	käbēn
cable	câble *m*	käb'əl
call ***(at port)***	cordage *m*	kôrdäzh
canal	canal *m*	känäl
captain	capitaine *m*	käpēten
captain's table	table *f* du commandant	täb(əl) dē kômäN-däN
coast	côte *f*	kôt
course	route *f*	ro͞ot
crew	équipage *m*	ākēpäzh
crossing	traversée *f*	träversā
cruise	croisière *f*	krô·äzyār
deck	pont *m*	pôN
– boat deck	pont *m* des embarcations	pôN dāzäNbärkä-syôN

– foredeck	plage *f* avant	pläzh äväN
– main deck	pont *m* principal	pôN preNsēpäl
– poop deck	plage *f* arrière	pläzh äryār
– promenade deck	pont-promenade *m*	pôN-prômenäd
– saloon deck	pont *m* de première classe	pôN də prəmyār kläs
– steerage	entrepont *m*	äNtrəpôN
– sun deck	sundeck *m*	sändek
– upper deck	pont *m* supérieur	pôN sēpārē·ār
deck chair	chaise *f* longue	shāz-lôNg
disembark	débarquer	dābärkā
dock *(noun)*	débarcadère *f*	dābärkädār
dock *(verb)*	aborder	äbôrdā
excursion	excursion *f* (à terre)	ekskērsyôN (ä tār)
excursion program	programme *m* d'excursion	prôgräm dekskērsyôN
farewell dinner	dîner *m* d'adieux	dēnā dädyā
ferry	ferry-boat *m*	ferē-bōt
– car ferry	ferry-boat *m*	ferē-bōt
– train ferry	ferry-boat *m*	ferē-bōt
first officer	premier officier *m*	prəmyā ôfēsyā
gangway	passerelle *f*	päserel
harbor	port *m*	pôr
harbor police	police *f* du port	pôlēs dē pôr
helm	gouvernail *m*	go͞overnä'ē
helmsman	pilote *m*	pēlôt
island	île *f*	ēl
jetty	môle *m*	môl
knot	nœud *m*	nā
lake	lac *m*	läk
land *(noun)*	terre *f*	tār
land *(verb)*	aborder, accoster	äbôrdā, äkôstā
landing place	endroit *m* de débarquement	äNdrô·ä də dābärkmäN
landing stage	débarcadère *m*	dābärkädār
lap rug	couverture *f* de laine	ko͞overtēr də lān
life belt	bouée *f* de sauvetage	bo͞o·ā də sōvtäzh
life jacket	gilet *m* de sauvetage	zhēlā də sōvtäzh
lighthouse	phare *m*	fär
mast	mât *m*	mä
mole	môle *m*	môl

ocean	océan *m*	ōsā·äN
passenger	passager *m*	päsäzhā
pier	jetée *f*	zhetā
place on deck	place *f* de pont	pläs də pôN
playroom	nurserie *f*	nārsrē
port *(land)*	port *m*	pôr
port *(side)*	bâbord *m*	bäbôr
port fees	taxe *f* portuaire	täks pôrtē·är
quay	quai *m*	kā
railing	bastingage *m*	bästeNgäzh
river	fleuve *m*	flāv
rope	cordage *m*	kôrdäzh
rough seas	mer *f* agitée	mār äzhētā
rudder	rame *f*	räm
sail	voile *f*	vô·äl
sailor	matelot *m*	mätlō
sea	mer *f*	mār
– on the high seas	en haute mer	äN ōt mār
seasickness	mal *m* de mer	mäl də mār
ship	bateau *m*	bätō
– freighter	cargo *m*	kärgō
– passenger ship	transatlantique *m*	träNsätläNtēk
– warship	bâtiment *m* de guerre	bätēmäN də gār
ship's doctor	médecin *m* de bord	mādəseN də bôr
shipboard party	fête *f* à bord	fāt ä bôr
shipping agency	agence *f* maritime	äzhäNs märētēm
shipping company	compagnie *f* de navigation	kôNpänyē də nävēgäsyôN
shore	rivage *m*	rēväzh
starboard	tribord *m*	trēbôr
steamer	paquebot *m*	päkbō
stern	poupe *f*	po͞op
steward	steward *m*	sto͞o·ärt
strait	détroit *m*	dātrô·ä
tourist class	classe *f* touriste	kläs to͞orēst
trug	remorqueur *m*	remôrkār
voyage	voyage *m* en bateau	vô·äyäzh äN bätō
wave	vague *f*	väg
yacht	yacht *m*	yôt (yäk)

AT THE BORDER

Passport Control

When do we get to the border?
Quand arriverons-nous à la frontière?
käNdärēverôN-nōō ä lä frôNtyār

***Your passport, please.**
Votre passeport, s'il vous plaît.
vôt(ər) päspôr, sēl vōō plā

***Your papers, please.**
Vos papiers, s'il vous plaît.
vō päpyā, sēl vōō plā

Here they are.
Tenez, s'il vous plaît.
tenā, sēl vōō plā

I'll be staying *a week (two weeks, until the . . .).*
Je resterai *une semaine (deux semaines, jusqu'à . . .).*
zhə resterā ēn smen (dā smen, zhēskä . . .)

I'm here *on business (on vacation).*
C'est un *voyage d'affaires (voyage touristique).*
seteN vô·äyäzh däfār (vô·äyäzh tōōrēstēk)

***I'm (We're)* visiting . . .**
Je visite (Nous visitons) . . .
zhə vēzēt (nōō vēzētôN) . . .

I'm traveling with the . . . group.
Je fais partie du groupe de . . .
zhə fā pärtē dē grōōp də . . .

I haven't got a vaccination certificate.
Je n'ai pas de certificat de vaccination.
zhə nā pä də sertēfēkä də väksēnäsyôN

What should I do?
Qu'est-ce qu'il faut faire?
keskēl fō fār

I *have (haven't)* had a *smallpox (cholera)* vaccination.
Je *(ne)* suis *(pas)* vacciné contre *la variole (le choléra).*
zhə (nə) sē·ē (pä) väksēnā kôNt(ər) lä värē·ôl (lə kôlārä)

Do I have to fill in this form?
Dois-je remplir ce formulaire?
dô·äzh räNplēr sə fôrmēlār

The children are entered in my passport.
Les enfants sont inscrits dans mon passeport.
lāzäNfäN sôNt eNskrē däN môN päspôr

Can I get my visa here?
Je peux avoir le visa ici?
zhə pāzävô·är lə vēzä ēsē

May I please phone my consulate?
Je peux téléphoner à mon consulat?
zhə pā tālāfōnā ä môN kôNsēlä

border	frontière *f*	frôNtyār
color of eyes	couleur *f* des yeux	ko͞olār dāzyā
color of hair	couleur *f* des cheveux	ko͞olār dā shevā
date of birth	date *f* de naissance	dät də nesäNs
departure	sortie *f*	sôrtē
distinguishing marks	signes *m/pl.* particuliers	sēn(yə) pärtēkēlyā
driver's license	permis *m* de conduire	permē də kôNdē·ēr
entry	entrée *f*	äNtrā
entry visa	visa *m* d'entrée	vēzä däNtrā
exit visa	visa *m* de sortie	vēzä də sôrtē
extend	prolonger	prōlôNzhā
height	taille *f*	tä'ē
identity card	carte *f* d'identité	kärt dēdäNtētā
insurance certificate	carte *f* d'assurance	kärt däsēräNs
international vaccination certificate	certificat *m* (international) de vaccination	sertēfēkä (eNternäsyônäl) də väksēnäsyôN
maiden name	nom *m* de jeune fille	nôN də zhān fē'ē
marital status	situation *f* de famille	sētē·äsyôN də fämē'ē
– single	célibataire	sälēbätār
– married	marié	märē·ā
– widowed	veuf *m*, veuve *f*	vāf, vāv
– divorced	divorcé	dēvôrsā
name	nom *m* de famille	nôN də fämē'ē
– first name	prénom *m*	prānôN
nationality	nationalité *f*	näsyônälētā
nationality plate	plaque *f* de nationalité	pläk də näsyônälētā
number	numéro *m*	nēmārō
occupation	profession *f*	prôfesyôN
passport	passeport *m*	päspôr
passport control	contrôle *m* des passeports	kôNtrôl dā päspôr
place of birth	lieu *m* de naissance	lēyā də nesäNs
place of residence	domicile *m*	dômēsēl
renew	prolonger; renouveler	prōlôNzhā; reno͞ovlā
signature	signature *f*	sēnyätēr
valid	valable	väläb'əl

Customs Control

***Do you have anything to declare?**
Avez-vous quelque chose à déclarer?
ävā-vo͞o kelke shōz ä dāklärā

I only have articles for my personal use.
Je n'ai que des objets personnels.
zhə nā ke dāzôbzhā persônel

That isn't mine.
Ce n'est pas à moi.
sə nā päzä mô·ä

***Please open ...**
Ouvrez ..., s'il vous plaît.
o͞ovrā ..., sēl vo͞o plā

This is a *present (souvenir)*.
C'est un *cadeau (souvenir de voyage)*.
seteN kädō (so͞ovenēr də vô·äyäzh)

I have ... *cigarettes (a bottle of perfume)*.
J'ai ... *cigarettes (du parfum)*.
zhā ... sēgäret (dē pärfeN)

That's my suitcase.
C'est ma valise.
sā mä välēz

***What's in here?**
Qu'est-ce qu'il y a là-dedans?
keskēlyä lä dedäN

That's all.
C'est tout.
sā to͞o

***All right!**
D'accord.
däkôr

I'd like to declare this.
Je voudrais déclarer ça.
zhə vo͞odrā dāklärā sä

Do I have to pay duty on this?
Dois-je déclarer ça?
dô·äzh dāklärā sä

How much can I bring in duty free?
J'ai droit à combien, en franchise?
zhā drô·ä ä kôNbyeN, äN fräN-shēz

What do I have to pay for it?
Combien je dois payer pour ça?
kôNbyeN zhə dô·ä pāyā po͞or sä

border, frontier	frontière *f*	frôNtyār
border crossing	passage *m* de la frontière	päsäzh də lä frôNtyār
customs	douane *f*	do͞o·än
customs control	passage *m* de la douane	päsäzh də lä do͞o·än
customs examination	contrôle *m* de douane	kôNtrôl də do͞o·än
customs office	bureau *m* de douane	bērō də do͞o·än
customs officer	douanier *m*	do͞o·änyā
duty	droits *m/pl.* de douane	drô·ä də do͞o·än
– export duty	droits *m/pl.* de sortie	drô·ä də sôrtē
– import duty	droits *m/pl.* d'entrée	drô·ä däNtrā

ACCOMMODATION

Checking it out

Where is the . . . *hotel (pension)*?
Où est *l'hôtel . . . (la pension. . .)*?
o͞o ā lôtel . . . (lä päNsyôN. . .)

Can you recommend a good hotel?
Pourriez-vous me recommander un bon hôtel?
po͞orē·ā-vo͞o mə rekômäNdā eN bônôtel

***Is (Are)* there . . . near here?**
Y a-t-il près d'ici . . .?
ēyätēl prā dēsē . . .

accommodations	un logis	eN lōzhē
apartments	des appartements	dāzäpärtəmäN
a boarding house	une pension	ēn päNsyôN
bungalows	des bungalows	dā beNgälō
a camping site	un terrain de camping	eN tereN də käNpēng
a hotel	un hôtel	eNôtel
an inn	une auberge	ēn ōbärzh
a motel	un motel	eN môtel
a pension	une pension	ēn päNsyôN
rooms in private homes	des chambres chez l'habitant	dā shäNb(ər) shā läbētäN
a youth hostel	une auberge de jeunesse	ēn ōbärzh də zhānes

– near the beach.
– près de la plage.
– prā dəlä pläzh

– in a quiet place (centrally located).
– dans un site *tranquille (central).*
– däNzeN sēt träNkēl (säNträl)

How *are the prices (is the food)* there?
Comment *sont les prix (est la nourriture)*?
kômäN sôN lā prē (ā lä no͞orētēr)

> *Only the most modern European hotels have bathrooms attached to every room, and most rooming houses and pensions will require guests to share a bathroom down the hall with others.*

Checking in

I reserved a room here.
J'ai retenu chez vous une chambre.
zhā retenē shā vo͞o ēn shäNb(ər)

. . . six weeks ago.
. . . il y a six semaines.
. . . ēlyä sē smen

The . . . travel agency reserved a room for *me (us)*.
L'agence de voyage . . . a fait retenir pour *moi (nous)* une chambre.
läzhäNs də vô·äyäzh . . . ä fā retenēr po͞or mô·ä (no͞o) ēn shäNb(ər)

Have you got a *single (double)* room available?
Vous avez une chambre pour *une personne (deux personnes)*?
vo͞ozävā ēn shäNb(ər) po͞or ēn persôn (po͞or dā persôn)

I'd like to have...	Je voudrais ...	zhə vo͞odrā ...
– an apartment	un appartement	eNäpärtəmäN
– bungalow	un bungalow	eN beNgälō
– double room	une chambre à deux lits	ēn shäNbrä dā lē
– an efficiency apartment	une location	ēn lôkäsyôN
– a quiet room	une chambre calme	ēn shäNb(ər) kälm
– a room	une chambre	ēn shäNb(ər)
– on the *first (second)* floor	au premier (deuxième) étage	ō prəmyer (dāzyām) ātäzh
– with balcony	avec balcon	ävek bälkôN
– with *bath (shower)*	avec bain (douche)	ävek beN (do͞osh)
– with hot and cold running water	avec eau courante chaude et froide	ävek ō ko͞oräNt shôd ā frô·äd
– with terrace	avec terrasse	ävek teräs
– with toilet	avec W.-C.	āvek do͞obləvā-sā

. . . for *one night (two nights, one week, four weeks)*.
. . . pour *une nuit (deux jours, une semaine, quatre semaines)*.
. . . po͞or ē·nē·ē (dā zho͞or, ēn smen, kät(ər) smen)

> *Careful! Buildings in all European countries – including Britain – use a different numbering system for the floors. The bottom floor is called the ground floor (in French* le rez-de-chaussée), *the second (American) floor is called the first floor* (le premier étage), *the third floor the second floor* (le deuxième étage), *and so on.*

Can I have a look at the room?
Puis-je voir la chambre?
pē·ēzh vô·är lä shäNb(ər)

I like it.
Elle me plaît.
el mə plā

***I'll (We'll)* take it.**
Je la prends (Nous la prenons).
zhə lä präN (no͞o lä prenôN)

Could you show me another room?
Pouvez-vous me montrer encore une autre chambre?
po͞ovā-vo͞o mə môNtrā äNkôr ēnôt(ər) shäNb(ər)

Could you put in *an extra bed (a crib)?*
Pouvez-vous mettre *encore un lit (un lit d'enfant)* dans la chambre?
po͞ovā-vo͞o meträNkôr eN lē (eN lē däNfäN) däN lä shäNb(ər)

Price

How much is the room per *day (week)?*
Quel est le prix de la chambre par *jour (semaine)?*
kel ā lə prē də lä shäNb(ər) pär zho͞or (smen)

– with breakfast.
– avec petit déjeuner.
– ävek pətē dāzhānā

– with two meals a day.
– avec demi-pension.
– ävek dəmē-päNsyôN

– American plan.
– avec pension complète.
– ävek päNsyôN kôNplet

Is *everything (service)* included?
Tout (Le service) est compris?
to͞o (lə servēs) ā kôNprē

What's the *single room surcharge (seasonal surcharge)?*
Pour une *chambre individuelle, le supplément (La taxe saisonnière)* c'est combien?
po͞or *e*n shäNbreNdēvēdē·el lə sēplämäN (lä täks sāzônyār) sā kôNbyeN

Are there reduced rates for children?
Y a-t-il une réduction pour enfants?
ēyätēl ēn rādēksyôN po͞or äNfäN

How much is that altogether?
Ça fait combien en tout?
sä fā kôNbyeN äN to͞o

How much deposit do I have to pay?
Quel accompte désirez-vous?
kel äkôNt dāzērā-vo͞o

Registration, Luggage

I'd like to *register (check in).*
Je voudrais remplir la fiche (d'hôtel).
zhə vo͞odrā räNplēr lä fēsh dôtel

Do you need our passports?
Est-ce qu'il vous faut nos passeports?
eskēl vo͞o fō nō päspôr

When do you want back the registration form?
On doit vous remettre la fiche d'hôtel quand?
ôN dô·ä vo͞o remet(ər) lä fēsh dôtel käN

What do I have to fill out here?
Qu'est-ce qu'il faut mettre ici?
keskēl fō metrēsē

***I just need your signature.**
Votre signature suffit.
vôt(ər) sēnyätēr sēfē

Would you have my luggage picked up?
Pouvez-vous envoyer chercher mes bagages?
po͞ovā-vo͞ozäNvô·äyā shārshā mā bägäzh

It's still at the *station (airport).*
Ils sont encore *a la gare (à l'aéroport).*
ēl sôNtäNkôr ä lä gär (ä lä·ārōpôr)

Here's the baggage check.
Voici le bulletin d'enregistrement.
vô·äsē lə bēlteN däNrezhēstrəmäN

Where's my luggage?
Où sont mes bagages?
o͞o sôN mā bägäzh

Is my baggage already up in the room?
Mes bagages sont-ils déjà dans la chambre?
mā bägäzh sôNtēl dāzhä däN lä shäNb(ər)

Can I leave my luggage here?
Puis-je laisser mes bagages ici?
pē·ēzh lāsā mā bägäzh ēsē

Would you put these valuables in the safe?
Pourriez-vous garder ces objets de valeur dans votre coffre-fort?
po͞orē·ā-vo͞o gärdā sezôbzhā də välär däN vôt(ər) kôf(ər)-fôr

Do you have a *garage (parking lot)?*
Avez-vous *un garage (un parking)?*
ävā-vo͞ozeN gäräzh (eN pärkēng)

Reception, Desk Clerk

Where is room 308?
Où est la chambre numéro trois cent huit?
o͞o ā lä shäNb(ər) nēmārō trô·ä säNē·ēt

The key, please.
La clé, s'il vous plaît!
lä klā, sēl vo͞o plā

Number . . ., please.
Numéro . . ., s'il vous plaît.
nēmārō . . ., sēl vo͞o plā

Has anyone asked for me?
Quelqu' un m'a-t-il demandé?
kelkeN mätēl dəmäNdā

Is there any mail for me?
Y a-t-il du courrier pour moi?
ēyätel dē ko͞oryā po͞or mô·ä

What time does the mail come?
Quand arrive le courrier?
käNdärēv lə ko͞oryā

Do you have any *stamps (picture postcards)?*
Avez-vous des *timbres-postes (cartes postales)?*
ävā-vo͞o dā teNb(ər)-pôst (kärt pôstäl)

What's the postage on a *letter (postcard)* to the United States?
Combien coûte *une lettre (une carte postale)* pour les États-Unis?
kôNbyeN ko͞ot ēn let(ər) (ēn kärt pôstäl) po͞or lāzātäzēnē

Where can I *get (rent)* . . .?
Je peux *avoir (louer)* . . . où?
zhə pāzävô·är (pā lo͞o·ā) . . . o͞o

Where do I sign up for the excursion to . . .?
Je peux m'inscrire où, pour l'excursion à . . .?
zhə pā meNskrēr o͞o, po͞or lekskērsyōN ä . . .

Where can I *make a phone call (change some money)?*
Je peux *téléphoner (changer de l'argent)* où?
zhə pā tālāfōnā (shäNzhā·də lärzhäN) o͞o

I'd like to place a long distance call to . . .
Je voudrais une communication pour . . .
zhə vo͞odrā ēn kômēnēkäsyôN po͞or . . .

I'm expecting a long distance call from the United States.
J'attends un appel des États-Unis.
zhätäN eNäpel dāzātäzēnē

Where can I get an American newspaper?
Où peut-on acheter des journaux américains?
o͞o pātôN äshtā dā zho͞ornō ämārēkeN

Where *is (are)* . . .?
Où *est (sont)* . . .?
o͞o ā (sôN) . . .

Could you get me . . .?
Pouvez-vous me procurer . . .?
po͞ovā-vo͞o mə prôkērā . . .

What's the voltage here?
Le courant, c'est du combien ici?
lə ko͞oräN, sā dē kôNbyeN ēsē

> *Electric current: In general (as in most of Europe) it is 220 volts, but in some places it is still 110 volts. You'll need the European circular two pin adaptor plugs as well as an adaptor if your appliance doesn't have a built-in converter switch.*

I'll be back in *ten minutes (a couple of hours).*
Je reviendrai dans *dix minutes (deux heures).*
zhə revyeNdrā däN dē mēnēt (dāzār)

We're going *down to the beach (into town).*
Nous allons *à la plage (en ville).*
no͞ozälôN älä pläzh (äN vēl)

I'll be in the *lounge (bar).*
Je suis *au salon (au bar).*
zhə sē·ē ō sälôN (ō bär)

I *lost my key (left my key in the room).*
J'ai *perdu la clé (laissé la clé dans la chambre).*
zhā perde lä klā (lesā lä klā däN lä shäNb(ər)

What time are meals served?
Quelles sont les heures de repas?
kel sôN lāzār də repä

Where's the dining room?
Où est la salle à manger?
o͞o ā lä säl ä mäNzhā

Can we have breakfast in the room?
Pouvons-nous prendre le petit déjeuner dans la chambre?
po͞ovôN-no͞o präNd(ər) lə pətē dāzhānā däN lä shäNb(ər)

Could we have breakfast at seven tomorrow morning, please?
Pouvons-nous prendre le petit déjeuner demain à sept heures?
po͞ovôN-no͞o präNd(ər) lə pətē dāzhānā dəmeN ä setār

I'd like a box lunch tomorrow morning, please.
Pour demain matin un panier-repas, s'il vous plaît.
po͞or dəmeN mäteN eN pänyā-repä, sēl vo͞o plā

Please wake me at 7:30 tomorrow.
Réveillez-moi demain à sept heures et demie.
rāvāyā-mô·ä dəmeN ä setār ā dəmē

Maid

Come in!
Entrez!
äNtrā

Just a moment, please!
Un instant, s'il vous plaît.
eNeNstäN, sēl vo͞o plā

Could you wait another *five (ten)* minutes?
Pourriez-vous attendre encore *cinq (dix)* minutes?
po͞orē·ā-vo͞o ätäNdräNkôr seNk (dē) mēn*ē*t

We'll be going out in another *quarter hour (half hour)*.
Nous partons dans *un quart d'heure (une demi-heure)*.
no͞o pärtôN däNseN kär d*ā*r (*ē*n dəmē-*ā*r)

Please bring *me (us)* ...
Apportez-*moi (-nous)*, s'il vous plaît ...
äpôrtā-mô·ä (-no͞o), sēl vo͞o plā ...

another blanket	encore une couverture .	äNkôr *ē*n ko͞overt*ē*r
another towel	encore une serviette ...	äNkôr *ē*n servyet
an ash tray	un cendrier	eN säNdrē·ā
a blanket	une couverture de laine	*ē*n ko͞overt*ē*r də lān
breakfast	le petit déjeuner	lə pətē dāzh*ā*nā
a bar of soap	un morceau de savon ..	eN môrsō də sävôN
a couple of clothes hangers	quelques cintres	kelke seNt(ər)

How does this thing work?
Comment est-ce que cela fonctionne?
kômäNteske səlä fôNksyôn

Is our room ready?
Notre chambre est déjà faite?
nôt(ər) shäNbrā dāzhä f*ā*t

Would you have these things laundered for me?
Pouvez-vous faire laver ce linge?
po͞ovā-vo͞o f*ā*r lävā sə leNzh

Thanks very much!
Merci beaucoup!
mersē bōko͞o

This is for you.
C'est pour vous.
sā po͞or vo͞o

Complaints

I'd like to speak to the manager, please.
Je voudrais parler au gérant, s'il vous plaît.
zhə vo͞odrā pärlā ō zhāräN, sēl vo͞o plā

There's no . . .
Il manque . . .
ēl mäNk . . .

There are no . . .
Il manque . . .
ēl mäNk . . .

. . . doesn't work.
. . . ne fonctionne pas.
. . . nə fôNksyôn pä

There's no light in my room.
Dans ma chambre il n'y a pas de lumière.
däN mä shäNbrēlnyä pä də lēmyār

This bulb has burned out.
Cette ampoule est grillée.
set äNpo͞ol ā grēyā

The socket is broken.
La prise de courant ne marche pas.
lä prēz də ko͞oräN nə märsh pä

The fuse has blown.
Le plomb a sauté.
lə plôN ä sôtā

The *bell (heating)* doesn't work.
La sonnette (Le chauffage) ne marche pas.
lä sônet (lə shôfäzh) nə märsh pä

The key doesn't fit.
La clé ne va pas.
lä klā nə vä pä

The rain comes in.
La pluie rentre.
lä plē·ē räNt(ər)

This window *won't shut properly (won't open).*
Cette fenêtre *ferme mal (ne s'ouvre pas).*
set fenāt(ər) fārm·mäl (nə so͞ov(ər) pä)

There's no *(hot)* water.
Il n'y a pas d'eau *(chaude).*
ēl nyä pä dō (shōd)

The faucet drips.
Le robinet goutte.
lə rôbēnā go͞ot

The toilet won't flush.
La chasse d'eau ne marche pas.
lä shäs dō nə märsh pä

There's a leak in this pipe.
Il y a une fuite.
ēlyä ēn fē·ēt

The drain is stopped up.
Le lavabo est bouché.
lə läväbō ā bo͞oshā

Checking out

I'll be leaving tomorrow.
Je pars demain.
zhə pär dəmeN

We're continuing on tomorrow.
Nous continuerons notre voyage demain.
no͞o kôNtēn*ē*·ərôN nôt(ər) vô·äyäzh dəmeN

Would you please make up my bill?
Préparez la note, s'il vous plaît.
prāpärā lä nôt, sēl vo͞o plā

Could I please have *my (our)* bill?
Je peux avoir *ma (notre)* note, s'il vous plaît?
zhə p*ā*zävô·är mä (nôtər) nôt, sēl vo͞o plā

Please wake me tomorrow morning.
Réveillez-moi demain matin, s'il vous plaît.
rāvāyā-mô·ä dəmeN mäteN, sēl vo͞o plā

Please order a taxi for me tomorrow morning at 8.
Appelez un taxi pour *demain (huit heures)*, s'il vous plaît.
äplā eN täksē po͞or dəmeN (*ē*·ēt*ā*r), sēl vo͞o plā

Would you have my luggage taken to the *station (airport)?*
Pouvez-vous faire porter mes bagages *à la gare (à l'aéroport)?*
po͞ovā-vo͞o fār pôrtā mā bägäzh ä lä gär (ä lä·ārōpôr)

When does the *bus (train)* to . . . leave?
Quand part *l'autobus (le train)* pour . . .?
käN pär lôtōb*ē*s (lə treN) po͞or . . .

Please forward my mail.
Faites-moi suivre mon courrier, s'il vous plaît.
fāt-mô·ä s*ē*·ēv(ər) môN ko͞oryā, sēl vo͞o plā

Thanks for everything!
Merci infiniment pour tout!
mersē eNfēnēmäN po͞or to͞o

We had a very good *time (rest)* here.
Ça a été très agréable ici.
sä ä ātā trāzägrā·äb'əl ēsē

accommodations	logis *m*	lôzhē
adapter plug	fiche *f* intermédiaire	fēsh eNtermādyār
air conditioning	climatisation *f*	klēmätēzäsyôN
alternating current	courant *m* alternatif	ko͞oräN älternätēf
American plan	pension *f* complète	päNsyôN kôNplet
apartment	appartement *m*, studio *m*	äpärtəmäN, st*ē*dē·ō
apartment building	immeuble *m* de studios	ēm*ā*b'əl də st*ē*dē·ō
armchair	fauteuil *m*	fōt*ā*'ē
arrival	arrivée *f*	ärēvā
ash tray	cendrier *m*	säNdrē·ā
balcony	balcon *m*	bälkôN
basement	sous-sol *m*	so͞o-sôl
bathroom	salle *f* de bains	säl də beN
bed	lit *m*	lē
– blanket	couverture *f* (de laine)	ko͞overt*ē*r (də lān)
– crib	lit *m* d'enfant	lē däNfäN
– mattress	matelas *m*	mätlä
– pillow	oreiller *m*	ôrāyā
bed and two meals	demi-pension *f*	dəmēpäNsyôN
bed linen	draps *m/pl.* de lit	drä də lē
– cover	housse *f* d'édredon	ho͞os dādredôN
– pillowcase	taie *f* d'oreiller	tā dôrāyā
bed rug	descente *f* de lit	desäNt də lē
bedside table	table *f* de nuit	täb'əl də n*ē*·ē
bell	sonnette *f*	sônet
bill	note *f*	nôt
breakfast	petit déjeuner *m*	pətē dāzh*ā*nā
– eat breakfast	prendre son petit déjeuner	präNd(ər) sôN pətē dāzh*ā*nā
bucket	seau *m*	sō
carpet	tapis *m*	täpē
category	catégorie *f*	kätāgôrē
ceiling	plafond *m*	pläfôN
cellar	cave *f*	käv
central heating	chauffage *m* central	shôfäzh säNträl
chair	chaise *f*	shāz
check-in	déclaration *f* de séjour	dākläräsyôN də sāzho͞or

closet	placard *m*	pläkär
clothes hanger	cintre *m*	seNt(ər)
complaint	réclamation *f*	rāklämäsyôN
concierge	concierge *m*; portier *m*	kôNsyārzh; pôrtyā
corridor	corridor *m*; couloir *m*	kôrēdôr; ko͞olō·är
curtain	rideau *m*	rēdō
day bed	canapé-lit *m*	känäpā-lē
deck chair	chaise *f* longue	shāz-lôNg
departure	départ *m*	dāpär
deposit	acompte *m*; arrhes *f/pl.*	äkôNt; är
dining room	salle *f* à manger	säl ä mäNzhā
dinner	dîner *m*	dēnā
door	porte *f*	pôrt
door handle	poignée *f*	pô·änyā
drapery	rideau *m*	rēdō
drawer	tiroir *m*	tērô·är
elevator	ascenseur *m*	äsäNsär
entrance	entrée *f*	äNtrā
exit	sortie *f*	sôrtē
extension cord	rallonge *f*	rälôNzh
extra week	semaine *f* supplémentaire	smen sēplāmäNtār
fan	ventilateur *m*	väNtēlätär
faucet	robinet *m* d'eau	rôbēnā dō
fireplace	cheminée *f*	shemēnā
floor	étage *m*	ātäzh
front desk	réception *f*	rāsepsyôN
front door	porte *f* d'entrée	pôrt däNtrā
fuse	fusible *m*	fēzēb'əl
garden umbrella	parasol *m*	päräsôl
grill room	grill-room *m*	grēl-ro͞om
guest house	pension *f*	päNsyôN
hall	hall *m* d'hôtel	äl dôtel
head clerk	chef *m* de réception	shef də rāsepsyôN
heating	chauffage *m*	shôfäzh
hotel	hôtel *m*	ôtel
– beach hotel	hôtel *m* de la plage	ôtel dəlä pläzh
hotel restaurant	restaurant *m* d'hôtel	restôräN dôtel
house	maison *f*	māzôN
house key	clé *f* de la maison	klā dəlä māzôN

inquiry	renseignement *m*	räNsen(yə)mäN
key	clé *f*	klā
kitchen	cuisine *f*	kē̆·ēzēn
kitchenette	coin *m* cuisine	kô·eN kē̆·ēzēn
lamp	lampe *f*	läNp
laundry	linge *m*	leNzh
– do laundry	laver	lävā
– dry	sècher	sāshā
– iron	repasser	repäsā
light bulb	ampoule *f* (électrique)	äNpo͞ol ālektrēk
lights	éclairage *m*	āklārāzh
lobby	vestibule *m*; hall *m*	vestēbē̆l; äl
lock	serrure *f*	serē̆r
– lock up	fermer à clé	fermā ä klā
– unlock	ouvrir (avec une clé)	o͞ovrēr (avek ē̆n klā)
lunch	déjeuner *m*	dāzhā̆nā
maid	femme *f* de chambre	fām də shäNb(ər)
mirror	miroir *m*, glace *f*	mērô·är, gläs
move	déménager	dāmānäzhā
move in	emménager	äNmānäzhā
move out	déménager	dāmānäzhā
night's lodging	nuitée *f*	nē̆·ētā
pail	seau *m*	sō
patio	cour *f* intérieure	ko͞or eNtārē·ā̆r
pension	pension *f*	päNsyôN
plug	fiche *f*, prise *f* (d'électricité)	fēsh, prēz (dālektrēsētā)
pot	pot *m*	pô
price	prix *m*	prē
private beach	plage *f* privée	pläzh prēvā
radiator	radiateur *m*	rādē·ätā̆r
reading lamp	lampe *f* de chevet	läNp də shevā
reception desk	réception *f*	rāsepsyôN
refrigerator	réfrigérateur *m*	rāfrēzhārätā̆r
registration	déclaration *f* de séjour	dākläräsyôN də sāzho͞or
rent *(noun)*	loyer *m*	lô·äyā
rent *(verb)*	louer	lo͞o·ā

rest room	toilettes *f/pl.*	tô·älet
– ladies' room	toilettes *f/pl.* pour dames	tô·älet po͞or däm
– men's room	toilettes *f/pl.* pour messieurs	tô·älet po͞or mesy*ā*
room	pièce *f*	pyās
– bedroom	chambre *f* à coucher	shäNbrä ko͞oshā
– living room	séjour *m*	sāzho͞or
– nursery	chambre *f* d'enfants	shäNb(ər) däNfäN
season	saison *f*	sāzôN
service (charge)	service *m*	servēs
shower	douche *f*	do͞osh
sink	lavabo *m*	läväbō
socket	prise *f*	prēz
staircase	escalier *m*	eskälyā
stairwell	cage *f* d'escalier	käzh deskälyā
stove	fourneau *m*	fo͞ornō
swimming pool	piscine *f*	pēsēn
switch	interrupteur *m*	eNter*ē*pt*ā*r
table	table *f*	täb'əl
tablecloth	nappe *f*	näp
telephone	téléphone *m*	tālāfôn
terrace	terrasse *f*	teräs
toilet paper	papier *m* hygiénique	päpyā ēzhē·änēk
tour guide	guide *m*	gēd
travel agency	agence *f* de voyage	äzhäNs də vô·äyäzh
vacate the room	libérer la chambre	lēbārā lä shäNb(ər)
ventilation	aération *f*	ä·āräsyôN
voltage	voltage *m*	vôltäzh
wall	mur *m*	m*ē*r
water	eau *f*	ō
– cold water	eau *f* froide	ō frô·äd
– hot water	eau *f* chaude	ō shōd
water glass	verre *f* à eau	vār ä ō
window	fenêtre *f*	fenāt(ər)
windowpane	vitre *f*	vēt(ər)

Camping, Youth Hostels

Is there a *camping site (youth hostel)* near here?
Y a-t-il *un terrain de camping (une auberge de jeunesse)?*
ēyätēl eN tereN də käNpēng (ēnōbārzh də zhānes)

Can we camp here?
Pouvons-nous camper ici?
po͞ovôN-no͞o käNpā ēsē

Is the site guarded at night?
Le terrain est-il gardé la nuit?
lə tereN ātēl gärdā lä nē·ē

Do you have room (for another tent)?
Y a-t-il encore de la place (pour une tente)?
ēyätēl äNkôr dəlä pläs (po͞or ēn täNt)

How much does it cost to stay overnight?
Combien coûte une nuit?
kôNbyeN ko͞ot ēn nē·ē

How much is it for the *car (trailer)?*
Quels sont les frais pour *l'auto (la caravane)?*
kel sôN lā frā po͞or lôtō (lä kärävän)

I'll be staying . . . *days (weeks).*
Je reste . . . *jours (semaines).*
zhə rest . . . zho͞or (smen)

Can we . . . here?
Peut-on . . . ici?
pāt-ôN . . . ēsē

Is there a grocery store near here?
Y a-t-il près d'ici un magasin d'alimentation?
ēyätēl prā dēsē eN mägäzeN dälēmäNtäsyôN

Can I *rent bottled gas (exchange gas bottles)* here?
Je peux *emprunter (échanger)* ici des bouteilles de gaz?
zhə pāzäNpreNtā (āshäNzhā) ēsē dā bo͞otā'ē də gäz

Where are the *rest rooms (wash rooms)?*
Où sont les *toilettes (lavabos)?*
o͞o sôN lā tô·älet (läväbō)

Are there any electrical connections here?
Y a-t-il l'électricité?
ēyätēl lālektrēsētā

Can we drink the water?
L'eau est potable?
lō ā pôtāb'əl

Can I rent . . .?
Je peux emprunter . . .?
zhə pāzäNpreNtā . . .

Where can I . . .?
Où peut-on . . .?
o͞o pātôN . . .

advance reservation	réservation *f*	rāzerväsyôN
camp bed	lit *m* pliant	lē plē·äN
camping	camping *m*	käNpēng
camping ID	carte de l'A.C.C.F.	kärt dəlä·sā·sā·ef
camp out	faire du camping	fār dē käNpēng
camp site	terrain *m* de camping	tereN də käNpēng
check-in	déclaration *f* de séjour	dāklärasyôN də sāzhōōr
check-out	déclaration *f* de départ	dāklärasyôN də dāpär
cook	préparer les repas	prāpärā lā repä
cooking utensils	gamelle *f*; ustensiles *m/pl.* de cuisine	gämel; ēstäNsēl də kē·ēzēn
day room	salle *f* commune	säl kômēn
dishes	vaisselle *f*	vāsel
dormitory	dortoir *m*	dôrtô·är
drinking water	eau *f* potable	ō pôtäb'əl
get	avoir	ävô·är
go swimming	se baigner	sə bānyā
hostel parents	parents *m/pl.* aubergistes	päräN ōberzhēst
– hostel mother	mère *f* aubergiste	mār ōbārzhēst
– hostel father	père *m* aubergiste	pār ōbārzhēst
iron	repasser	repäsā
membership card	carte *f* de membre	kärt də mäNb(ər)
park	stationner	stäsyônā
playground	terrain *m* de jeux	tereN də zhā
recreation room	salle *f* commune	säl komēn
rent	prêter	prātā
rental fee	prix *m* de location	prē də lôkäsyôN
sleeping bag	sac *m* de couchage	säk də kōōshäzh
take a bath	prendre un bain	präNdreN beN
tent	tente *f*	täNt
trailer	caravane *f*	käräván
usage fee	frais *m/pl.* d'utilisation	frā dētēlēzäsyôN
wash	laver	lävā
youth group	groupe *m* de jeunes	grōōp də zhān
youth hostel	auberge *f* de jeunesse	ōbārzh də zhānes
youth hostel card	carte *f* d'A.J.	kärt dä·zhē

EATING AND DRINKING

Ordering

Is there a *good (Chinese, seafood)* restaurant here?
Y a-t-il ici un *bon restaurant (restaurant chinois, restaurant de poisson et crustacés)?*
ēyätēl ēsē eN bôN restôräN (restôräN shēnô·ä, restôräN də pô·äsôN ā krēstäsā)

Would you please reserve a table for four at eight P.M.?
Réservez une table de quatre personnes pour 8 heures, s'il vous plaît.
rāzervā ēn täb'əl də kät(ər) persôn po͞or ē·ētär, sēl vo͞o plā

Is this *table (seat)* taken?
Cette *table (place)* est-elle réservée?
set·täb'əl (pläs) ātel rāzervā

I'd like a meal.
Je voudrais commander un plat.
zhə vo͞odrā kômäNdā eN plä

Waiter!
Garçon!
gärsôN

Waitress!
Madame!
mädäm

Is this your table?
Faites-vous le service ici?
fāt-vo͞o lə servēs ēsē

We'd like a drink.
Nous voudrions commander des boissons.
no͞o vo͞odrē·ôN kômäNdā dā bô·äsôN

Could I see the *menu (wine list)*, please?
La *carte (carte des vins/boissons)*, s'il vous plaît.
lä kärt (kärt dā veN/bô·äsôN), sēl vo͞o plā

What can we have right away?
Que pouvez-vous nous servir tout de suite?
ke po͞ovā-vo͞o no͞o servēr to͞otsē·ēt

Do you have . . .?
Avez-vous . . .
ävā-vo͞o

Do you have *vegetarian (diet)* food too?
Avez-vous aussi des menus *végétariens (diététiques)*?
ävā-vo͞o ôsē dā menē vāzhātärē·eN (dē·ātātēk)

Please bring us *one portion (two portions)* of . . . .
Apportez-nous *un(e) . . . (deux . . .), s'il vous plaît.*
äpôrtā-no͞o eN (ēn) . . . (dā . . .), sēl vo͞o plā

A *cup (pot, glass, bottle)* of . . ., please.
Une tasse (un pot, un verre, une bouteille) de . . ., s'il vous plaît.
ēn täs (eN pô, eN vār, ēn bo͞otā'ē) də . . ., sēl vo͞o plā

Table Service

ash tray	cendrier *m*	säNdrē·ā
bottle	bouteille *f*	bo͞otā'ē
bowl	terrine *f*	terēn
bread basket	corbeille *f* à pain	kôrbā'ē ä peN
carafe	carafe *f*	käräf
corkscrew	tire-bouchon *m*	tēr-bo͞oshôN
cruet stand	huilier *m*	ē̆·ēlēyā
cup	tasse *f*	täs
– saucer	soucoupe *f*	so͞oko͞op
cutlery	couvert *m*	ko͞ovār
decanter	carafe *f*	käräf
egg cup	coquetier *m*	kôketyā
fork	fourchette *f*	fo͞orshet
glass	verre *m*	vār
– water glass	verre *m* à eau	vār ä ō
– wine glass	verre *m* à vin	vār ä veN
knife	couteau *m*	ko͞otō
mustard jar	moutardier *m*	mo͞otärdyā
napkin	serviette *f*	servyet
pepper mill	moulin *m* à poivre	mo͞oleN ä pô·äv(ər)
pepper shaker	poivrier *m*	pô·ävrēyā
pitcher	pichet *m*	pēshā
– cream pitcher	pot *m* à lait	pōtä lā
plate	assiette *f*	äsyet
– bread plate	petite assiette *f*	pətēt äsyet
– soup plate	assiette *f* à soupe	äsyet ä so͞op
pot	pot *m*	pô
– coffee pot	cafetière *f*	käfetyār
– tea pot	théière *f*	tā·ēyār
salt shaker	salière *f*	sälēyār
serving dish	plat *m*	plä
silverware	argenterie *f*	ärzhäNtərē
spoon	cuiller *f*	kē̆·ēyār
– soup spoon	cuiller *f* à soupe	kē̆·ēyār ä so͞op
– teaspoon	petite cuiller *f*	pətēt kē̆·ēyār
sugar bowl	sucrier *m*	sē̆krēyā
tablecloth	nappe *f*	näp
toothpick	cure-dent *m*	kē̆r-däN
tray	plateau *m*	plätō

Breakfast

bread	pain *m*	peN
– dark bread	pain *m* bis	peN bē(s)
– rye bread	pain *m* de seigle	peN də sāg'əl
– white bread	pain *m* blanc	peN bläN
– whole wheat bread	pain *m* complet	peN kôNplā
breakfast	petit déjeuner *m*	pətē dāzh*ā*ṅā
butter	beurre *m*	b*ā*r
cereal	céréales *f/pl.*	sārā·äl
coffee	café *m*	käfā
– black	– noir	nô·är
– decaffeinated	– décaféiné	dākäfā·ēnā
– with cream	– au lait	ō lā
– with sugar	avec du sucre	ävek d*ē* s*ē*k(ər)
cold cuts	tranches *f/pl.* de charcuterie	träNsh də shärk*ē*tərē
egg	œuf *m*	*ā*f
– hard-boiled	– dur	– d*ē*r
– soft-boiled	– à la coque	– älä kôk
– ham & eggs	œufs *m/pl.* au jambon	*ā* ō zhäNbôN
– fried eggs	œufs *m/pl.* sur le plat	*ā* s*ē*r lə plä
– poached eggs	œufs *m/pl.* pochés	*ā* pôshā
– scrambled eggs	œufs *m/pl.* brouillés	*ā* bro͞oyā
fruit juice	jus *m* de fruits	zh*ē* də fr*ē*·ē
– orange juice	jus *m* d'orange	zh*ē* dôräNzh
– tomato juice	jus *m* de tomate	zh*ē* də tômät
honey	miel *m*	myel
hot chocolate	chocolat *m*	shôkōlä
jam	confiture *f*	kôNfētēr
milk	lait *m*	lā
oatmeal	bouillie *f* d'avoine	bo͞oyē dävô·än
roll	petit pain *m*	pətē peN
sausage	saucisse *f*	sôsēs
slice	tranche *f*	träNsh
tea	thé *m*	tā
– with lemon	– au citron	ō sētrôN
– with milk	– au lait	ō lā
toast	toast *m*	tōst
zwieback	biscotte *f*	bēskôt

On the European continent, breakfast is generally a simple affair, consisting of coffee or tea, rolls, butter, jam, and occasional cold cuts.

Lunch and Dinner

***I'd (We'd)* like to have . . .**
Je voudrais (On voudrait) . . .
zhə vo͞odrā (ôN vo͞odrā) . . .

Would you bring us . . .
Pouvez-vous nous apporter. . .?
po͞ovā-vo͞o no͞ozäpôrtā

Please pass . . .
Voudriez-vous me passer . . .
vo͞odrē·ā-vo͞o mə päsā . . .

What's the name of this dish?
Comment s'appelle ce plat?
kômäN säpel sə plä

***Would you like seconds on anything?**
Désirez-vous encore quelque chose?
dāzērā-vo͞o äNkôr kelke shōz

Yes, please.
Oui, s'il vous plaît.
o͞o·ē, sēl vo͞o plā

Yes, indeed!
Volontiers.
vôlôNtyā

Just a little.
Un tout petit peu.
eN to͞o pətē pā̆

Thanks, that's enough.
Merci, c'est assez.
mersē, setäsā

No, thanks.
Non, merci.
nôN, mersē

I've had enough.
Je n'ai plus faim.
zhə nā plē̆ feN

Nothing more, thanks.
Plus rien, merci!
plē̆ rē·eN, mersē

***Did you like it?**
C'était bon?
sātā bôN

Delicious!
Délicieux!
dālēsyā̆

***This dish (The wine)* is delicious!**
Ce plat (Le vin) est excellent!
sə plä (lə veN) ātekseläN

***Empty your glass!**
Videz votre verre!
vēdā vôt(ər) vār

Cheers!
À votre santé!
ä vôt(ər) säNtā

I'am not allowed to have any alcohol (I don't care for alcohol).
L'alcool m'est défendu (Je ne prends pas d'alcool).
lälkôl mā dāfäNdē̆ (zhə nə präN pä dälkôl)

To wish the others at the table an enjoyable meal, say Bon appétit! *Before taking the first drink, you can propose a drink to the health of the company by saying* À votre santé! *or simply* Santé!

Cooking

baked	cuit au four	kē·ē ō fo͞or
boiled	cuit; bouilli	kē·ē; bo͞oyē
cold	froid	frô·ä
deep fried	frit	frē
fat	gras	grä
fresh	frais	frā
fried	sauté	sôtā
grilled	grillé	grēyā
hard	dur	dēr
hot	chaud	shō
hot *(spicy)*	épicé; piquant	āpēsā; pēkäN
juicy	juteux	zhēta
lean	maigre	māg(ər)
medium (done)	à point	ä pô·eN
pickled	salé	sälā
rare	saignant	senyäN
raw	cru	krē
roasted	rôti	rôtē
salted	salé	sälā
seasoned	assaisonné	äsāzônā
smoked	fumé	fēmā
soft	tendre	täNd(ər)
steamed	étuvé; cuit à la vapeur	ātēvā; kē·ē älä väpār
stewed	braisé	brāzā
stuffed	farci	färsē
stuffing	farce *f*	färs
tender	tendre	täNd(ər)
tough	coriace	kôryäs
well done	bien cuit	byeN kē·ē

Ingredients

bacon	lard *m*	lär
bay leaves	feuilles *f/pl.* de laurier	fā'ē də lôryā
butter	beurre *m*	bār
capers	câpres *f/pl.*	käp(ər)

caraway	cumin *m*	kēmeN
chives	civette *f*	sēvet
cinnamon	cannelle *f*	känel
cloves	clous *m/pl.* de girofle	klo͞o də zhērôf'əl
currants	raisins *m/pl.* de corinthe	rāzeN də kôreNt
fat	graisse *f*	grās
garlic	ail *m*	ä'ē
ginger	gingembre *m*	zheNzhäNb(ər)
herbs	fines herbes *f/pl.*	fēnzārb
horseradish	raifort *m*	rāfôr
jelly *(aspic)*	gélatine *f*, aspic *m*	zhālätēn, äspēk
jelly *(fruit)*	gelée *f*	zhelā
ketchup	ketchup *m*	ketshəp
lard	saindoux *m*	seNdo͞o
lemon	citron *m*	sētrôN
margarine	margarine *f*	märgärēn
mayonnaise	mayonnaise *f*	mäyônāz
mayonnaise sauce	sauce *f* mayonnaise	sôs mäyônāz
mushrooms	champignons *m/pl.*	shäNpēnyôN
mustard	moutarde *f*	mo͞otärd
nutmeg *(powder)*	muscade *f*	məskäd
oil	huile *f*	ē·ēl
olives	olives *f/pl.*	ôlēv
onion	oignon *m*	ônyôN
paprika	paprika *m*	päprēkä
parsley	persil *m*	persē
pepper	poivre *m*	pô·äv(ər)
pickles	cornichons *m/pl.*	kôrnēshôN
raisins	raisins *m/pl.* secs	rāzeN sek
rosemary	romarin *m*	rōmäreN
sage	sauge *f*	sôzh
salt	sel *m*	sel
sauce	sauce *f*; jus *m*	sôs, zhē
– cream sauce	sauce *f* à la crème	sôs älä krām
– gravy	jus *m* de rôti	zhē də rôtē
seasoning (spice)	épice *f*	āpēs
thyme	thym *m*	teN
vanilla	vanille *f*	vänē'ē
vinegar	vinaigre *m*	vēnāg(ər)
wine	vin *m*	veN

THE MENU

Appetizers

ailloli *m*	ä·ēyôlē	**garlic mayonnaise**
anchois *m/pl.*	äNshô·ä	**anchovies**
anguille *f* fumée	äNgē'ē fēmā	**smoked eel**
artichaut *m*	ärtēshō	**artichoke**
– cœur d'artichaut	kār därtēshō	**heart of artichoke**
– lyonnais	lē·ônā	**boiled artichoke**
assiette *f* anglaise	äsyet äNglāz	**cold cuts**
beurre *f* d'anchois	bār däNshô·ä	**anchovy butter**
canapé *m*	känäpā	**appetizer**
crabes *m/pl.*	kräb	**crab**
crevettes *f/pl.*	krevet	**shrimp**
croque-monsieur *m*	krôk-məsyā	**grilled ham and cheese sandwich**
croûte *f* au fromage	kro͞ot ō frômäzh	**cheese pastry**
écrevisses *f/pl.*	ākrevēs	**crayfish**
escargots *m/pl.*	eskärgō	**snails**
homard *m*	ômär	**lobster**
huîtres *f/pl.*	ē·ēt(ər)	**oysters**

> *A simple way of selecting your meal in a French restaurant is to choose from the* menu. *This full course meal is generally very good and cheaper than if you order* à la carte. *Don't get confused: the word for menu in French is* la carte.

jambon *m*	zhäNbôN	**ham**
– blanc	– bläN	**– boiled**
– fumé	– fēmā	**– smoked**
– cru	– krē	**– raw**
pâté *m* de foie gras	pätā də fô·ä grä	**goose liver pâté**
pâté *m* en croute	pätā eN kro͞ot	**paté in crust**
salade *f* niçoise	säläd nēsô·äz	**vegetable salad**
salade *f* de tomates	säläd də tômät	**tomato salad**
saucisson *m*	sôsēsôN	**French salami**
viande *f* froide	vyäNd frô·äd	**cold meat**
vol-au-vent *m*	vôl-ô-väN	**puff pastry pie**

Soups

bisque *f*	bēsk	**shellfish soup**
bouillabaisse *f*	bo͞oyäbās	**bouillabaisse**
consommé *m*	kôNsômā	**bouillon, broth**
crème *f* d'asperges	krām däspārzh	**cream of asparagus soup**
garbure *f*	gärbēr	**vegetable soup with goose meat**
potage *m*	pôtäzh	**soup**
– à la printanière	– älä preNtänyār	**vegetable soup**
– de gibier	– də zhēbyā	**game soup**
– de volaille	– də vôlä'ē	**chicken broth**
– julienne	– zhēlyen	**julienne**
– Saint-Germain	– seN zhermeN	**pea soup**
potée *f*	pôtā	**hot pot**
soupe *f*	so͞op	**soup**
– à l'ail	– ä lä'ē	**garlic soup**
– à l'oignon	– ä lônyôN	**onion soup**
– aux choux	ō sho͞o	**cabbage soup**
– aux lentilles	ō läNtē'ē	**lentil soup**
– de poissons	– də pô·äsôN	**fish soup**
vichyssoise *f*	vēshēsô·äz	**vichyssoise**

Noodles

plat *m* de macaronis *or* de nouilles	plä də mäkärōnē, də no͞o'ē	**dish with macaroni *or* noodles**
– à la crème fraîche	– älä krām frāsh	**with cream**
– à la sauce tomate	– älä sôs tômät	**with tomato sauce**
– au gratin	– ō gräteN	**au gratin *(baked cheese)***
– au parmesan	– ō pärmezäN	**with permesan cheese**

Fish

aiglefin *m*	āgləfeN	**haddock**
anguille *f*	äNgē'ē	**eel**
barbeau *m*	bärbō	**mullet**
brochet *m*	brôshā	**pike**
cabillaud *m*	käbēyō	**cod(fish)**
carpe *f*	kärp	**carp**
colin *m*	kôleN	**hake**
dorade *f*	dôräd	**gilthead**
esturgeon *m*	estērzhôN	**sturgeon**
hareng *m*	äräN	**herring**
maquereau *m*	mäkərō	**mackerel**
morue *f*	môrē	**cod(fish)**
perche *f*	pārsh	**perch**
plie *f*	plē	**plaice**
poisson *m*	pô·äsôN	**fish**
– d'eau douce	– dō do͞os	**freshwater fish**
– de mer	– də mār	**saltwater fish**
sandre *f*	säNd(ər)	**pike, perch**
saumon *m*	sômôN	**salmon**
sole *f*	sôl	**sole**
tanche *f*	täNsh	**tench**
thon *m*	tôN	**tuna**
truite *f*	trē·ēt	**trout**
turbot *m*	tērbō	**turbot**
– à la meunière	– älä mānyār	**– fried**
– au bleu	– ō blā	**– steamed**

Sea Food

coquillages *m/pl.*	kôkēyäzh	**shellfish**
coquilles *f/pl.* Saint-Jacques	kôkē'ē seN zhäk	**scallops**
crabes *f/pl.*	kräb	**hard-shell crabs**
crevettes *f/pl.*	krevet	**shrimps**
écrevisse *f*	ākrevēs	**crayfish**
homard *m*	ômär	**lobster**
huître *f*	ē·ēt(ər)	**oyster**
langouste *f*	läNgo͞ost	**spiny lobster**
moules *f/pl.*	mo͞ol	**mussels**

Poultry

abattis *m* d'oie	äbätē dô·ä	**goose giblets**
bécasse *f*	bākäs	**woodcock**
blanc *m* de poulet	bläN də po͞olā	**chicken breast**
caille *f*	kä'ē	**quail**
canard *m*	känär	**duck**
– sauvage	– sôväzh	**wild duck**
coq *m* au vin	kôk ō veN	**stewed chicken in red wine**
dinde *f*	deNd	**turkey**
– aux marrons	– ō märôN	**– with sweet roasted chestnuts**
faisan *m*	fāzäN	**pheasant**
oie *f*	ô·ä	**goose**
perdrix *f*	perdrē	**partridge**
pigeon *m*	pēzhôN	**pigeon**
poule *f*	po͞ol	**chicken**
poulet *m* de grain	po͞olā də greN	**broiler**
poulet *m* rôti	po͞olā rôtē	**roast chicken**

Meat

agneau *m*	änyō	**lamb**
bœuf *m*	bəf	**beef**
cerf *m*	sār	**stag**
chevreau *m*	shevrō	**goat kid**
chevreuil *m*	shevrə'ē	**venison**
gibier *m*	zhēbyā	**game**
lapin *m*	läpeN	**rabbit**
lièvre *m*	lē·āv(ər)	**wild rabbit**
mouton *m*	mo͞otôN	**lamb**
porc *m*	pôr	**pork**
sanglier *m*	säNglēyā	**wild boar**
veau *m*	vō	**veal**

aloyau *m*	älô·äyō	**sirloin**
bifteck *m*	bēftek	**steak**
– à cheval	– ä sheväl	**– with egg**
blanquette *f* de veau	bläNket dә vō	**veal stew**
bœuf *m* à la mode	b*ā*f älä môd	**braised beef with carrots**
– bourguignon	– bo͞orgēnyôN	**beef stew with mushrooms and red wine**
cervelle *f*	servel	**brains**
– en beignet	– servel äN benyā	**baked brains**
châteaubriand *m*	shätôbrē·äN	**châteaubriand steak**
civet *m*	sēvā	**ragout**
– de lièvre	– sēvā dә lē·āv(әr)	**jugged hare**
côtelette *f*	kôtlet	**chop**
cochon *m* de lait à la broche	kôshôN dә lā älä brôsh	**suckling pig on a spit**
cuisse *f*	k*ē*·ēs	**leg**
cuisses *f/pl.* de grenouilles	k*ē*·ēs dә greno͞o'ē	**grenouilles legs**
couscous	ko͞osko͞os	**couscous *(vegetables and semolina with meat or chicken)***
daube *f* de mouton	dôb dә mo͞otôN	**stewed lamb**
entrecôte *f*	äNtr(ә)kôt	**steak**
épaule *f*	āpôl	**shoulder**
escalope *f*	eskälôp	**schnitzel**
– à la viennoise	– älä vē·enô·äz	**Wiener schnitzel**
estouffade de bœuf	esto͞ofäd dә b*ā*f	**stewed beef (ragout)**
étuvée *f* de veau	ät*ē*vā dә vō	**leg of veal, stewed**
faux-filet *m*	fō-fēlā	**rump steak**
filet *m*	fēlā	**tenderloin, fillet**
foie *f*	fô·ä	**liver**
fricandeau *m*	frēkäNdō	**larded roast veal**
fricassé *m*	frēkäsā	**fricassee**
gigot *m*	zhēgō	**leg**
– d'agneau	– zhēgō dänyō	**leg of lamb, roast**
grillade *f*	grēyäd	**grilled meat**
– de porc	– dә pôr	**grilled pork**

hachis *m*	äshē	**roast forcemeat**
haricot *m* de mouton	ärēkō də mo͞otôN	**lamb stew with white beans**
jambonneau *m*	zhäNbônō	**trotters, pickled pork**
langue *f*	läNg	**tongue**
– de bœuf Valenciennes	– də bā̈f väläNsyen	**smoked tongue of beef**
miroton *m*	mērōtôN	**stewed beef with sauce of onions**
oiseaux *m/pl.* sans tête	ô·äzō säN tāt	**collared veal *(filled)***
pâté *m*	pätā	**paté**
petit salé *m*	pətē sälā	**salted meat**
poitrine *f*	pô·ätrēn	**brisket**
pot-au-feu *m*	pôtōfā̈	**stew *(vegetables and meat)***
quenelles *f/pl.*	kenel	**fish or chickenballs**
ragoût *m*	rägo͞o	**ragout, hash**
ris *m* de veau	rē də vō	**veal and rice**
rognonnade *f* de veau	rônyônäd də vō	**roast veal loin**
rognons *m/pl.*	rônyôN	**kidneys**
rôti *m*	rôtē	**joint**
saucisses *f/pl.*	sôsēs	**sausages**
selle *f*	sel	**saddle**
– de chevreuil	– də shevrā̈'ē	**saddle of venison**
sauté *m* de lapin au vin blanc	sôtā də läpeN ō veN bläN	**ragout of rabbit, stewed in white wine**
tripes *f/pl.*	trēp	**tripe**

Vegetables

artichauts *m/pl.*	ärtēshō	**artichokes**
asperge *f*	äspärzh	**asparagus**
aubergine *f*	ōberzhēn	**eggplant**
betteraves *f/pl.*	betəräv	**turnips**
– rouges	– ro͞ozh	**beets**
carottes *f/pl.*	kärôt	**carrots**
céleri *m*	sälerē	**celery**

céleri-rave	sālerē-räv	**celery root**
champignons *m/pl.*	shäNpēnyôN	**mushrooms**
chicorée *f*	shēkôrā	**curly endive, chicory**
chou *m*	shōō	**cabbage**
– blanc	– bläN	**white cabbage**
– de Bruxelles	– də brēsel	**Brussels sprouts**
– frisé	– frēzā	**savoy cabbage**
– rouge	– rōōzh	**red cabbage**
choucroute *f*	shōōkrōōt	**sauerkraut**
chou-fleur *m*	shōō-flār	**cauliflower**
chou-rave *m*	shōō-räv	**kohlrabi**
concombre *m*	kôNkôNb(ər)	**cucumber**
courge *f*	kōōrzh	**pumpkin, squash**
endives *f/pl.*	äNdēv	**Belgian endive**
épinards *m/pl.*	āpēnär	**spinach**
haricots *m/pl.*	ärēkō	**beans**
– verts	– vār	***French (string)* beans**
– beurre	– bār	**butter beans**
laitue *f*	lātē	**lettuce**
oignons *m/pl.*	ônyôN	**onions**
petits pois *m/pl.*	pətē pô·ä	**peas**
poivrons *m/pl.*	pô·ävrôN	**peppers**
scarole *f*	skärôl	**escarole**
pommes *f/pl.* de terre	pôm də tār	**potatoes**
– dauphine	dôfēn	**– croquettes**
– en robe des champs	äN rôb dā shäN	**– in their jackets**
– mousseline	mōōslēn	**mashed potatoes**
– rôties au four	rôtē ō fōōr	**baked potatoes**
– sautées	sôtā	**fried potatoes**
pommes *f/pl.*nature	pom nätēr	**boiled potatoes**
– frites	frēt	**French fries**
salade *f*	säläd	**salad**
tomates *f/pl.*	tômät	**tomatoes**

Cheese

bleu d'Auvergne	blā dōvārn(yə)	**blue cheese**
fromage *m*	frômäzh	**cheese**
– blanc	– bläN	**cottage cheese**
– aux fines herbes	– ō fēnzārb	**cheese with herbs**
– à pâte molle	– ä pät môl	**cream cheese**
– à tartiner	– ä tärtēnā	**cheese spread**
– de chèvre	– də shāv(ər)	**goat cheese**
– gruyère	– grēyār	**Swiss cheese, Gruyère (cheese)**

Desserts

clafoutis *m*	kläfo͞otē	**pudding with cherries**
crème *f*	krām	**mousse, pudding, custard**
– à la vanille	– älä vänē'ē	**vanilla custard**
– caramel	– kärämel	**caramel custard**
crêpe *f*	krāp	**crêpe *(thin pancake)***
– suzette	– sēzet	**crêpe suzette**
– fourrée	– fo͞orā	**– with filling**
glace *f*	gläs	**ice cream**
meringue *f*	mereNg	**meringue**
mousse *f* au chocolat	mo͞os ō shôkōlä	**chocolate mousse**
parfait *m*	pärfā	**frozen dessert**
pommes *f/pl.* meringuées	pôm mereNgā	**apple fritter**
riz *m* au lait	rē·ōlā	**rice pudding**
sabayon *m*	säbäyôN	**zabaglione *(wine mousse)***
soufflé *m* au chocolat	so͞oflā ō shôkōlä	**chocolate soufflé**

Fruit

ananas *m*	änänä	**pineapple**
abricot *m*	äbrēkō	**apricot**
airelles *f/pl.*	ārel	**blueberries**
– rouges	– ro͞ozh	**cranberries**
amandes *f/pl.*	ämäNd	**almonds**
banane *f*	bänän	**banana**
cacah(o)uètes *f/pl.*	käkä·o͞o·et	**peanuts**
cassis *m/pl.*	käsēs	**black currants**
cerises *f/pl.*	serēz	**cherries**
citron *m*	sētrôN	**lemon**
coco *m*	kôkō	**coconut**
coing *m*	kô·eN	**quince**
dattes *f/pl.*	dät	**dates**
figues *f/pl.*	fēg	**figs**
fraises *f/pl.*	frāz	**strawberries**
framboises *f/pl.*	fräNbô·äz	**raspberries**
fruits *m/pl.*	frē·ē	**fruit**
groseilles *f/pl.*	grôzā'ē	**red currants**
– à maquereau	– ä mäkərō	**gooseberries**
mandarine *f*	mäNdärēn	**tangerine**
marrons *m/pl.*	märôN	**chestnuts**
melon *m*	melôN	**(honeydew) melon**
mûres *f/pl.*	mēr	**blackberries**
noisettes *f/pl.*	nô·äzet	**hazelnuts**
noix *f/pl.*	nô·ä	**nuts**
orange *f*	ôräNzh	**orange**
pamplemousse *f*	päNpləmo͞os	**grapefruit**
pêche *f*	pāsh	**peach**
poire *f*	pô·är	**pear**
pomme *f*	pôm	**apple**
prune *f*	prēn	**plum**
raisins *m/pl.*	rāzeN	**grapes**
rhubarbe *f*	rēbärb	**rhubarb**

BEVERAGES

Wine

Bordeaux	Bordeaux	bôrdō
Burgundy	(vin de) Bourgogne	(veN də) bo͞orgôn(yə)
cider	cidre *m*	sēd(ər)
dessert wine	vin *m* de dessert	veN də desār
mulled wine	vin *m* chaud	veN shō
Muscatel	muscat *m*	m*ē*skä
red wine	vin *m* rouge	veN ro͞ozh
rosé wine	rosé *m*	rōzā
white wine	vin *m* blanc	veN bläN

Famous French wine

Beaujolais	bōzhôlā
Chablis	shäblē
Chateauneuf-du-Pape	shätōn*â*f-d*ē*-päp
Corbières	kôrbyār
Côtes de Provence	kōtdə prôväNs
Côtes du Rhône	kōtd*ē* rōn
Entre-deux-Mers	äNt(ər)-d*ā*-mār
Médoc	mādôk
Muscadet	m*ē*skädā
Saint-Emilion	seNtāmēlyôN
Sauternes	sôtārn

Beer

beer	bière *f*	byār
beer mug	chope *f* bière	shôp byār
dark beer	bière *f* brune	byār br*ē*n
a glass of beer	un verre de bière	eN vār də byār
light beer	bière *f* blonde	byār blôNd
malt liquor	bière *f* de malt	byār də mält

Other Alcoholic Beverages

alcoholic beverage	boisson *f* alcoolique	bô·äsôN älkôlēk
bitters	bitter *m*	bētär
brandy	eau-de-vie *f*	ōdvē
cognac	cognac *m*	kônyäk
gin	gin *m*	dzhēn
liqueur	liqueur *f*	lēkār
– apricot brandy	liqueur *f* d'abricot	lēkār däbrēkō
– cherry brandy	liqueur *f* de cerises	lēkār də serēz
punch	punch *m*	pôNtsh
rum	rhum *m*	rôm
vodka	vodka *m*	vôdkä
whiskey	whisky *m*	o͞o·ēskē

In virtually all European countries, when you order a whiskey, you are ordering Scotch whisky. *If you would prefer rye, bourbon, or some other beverage, you should say this when making your order.*

Non-Alcoholic Beverages

For coffee, tea, chocolate and milk, please see pp. 113–114.

fruit juice	jus *m* de fruits	zhē də frē·ē
– apple juice	jus *m* de pommes	zhē də pôm
– black currant juice	jus *m* de cassis	zhē də käsē
– grapefruit juice	jus *m* de pamplemousse	zhē də päNpləmo͞os
– orange juice	jus *m* d'orange	zhē dôräNzh
lemonade	limonade *f*	lēmônäd
milk shake	milk-shake *m*	mēlk-shāk
orangeade	orangeade *f*	ôräNzhäd
soda water	soda *m*; eau *f* de Seltz	sōdä; ō də sels
soft drink	boisson *f* non-alcoolisée	bô·äsôN nônälkôlēzā
tonic water	eau *f* tonique	ō tônēk
water	eau *f*	ō
– mineral water	– eau *f* minérale	ō mēnäräl
– carbonated	– gazeuse	– gäzāz
– non-carbonated	– non-gazeuse	– nôN-gäzāz

In the Café

In France, as in most of Europe, a café *is a great place to relax with a cup of coffee, meet friends, read the paper, or most popular of all, people-watch. If it's pastries and cakes you're interested in, you'll find the largest selection in a* pâtisserie *(bakery).*

I'd like . . .
Je voudrais . . .
zhə vo͞odrā

a piece of cake	un morceau de gâteau	eN môrsō də gätō
– of tart	– une tarte(lette)	ēn tärt(əlet)
a cup of coffee	un café	eN käfā
a cup of tea	un thé	eN tā
a dish of ice cream	une glace	ēn gläs
***– with (without)* whipped cream**	*– avec (sans)* Chantilly	– ävek (säN) shäNtēyē
a glass of orange juice	un verre de jus d'orange	eN vār də zhē dôräNzh
cake	gâteau *m*	gätō
candy	chocolat *m*, bonbon *m*	shôkōlä, bôNbôN
chocolate	chocolat *m*	shôkōlä
chocolate with ice cream	chocolat *m* glacé	shôkōlä gläsā
confectionery	pâtisserie *f* (fine)	pätēsərē (fēn)
cookies	petit gâteau *m* sec	pətē gätō sāk
– almond cookies	– aux amandes	– ōzämäNd
cream	crème *f*	krām
ice cream	glace *f*	gläs
– chocolate ice cream	glace *f* au chocolat	gläs ō shôkōlä
– strawberry ice cream	glace *f* à la fraise	gläs älä frāz
– vanilla ice cream	glace *f* à la vanille	gläs älä vänē'ē
– assorted ice cream	glace *f* panachée	gläs pänäshā
ice cream parlor	pâtissier glacier *m*	pätēsyā gläsyā
meringue	meringue *f*	māreNg

milk	lait *m*	lā
– ***cold (warm)*** **milk**	lait *m froid (chaud)*	lā frô·ä (shō)
– **evaporated milk**	lait *m* condensé	lā kôNdäNsā
sherbet	sorbet *m*	sôrbā
sugar	sucre *m*	sēk(ər)
– **cube sugar**	sucre *m* en morceaux	sēkräN môrsō
sundae	coupe *f* glacée	ko͞op gläsā
sweets	bonbons *m/pl.*	bôNbôN
tart	tarte *f*, gâteau *m*	tärt, gätō
– **fruit tart**	tarte *f* aux fruits	tärt ō frē·ē
tea ***(see p. 98)***	thé *m*	tā
wafers	gaufrettes *f/pl.*; cornet *m* de glace	gôfret; kôrnā də gläs
whipped cream	Chantilly *f*	shäNtēyē

Incidentally, nobody will expect you to know all the names of the different cakes, pies, pastries, tarts, cookies, candies and other tempting sweets available in this part of the world. Things are always on display in any café or bakery, which means all you have to do is walk up to the counter and use the universal language, in other words, point! Your cake or pastry will be delivered to your table.

Complaints, Paying the Check

We need another *portion (set of silverware, glass).*
Ici il manque encore *un plat (un couvert, un verre).*
ēsē ēl mäNk äNkôr eN plä (eN ko͞ovār, eN vār)

This isn't what I ordered.
Je n'ai pas commandé cela.
zhə nā pä kômäNdā səlä

I wanted . . .
J'ai commandé . . .
zhā kômäNdā

This is not fresh any more.
Ce n'est plus frais.
sə nā plē frā

This is . . .
C'est . . .
sā . . .

too fatty	trop gras	trō grä
too hard	trop dur	trō dēr
too hot *(temperature)*	trop chaud	trō shō
too hot *(spicy)*	trop épicé	trōāpēsā
too cold	trop froid	trō frô·ä
too salty	trop salé	trō sälā
too sour	trop aigre	trō āg(ər)
too tough	trop coriace	trō kôryäs

I'd like to pay. (The check, please!)
Garçon, l'addition s'il vous plaît.
gärsôN, lädēsyôN, sēl vo͞o plā

All together, please.
Je paie tout. (C'est moi qui règle.)
zhə pā to͞o (sā mô·ä kē rāg(əl)

Separate checks, please.
Nous payons séparément.
no͞o pāyôN sāpärāmäN

I don't think this is correct.
Cela ne me paraît pas exact.
səlä nə mə pärā päzegsäkt

We didn't have that.
Nous n'avons pas eu ça.
no͞o nävôN päzā sä

Thanks very much.
Merci beaucoup!
mersē bōko͞o

Keep the change.
C'est pour vous.
sā po͞or vo͞o

If you are pleased with the waiter's service, you can leave a small tip. Otherwise, the check includes the tip. The term taxe et service compris *on the menu means that tax and service charge are included in the price.*

DOWNTOWN

On the Street

Where is . . .?
Où est . . .?
o͞o ā . . .

the bus stop	l'arrêt d'autobus	lärā dôtōbēs
the Catholic Church	l'église catholique	lāglēz kätōlēk
the city hall	l'hôtel de ville	lôtel də vēl
the harbor	le port	lə pôr
the . . . Hotel	l'hôtel . . .	lôtel
the museum	le musée	lə mēzā
the police station	le commissariat de police	lə kômēsärē·ä də pôlēs
the post office	le bureau de poste	lə bērō də pôst
the Protestant Church	le temple	lə täNp'əl
. . . Square	la place	lä pläs . . .
. . . Street	la rue	lä rē . . .
the station	la gare	lä gär
the synagogue	la synagogue	lä sēnägôg
a taxi stand	une station de taxis	ēn stäsyôN də täksē

Is it far from here?
Est-ce loin d'ici?
es lô·eN dēsē

How far is it to the . . .?
Quelle est la distance d'ici *au (à la)* . . .?
kel ā lä dēstäNs dēsē ō (älä) . . .

How many minutes by foot?
Combien de minutes à pied?
kôNbyeN də mēnēt ä pyā

A good distance (Not far).
Assez (Pas) loin.
äsā (pä) lô·eN

Which direction is . . .?
Dans quelle direction se trouve. . .?
däN kel dēreksyôN sə tro͞ov . . .

What street is . . . on?
Dans quelle rue se trouve . . .?
däN kel rē sə tro͞ov . . .

There.
Là.
lä

Straight ahead.
Tout droit.
to͞o drô·ä

To the right.
À droite.
ä drô·ät

To the left.
À gauche.
ä gôsh

Bus, Taxi

Can I get there by bus?
Je peux y aller en autobus?
zhə pā ē·älā änôtōbēs

Which bus goes to (the) . . .?
Quel autobus va *à (au, à la)* . . .?
kel ôtōbēs vä ä (ō, älä) . . .

How many stops is it from here?
Combien d'arrêts y a-t-il?
kôNbyeN därā yätēl

Do I have to change?
Faut-il changer (d'autobus)?
fôtēl shäNzhā (dôtōbēs)

Where do I have to *get out (change)?*
Où faut-il *descendre (changer d'autobus)?*
o͞o fôtēl desäNd(ər) (shäNzhā dôtōbēs)

Would you please tell me when we get there?
Dites-moi quand nous serons à . . ., s'il vous plaît.
dēt-mō·ä käN no͞o serôN ä . . ., sēl vo͞o plā

A *one-way (transfer)* ticket to . . .
Un billet *simple (de correspondance)* pour . . .
eN bēyā seNp'əl (də kôrespôNdäNs) po͞or . . .

Where can I get a taxi?
Je peux prendre un taxi où?
zhə pā präNdreN täksē o͞o

Take me to . . .
Conduisez-moi *au (à la)* . . .
kôNdē·ēzā-mô·ä ō (älä) . . .

To the station, please.
À la gare, s'il vous plaît!
älä gär, sēl vo͞o plā

How much is the fare to . . .?
Ça fait combien *jusqu'à (jusqu'au, jusqu'à la)* . . .
sä fā kôNbyeN zhēskä (zhēskō, zhēskä lä) . . .

Could you show us some of the sights?
Pourriez-vous nous montrer quelques curiosités?
po͞orē·ā-vo͞o no͞o môNtrā kelke kērē·ōsētā

Please *wait (stop)* here a minute.
Attendez (Arrêtez-vous) ici un moment, s'il vous plaît.
ätäNdā (ärātā-vo͞o) ēsē eN mômäN, sēl vo͞o plā

Sightseeing and Excursions

Many museums and historic monuments as well as shops close for a few hours during lunchtime, so it's a good idea to take this into consideration when planning your day. Museums and other public monuments are usually closed on Tuesdays in France as well as on the public holidays.

Two tickets for the . . . tomorrow, please.
Pour demain deux places pour . . ., s'il vous plaît.
po͞or demeN dā pläs po͞or . . ., sēl vo͞o plā

Is lunch included?
Est-ce que le déjeuner est compris?
eske lə dāzhānā ā kôNprē

When do we get going?
Quelle est l'heure du départ?
kel ā lār dē dāpär

***When (Where)* do we meet?**
Quand (Où) nous retrouvons-nous?
käN (o͞o) no͞o retro͞ovôN-no͞o

Will we be seeing the . . . too?
Visitons-nous aussi . . .?
vēzētôN-no͞o ôsē . . .

Will we have some free time?
Avons-nous du temps à notre disposition?
ävôN-no͞o dē täN ä nôt(ər) dēspôzēsyôN

How much?
Combien?
kôNbyeN

Will we be able to do some shopping?
On peut faire du shopping?
ôN pā fār dē shôpēng

Will we be going to . . . too?
Est-ce qu'on va aussi à . . .?
eskôN vä osē ä . . .

How long will we stay in . . .?
Combien de temps resterons-nous à . . .?
kôNbyeN də täN restərôN-no͞ozä . . .

When do we get back?
Quand rentrerons-nous?
käN räNtrerôN-no͞o

What's worth seeing in . . .?
Quelles curiosités y a-t-il à . . .?
kel kērē·ōzētā yätēl ä . . .

When does . . . *open (close)*?
À quelle heure *ouvre (ferme)* . . .?
äkelār o͞ov(ər) (fārm) . . .

How much does the *admission (guided tour)* cost?
Combien coûte *l'entrée (la visite guidée)*?
kôNbyeN ko͞ot läNtrā (lä vēzēt gēdā)

Is there an English-speaking guide?
Y a-t-il un guide qui parle anglais?
ēyätēl eN gēd kē pärl äNglā

I'd like to see the . . .
J'aimerais voir . . .
zhāmerā vô·är . . .

Can we take a look at . . . today?
Peut-on visiter aujourd'hui . . .
p*ā*tôN vēzētā ōzhōōrd*ē*·ē . . .

the castle	le château	lə shätō
the cathedral	la cathédrale	lä kätādräl
the church	l'église	lāglēz
the fortress	la forteresse	lä fôrtəres
the exhibition	l'exposition	lekspōzēsyōN
the gallery	la galerie	lä gälerē
the memorial	le monument commémoratif	lə môn*ē*mäN kômemôrätēf
the museum	le musée	lə m*ē*zā
the palace	le palais	lə pälā
the zoo	le zoo	lə zô(ō)

When does the tour start?
À quelle heure commence la visite guidée?
äkel*ā*r kômäNs lä vēzēt gēdā

Can we take pictures?
On peut faire des photos?
ôN p*ā* fār dā fōtō

What is that *building (monument)*?
Quel *édifice (monument)* est-ce?
kel ādēfēs (môn*ē*mäN) es

Who *painted this picture (sculpted this statue)*?
De qui est *ce tableau (cette statue)*?
də kē·ā sə täblō (set stät*ē*)

What period does this . . . date from?
De quel siècle est . . .?
dəkel sēyāk'əl ā . . .

When was . . . built?
Quand a été bâti . . .?
käNdä ātā bätē . . .

Who built . . .?
Qui a bâti . . .?
kē ä bätē . . .

Where can I find . . .?
Où se trouve . . .?
ōō sə trōōv . . .

Is this . . .?
Est-ce que c'est . . .?
eske sā . . .

***This is where . . . *lived (was born, died)*.**
Ici *vécut (naquit, mourut)* . . .
ēsē vāk*ē* (näkē, mōōr*ē*) . . .

Vocabulary

airport	aéroport *m*	ä·ārōpôr
alley	ruelle *f*, allée *f*	rē·el, älā
amusement park	parc *m* d'attractions	pärk däträksyôN
area	région *f*	rāzhē·ôN
avenue	avenue *f*	ävənē
boat trip	promenade *f* en bateau	prômenäd äN bätō
botanical gardens	jardin *m* botanique	zhärdeN bôtänēk
bridge	pont *m*	pôN
building	édifice *m*, immeuble *m*	ādēfēs, ēmə̄b'əl
bus	autobus *m*	ôtōbēs
capital	capitale *f*	käpētäl
– national capital	capitale *f* nationale	käpētäl näsyônäl
castle	château *m*, château *m* fort	shätō shätō fôr
cathedral	cathédrale *f*	kätādräl
cave	caverne *f*	kävārn
cemetery	cimetière *m*	sēmetyār
church	église *f*	āglēz
churchyard	cimetière *m*	sēmetyār
city	ville *f*	vēl
city hall	hôtel *m* de ville	ôtel də vēl
consulate	consulat *m*	kôNsēlä
corner	coin *m*	kô·eN
countryside	paysage *m*	pā·ēzäzh
courthouse	palais *m* de Justice	pälā də zhēstēs
covered market	marché *m* couvert	märshā kōōvār
dead-end street	voie *f* sans issue	vô·ä säNzēsē
district	région *f*	rāzhē·ôN
ditch	fossé *m*	fôsā
downtown area	centre *m* (de la) ville	säNt(ər) (dəlä) vēl
embassy	ambassade *f*	äNbäsäd
environs	environs *m/pl.*	äNvērôN
excavations	fouilles *f/pl.*	fōō'ē
excursion	excursion *f*	ekskērsyôN
exhibition	exposition *f*	ekspōzēsyôN
factory	usine *f*	ēzēn
farmhouse	ferme *f*	fārm
fire department	pompiers *m/pl.*	pôNpyā

first-aid station	poste *m* de secours	pôst də səko͞or
fountain	fontaine *f*, jet *m* d'eau	fôNten, zhā dō
gallery	galerie *f*	gälerē
garden	jardin *m*	zhärdeN
gate	portail *m*	pôrtä'ē
government office	administration *f*	ädmēnēsträsyôN
grave	tombe *f*	tôNb
guide	guide *m*	gēd
harbor	port *m*	pôr
high-rise building	building *m*, tour *f*	bēldēng, to͞or
hiking path	sentier *m* de randonnée	säNtyā də räNdônā
hill	colline *f*	kôlēn
hospital	hôpital *m*	ôpētäl
house	maison *f*	māzôN
house number	numéro *m* de la maison	n*ē*mārō dəlä mā-zôN
landscape	paysage *m*	pā·ēzäzh
lane	ruelle *f*	r*ē*·el
last stop	terminus *m*	termēn*ē*s
library	bibliothèque *f*	bēblē·ôtāk
lost and found office	bureau *m* des objets trouvés	b*ē*rō dāzôbzhā tro͞ovā
main street	rue *f* principale	r*ē* preNsēpäl
memorial	monument *m* commémoratif	môn*ē*mäN kômāmôrätēf
military base	base *f* militaire	bäz mēlētār
ministry	ministère *m*	mēnēstār
moat	fossé *m*	fôsā
monument	monument *m*	môn*ē*mäN
mountain	montagne *f*	môNtän(yə)
mountain range	chaîne *f* de montagnes	shen də môNtän(yə)
motion picture theatre	cinéma *m*	sēnāmä
museum	musée *m*	m*ē*zā
national park	parc *m* national	pärk näsyōnäl
observatory	observatoire *m*	ôbservätô·är
old town	vieille ville *f*	vyā'ē vēl
open market	marché *m*	märshā

palace	palais *m*	pälā
park	parc *m*	pärk
part of town	quartier *m*	kärtyā
path	chemin *m*	shəmeN
pavillion	pavillon *m*	pävēyôN
pedestrian	piéton *m*	pyātôN
– pedestrian crossing	passage *m* clouté	päsäzh klo͞otā
police	police *f*	pôlēs
police station	commissariat *m* de police	kômēsärē·ä də pôlēs
policeman	agent *m* de police	äzhäN də pôlēs
port	port *m*	pôr
post office	bureau *m* de poste	bērō də pôst
power station	centrale *f* électrique	säNträl ālektrēk
public garden	parc *m*	pärk
public rest room	toilettes *f/pl.* publiques	tô·älet pēblēk
river	fleuve *m*	flāv
road	rue *f*	rē
road sign	panneau *m* de signalisation routière	pänō də sēnyälēzäsyôN ro͞otyār
ruin	ruine *f*	rē·ēn
school	école *f*	ākôl
sidewalk	trottoir *m*	trôtô·är
shop	magasin *m*	mägäzeN
shopping mall	centre *m* commercial	säNt(ər) kômersyäl
side road	rue *f* secondaire	rē sekôNdār
sightseeing	visite *f*	vēzēt
square	place *f*	pläs
stadium	stade *m*	städ
station	gare *f*	gär
stop	arrêt *m*	ärā
store	magasin *m*	mägäzeN
street	rue *f*	rē
suburb	faubourg *m*, banlieue *f*	fōbo͞or, bäNlēyā
suburban express train	train *m* de banlieue	treN də bäNlēyā
subway	métro *m*	mātrō
surroundings	environs *m/pl.*	äNvērôN

swimming area	piscine *f*	pēsēn
synagogue	synagogue *f*	sēnägôg
taxi	taxi *m*	täksē
taxi stand	station *f* de taxis	stäsyôN də täksē
temple	temple *m*	täNp'əl
throughway	passage *m*	päsäzh
tomb	tombe *f*	tôNb
tower	tour *f*	to͞or
town	ville *f*	vēl
traffic	circulation *f*	sērkēläsyôN
traffic light	feux *m/pl.*	fā
travel agency	agence *f* de voyage	äzhäNs də vô·äyäzh
university	université *f*	ēnēversētā
valley	vallée *f*	välā
village	village *m*	vēläzh
wall	mur *m*	mēr
waterfall	cascade *f*	käskäd
zebra crossing	passage *m* clouté	päsäzh klo͞otā
zoo	zoo *m*	zô(ō)

Religious Services

Where is the Catholic church?
Où est l'église catholique?
o͞o ā läglēz kätōlēk

Who's preaching the sermon?
Qui fait le sermon?
kē fā lə sermôN

What time *are services (is high mass)?*
Quand a lieu *le service religieux (la grand-messe)?*
käNdä lēyā lə servēs relēzhē·ā (lä gräNmes)

Is there a *wedding (christening)* today?
Y a-t-il aujourd'hui *un mariage (un baptème)?*
ēyätēl ōzho͞ordē·ē eN märē·äzh (eN bätām)

Do they have church concerts?
Il y a des concerts de musique religieuse?
ēlyā dā kôNsār də mēzēk relēzhē·āz

Please call a *clergyman (priest)!*
Faites venir un *curé (prêtre)*, s'il vous plaît.
fāt venēr eN kērā (prāt[ər]), sēl vo͞o plā

I am a	Je suis	zhə sē̄·ē
Christian	chrétien	krātyeN
Jew	juif	zhē̄·ēf
Catholic	catholique	kätōlēk
Methodist	méthodiste	mātōdēst
Moslem	musulman	mēzē̄lmäN
Protestant	protestant	prôtestäN

I don't belong to any religious denomination.
Je suis sans confession.
zhə sē̄·ē säN kôNfesyôN

abbey	abbaye *f*	äbā·ē
altar	autel *m*	ôtel
arch	arc *m*	ärk
baptism	baptême *m*	bätām
Baroque	baroque	bärôk
bell	cloche *f*	klôsh
candlestick	chandelier *m*	shäNdelēyā
cathedral	cathédrale *f*	kätādräl
(Roman) Catholic	catholique (romain)	kätōlēk (rômeN)
cemetery	cimetière *m*	sēmetyār
chapel	chapelle *f*	shäpel
choir	chœur m	kā̄r
Christ	le Christ	lə krēst
christening	baptême *m*	bätām
Christian	chrétien	krātyeN
Christianity	christianisme *m*	krēstyänēsm
church	église *f*	āglēz
churchyard	cimetière *m*	sēmetyār
circumcision	circoncision *f*	sērkôNsēzyôN
clergyman	*cath.* curé *m*;	kē̄rā;
	protest. pasteur *m*	pästā̄r
communion	communion *f*	kômē̄nyôN
confess	se confesser	sə kôNfesā
confession	confession *f*	kôNfesyôN
convent	couvent *m*	ko͞oväN
creed	profession *f* de foi	prôfesyôN də fô·ä
cross	croix *f*	krô·ä
crucifix	crucifix *m*	krē̄sēfēks

cupola	coupole *f*	ko͞opôl
denomination	confession *f*	kôNfesyôN
dome	coupole *f*	ko͞opôl
font	fonts *m/pl.* baptismaux	fôN bätēsmō
fresco	fresque *f*	fresk
God	Dieu *m*	dyā̆
Gospel	Evangile *m*	āväNzhēl
Gothic	gothique	gōtēk
grave	tombeau *m*	tôNbō
High Mass	grand-messe *f*	gräNmes
Islam	islamisme *m*	ēslämēsm
Jew	juif *m*	zhē̆·ēf
Jewish	juif	zhē̆·ēf
Judaism	judaïsme *m*	zhē̆dä·ēsm
mass	messe *f*	mes
monastery	couvent *m*	ko͞oväN
mosaic	mosaïque *f*	mōzä·ēk
Moslem	musulman *m*	mē̆zē̆lmäN
mosque	mosquée *f*	môskā
nave	nef *f*	nef
organ	orgue *m*	ôrg
pastor	*cath.* curé *m*; *protest.* pasteur *m*	kerā; pästā̆r
pillar	pilier *m*	pēlēyā
portal	portail *m*	pôrtä'ē
priest	prêtre *m*	prāt(ər)
procession	procession *f*	prôsesyôN
Protestant	protestant	prôtestäN
pulpit	chaire *f*	shār
rabbi	rabbin *m*	räbeN
religion	religion *f*	relēzhē·ôN
religious	religieux	relēzhē·ā̆
Romanesque	roman	rômäN
rosary	rosaire *m*	rōzār
sacristan, sexton	sacristain *m*	säkrēsteN
sacristy	sacristie *f*	säkrēstē
sermon	sermon *m*	sārmôN
service	office *m* religieux	ôfēs relēzhē·ā̆
Stations of the Cross	stations *f/pl.* du chemin de croix	stäsyôN dē̆ shəmeN də krô·ä

Star of David	étoile *f* de David	ātô·äl də dävēd
statue	statue *f*	stätē̆
synagogue	synagogue *f*	sēnägôg
tomb	tombeau *m*	tôNbō
tower	tour *f*	to͞or
vestibule	porche *m*	pôrsh

GOING SHOPPING

General Words and Phrases

Where can I *get (buy)* . . .?
Où est-ce que je peux *trouver (acheter)* . . .?
o͞o eske zhə pǟ tro͞ovā (äshtā) . . .

I need . . .
J'ai besoin de . . .
zhā bezô·eN də

Is there a *leather (china)* shop here?
Y a-t-il un magasin *de cuir (de porcelaine)?*
ēyätēl eN mägäzeN də kē̆·ēr (də pôrsəlen)

Have you got . . .?
Avez-vous . . .?
ävā-vo͞o . . .

***I'd (We'd)* like . . .**
Je voudrais (Nous voudrions) . . .
zhə vo͞odrā (no͞o vo͞odrē·ôN) . . .

Please show me . . .
Montrez-moi . . ., s'il vous plaît.
môNtrā-mô·ä . . . sēl vo͞o plā

Please give me . . .
Donnez-moi . . ., s'il vous plaît.
dônā-mô·ä . . ., sēl vo͞o plā

a bag	un sac	eN säk
a bottle	une bouteille	ēn bo͞otā'ē
a box	une boîte	ēn bô·ät
a few	quelques	kelke
a jar	un verre	eN vār
a pound	une livre	ēn lēv(ər)
a *pack (packet)*	un paquet	eN päkā
a pair	une paire	ēn pār
a piece	un morceau	eN môrsō
a quart	un litre	eN lēt(ər)
a quarter pound	un quart	eN kär
a roll	un rouleau	eN ro͞olō
a tube	un tube	eN tē̆b
two pounds	un kilo	eN kēlō
a yard	un mètre *(approx.)* *(=0,914 m)*	eN māt(ər)

That's plenty.
C'est assez.
set äsā

A little more.
Encore un peu.
äNkôr eN *pā*

Even more.
Davantage.
däväNtäzh

Can you order it for me?
Pouvez-vous le commander?
po͞ovā-vo͞o lə kômäNdā

When will you get it in?
Quand est-ce que vous l'aurez?
käNdeske vo͞o lôrā

Can I exchange it?
Je peux l'échanger?
zhə *pā* lāshäNzhā

I don't like the *shape (color).*
La *forme (couleur)* ne me plaît pas.
lä fôrm (ko͞o*lār*) nə mə plā pä

This is . . .	C'est . . .	sā . . .
too big	trop grand	trō gräN
too dark	trop foncé	trō fôNsā
too expensive	trop cher	trō shār
too *light (pale)*	trop clair	trō klār
too narrow	trop étroit	trōpātrô·ä
too small	trop petit	trō pətē
too wide	trop large	trō lärzh
too much	trop	trō

This is not enough.
Ce n'est pas assez.
sə nā päzäsā

Have you got something a little *nicer (less expensive)?*
Vous avez quelque chose *de mieux (de moins cher)?*
vo͞ozävā kelke shōz də my*ā* (də mô·eN shār)

I like that.
Cela me plaît.
səlä mə plā

I'll take it.
Je *le (la, les)* prends.
zhə lə (lä, lā) präN

How much is that?
Ça coûte combien?
sā ko͞ot kôNbyeN

Thanks, that'll be all.
Merci, c'est tout.
mersē, sā to͞o

Can you send my stuff to the . . . Hotel please?
Pouvez-vous m'envoyer la marchandise à l'hôtel . . ., s'il vous plaît?
po͞ovā-vo͞o mäNvô·äyā lä märshäNdēz ä lôtel . . ., sēl vo͞o plā

Do you take *credit cards (traveller's cheques)?*
Vous acceptez *des cartes de crédit (des chèques de voyage)?*
vo͞ozäkseptā dā kärt də krādē (dā shek də vô·äyäzh)

Stores

antique shop	magasin *m* d'antiquités	mägäzeN däNtēkētā
art gallery	galerie *f*	gälerē
bakery	boulangerie *f*	bo͞oläNzhərē
barber shop	coiffeur *m*	kô·äf*ā*r
beauty parlor	institut *m* de beauté ...	eNstēt*ē* də bōtā
bookshop	librairie *f*	lēbrārē
butcher shop	boucherie *f*	bo͞osherē
candy store	confiserie *f*	kôNfēzerē
china shop	magasin *m* de porcelaine	mägäzeN də pôrsəlen
cigar store	bureau *m* de tabac	b*ē*rō də täbä
clothes dyer	teinturerie *f*	teNt*ē*rerē
cobbler shop	cordonnerie *f*	kôrdônərē
cosmetic salon	institut *m* de beauté ...	eNstēt*ē* də bōtā
dairy	crèmerie *f*	krāmerē
department store	grand magasin *m*	gräN mägäzeN
dressmaker's shop ...	tailleur *m* pour dames .	täy*ā*r po͞or däm
drug store *(cosmetics & sundries)*	droguerie *f*	drôgerē
drug store *(prescription pharmacy)*	pharmacie *f*	färmäsē
dry cleaner's	nettoyage *m* à sec	netô·äyäzh ä sek
electrical shop	magasin *m* d'électroménager	mägäzeN dālektrōmānäzhā
fashion boutique	magasin *m* de haute couture	mägäzeN də ōt ko͞ot*ē*r
fish market	poissonnerie *f*	pô·äsônrē
flower shop	magasin *m* de fleurs ...	mägäzeN də fl*ā*r
fruit market	épicerie *f*, marché *m* ...	āpēsərē, märshā
furrier	pelleterie *f*	peletərē
furniture store	magasin *m* de meubles .	mägäzeN də m*ā*b'əl
grocery store	épicerie *f*	āpēsərē
haberdashery	mercerie *f*	mārserē
hardware store	quincaillerie *f*	keNkäyerē
hat shop	chapellerie *f*	shäpelerē
jewelry store	bijouterie *f*	bēzho͞otərē

laundromat	laverie *f* automatique	läverē ôtōmätēk
laundry	blanchisserie *f*	bläNshēsərē
leather goods store	maroquinerie *f*	märôkēnərē
lingerie shop	magasin *m* de lingerie	mägäzeN də leN-zhərē
liquor store	vins et spiritueux	veN ā spērētē·ā
music store	magasin *m* de musique	mägäzeN də mēzēk
newsdealer	marchand *m* de journaux	märshäN də zhōōrnō
optician	opticien *m*	ôptēsyeN
perfume shop	parfumerie *f*	pärfēmərē
pet shop	magasin *m* d'animaux	mägäzeN dänēmō
photo shop	photographe *m*	fōtōgräf
photographer's studio	photographe *m*	fōtōgräf
poultry shop	commerce *m* de volaille(s)	kômers də vôlä'ē
real estate agency	agence *f* immobilière	äzhäNs ēmôbēlēyār
record store	magasin *m* de disques	mägäzeN də dēsk
second-hand book-shop	librairie *f* d'occasion	lēbrārē dôkäzyôN
self-service	libre-service *m*	lēb(ər)-servēs
shoemaker's shop	cordonnerie *f* !	kôrdônərē
shoe store	magasin *m* de chaussures	mägäzeN də shōsēr
souvenir shop	magasin *m* de souvenirs *m/pl.*	mägäzeN də sōōvənēr
sporting goods store	magasin *m* de sport	mägäzeN də spôr
stationery store	papeterie *f*	päpātərē
super market	supermarché *m*	sēpermärshā
tailor shop	tailleur *m*	täyär
textile store	magasin *m* de tissu	mägäzeN də tēsē
toy store	magasin *m* de jouets	mägäzeN də zhōō·ā
travel agency	agence *f* de voyage	äzhäNs də vô·äyäzh
vegetable market	marchand *m* de légumes	märshäN də lāgēm
watchmaker's shop	horlogerie *f*	ôrlôzhərē
wine shop	marchand *m* de vin	märshäN də veN

Flowers

bouquet	bouquet *m* de fleurs	bo͞okā də flár
chrysanthemums	chrysanthèmes *m/pl.*	krēsäNtām
flower pot	pot *m* de fleurs	pô də flár
flowers	fleurs *f/pl.*	flár
gladioli	glaïeuls *m/pl.*	gläyál
lilacs	lilas *m*	lēlä
orchids	orchidées *f/pl.*	ôrkēdā
roses	roses *f/pl.*	rōz
tulips	tulipes *f/pl.*	tēlēp
vase	vase *m*	väz
violets	violettes *f/pl.*	vē·ôlet

Bookshop

autobiography	autobiographie *f*	ôtōbē·ōgräfē
biography	biographie *f*	bē·ōgräfē
book	livre *m*	lēv(ər)
catalogue	catalogue *m*	kätälôg
children's book	livre *m* pour enfants	lēv(ər) po͞or äNfäN
city map	plan *m* de la ville	pläN dəlä vēl
detective novel	roman *m* policier	rômäN pôlēsyā
dictionary	dictionnaire *m*	dēksyônār
guide book	guide *m* touristique	gēd to͞orēstēk
map	carte *f* géographique	kärt zhē·ōgräfēk
novel	roman *m*	rômäN
paperback	livre *m* de poche	lēv(ər) də pôsh
phrase book	guide *m* de conversation	gēd də kôNverzäsyôN
poetry book	recueil *m* de poésie	rekā'ē də pō·äzē
record	disque *m*	dēsk
reference book	ouvrage *m* de référence	o͞ovräzh də rāfäräNs
road map	carte *f* routière	kärt ro͞otyār
story book	livre *m* de contes	lēv(ər) də kôNt
text book	manuel *m*	mänē·el
thriller	roman *m* policier	rômäN pôlēsyā
translation	traduction *f*	trädēksyôN
travel reading	lecture *f* de voyage	lektēr də vô·äyäzh
volume	volume *m*	vôlēm

Photo Shop

Would you please develop this film?
Développez-moi ce rouleau, s'il vous plaît.
dāvālôpā-mô·ä sə ro͞olō, sēl vo͞o plā

One *print (enlargement)* of each negative, please.
Une épreuve (Un agrandissement) de chaque négatif, s'il vous plaît.
ēn āprāv (eNägräNdēs·mäN) də shäk nāgätēf, sēl vo͞o plā

– three by four (inches).
– sept (sur) dix.
– set (sēr) dēs

– three and a half by three and a half.
– neuf (sur) neuf.
– nāf (sēr) nāf

– three and a half by five and a half (inches).
– neuf (sur) treize.
– nāf (sēr) trāz

Could you retouch this for me?
Est-ce que vous pouvez retoucher un peu?
eske vo͞o po͞ovā reto͞oshā eN pā

I'd like . . .
Je voudrais . . .
zhə vo͞odrā . . .

– a cartridge film.
– un film à châssis.
– eN fēlm ä shäsē

– a super eight color film.
– un film en couleurs super huit.
– eN fēlm äN ko͞olār sēpär ē·ēt

– a sixteen millimeter color film.
– un film en couleurs seize mm.
– eN fēlm äN ko͞olār sāz mēlēmāt(ər)

– a black and white eight millimeter film.
– un film noir et blanc huit millimètres.
– eN fēlm nô·är ā bläN ē·ē mēlēmāt(ər)

– a thirty-five millimeter film.
– un film trente cinq millimètres.
– eN fēlm träNt seNk mēlēmāt(ər)

– a film for color slides.
– une pellicule de diapositives.
– ēn pelēkēl də dē·äpôzētēv

– a *twenty (thirty-six)* exposure film.
– une pellicule de *vingt (trente-six)* poses.
– ēn pelēkēl də veN (träNt-sēs) pōz

Would you please put the film in the camera for me?
Vous pourriez me mettre la pellicule dans l'appareil, s'il vous plaît?
vo͞o po͞orē·ā mə met(ər) lä pelēkēl däN läpärā'ē, sēl vo͞o plā

camera	appareil *m* photographique	äpärä'ē fōtōgräfēk
color film	pellicule *f* en couleurs	pelēk*ē*l äN ko͞ol*ā*r
color negative film	pellicule *f* négative en couleurs	pelēk*ē*l nāgätēv äN ko͞ol*ā*r
develop	développer	dāvelôpā
development	développement *m*	dāvelôpmäN
diaphragm	diaphragme *m*	dē·äfrägm
8-mm film	film *m* de huit millimètres	fēlm də *ē*·ē mēlēmāt(ər)
enlargement	agrandissement *m*	ägräNdēsmäN
exposure	exposition *f*	ekspōzēsyôN
exposure meter	posemètre *m*	pōzmāt(ər)
film	film *m*, pellicule *f*	fēlm, pelēk*ē*l
film *(take moving pictures)*	filmer	fēlmā
flash bulb	ampoule *f* flash	äNpo͞ol fläsh
flash cube	cube *m* flash	k*ē*b fläsh
lens	objectif *m*	ôbzhektēf
movie camera	caméra *f*	kämārä
negative	négatif *m*	nāgätēf
paper	papier *m*	päpyā
– glossy *(matte)*	– brillant *(mat)*	– brēyäN (mä)
photo, picture	photo(graphie) *f*	fōtō(gräfē)
photograph *(verb)*	prendre des photos	präNd(ər) dā fōtō
print	épreuve *f*	āpr*ā*v
– color print	épreuve *f* en couleurs	āpr*ā*v äN ko͞ol*ā*r
reversal film	film *m* inversible	fēlm eNversēb'əl
roll film	pellicule *f*, rouleau *m*	pelēk*ē*l, ro͞olō
shutter	obturateur *m*	obt*ē*rät*ā*r
shutter (release)	déclencheur *m*	dākläNsh*ā*r
– automatic shutter	déclencheur *m* automatique	dākläNsh*ā*r ôtōmätēk
slide	diapositive *f*	dē·äpōzētēv
slide frame	petit cadre *m* pour diapositives	pətē käd(ər) po͞or dē·äpōzētēv
snapshot	instantané *m*	eNstäNtänā
take a picture	prendre une photo	präNdr*ē*n fōtō
tripod	pied *m*	pyā
view finder	viseur *m*	vēz*ā*r
yellow filter	filtre *m* jaune	fēlt(ər) zhōn

Jeweler

amber	ambre *m* jaune	äNb(ər) zhōn
bracelet	bracelet *m*	bräslā
brooch	broche *f*	brôsh
costume jewelry	bijoux *m/pl.* fantaisie	bēzho͞o fäNtāzē
cufflinks	boutons *m/pl.* de manchette	bo͞otôN də mäNshet
diamond	brillant *m*	brēyäN
ear clips	clips *m/pl.*	klēp
earrings	boucles *f/pl.* d'oreille	bo͞ok'əl dôrā'ē
emerald	émeraude *f*	āmerōd
gold	or *m*	ôr
gold plated	doré	dôrā
jewelry	parure *f*	pärēr
necklace	chaîne *f*	shen
pearls	perles *f/pl.*	pārl
pendant	pendant *m*	päNdäN
ring	bague *f*	bäg
ruby	rubis *m*	rēbē
sapphire	saphir *m*	säfēr
silver	argent *m*	ärzhäN
silver plated	argenté	ärzhäNtā
wedding ring	alliance *f*	älyäNs

Clothing

May I try it on?
Je peux l'essayer?
zhə pā lesāyā

I take a size ...
Je fais du ...
zhə fā dē ...

This is ...
C'est ...
sā ...

too long	trop long	trō lôN
too short	trop court	trō ko͞or
too tight	trop étroit	trōpātrô·ä
too wide	trop large	trō lärzh

Can it be altered?
On peut faire des retouches?
ôN pā fār dā reto͞osh

... fits just fine (doesn't fit).
... me va bien (ne me va pas).
... mə vä byeN (nə mə vä pä)

apron	tablier *m*	täblēyā
bathing cap	bonnet *m* de bain	bônā də beN
bathing trunks/suit	maillot *m* de bain	mäyō də beN
bathrobe	peignoir *m*	penyô·är
belt	ceinture *f*	seNtēr
bikini	bikini *m*	bēkēnē
blouse	chemisier *m*	shemēzyā
blue jeans	blue-jeans *m/pl.*	bloodzēn
bra, brassière	soutien-gorge *m*	sootyeN-gôrzh
cap	casquette *f*	käsket
cardigan	veste *f* de tricot	vest də trēkō
coat	manteau *m*	mäNtō
corset	corselet *m*; corset *m*	kôrsəlā, kôrsā
dress	robe *f*	rôb
dressing gown	robe *f* de chambre	rôb də shäNb(ər)
fur coat	(manteau *m* de) fourrure *f*	(mäNtō də) foorēr
fur jacket	veste *f* de fourrure	vest də foorēr
garter belt	porte-jarretelles *f*	pôrt-zhärtel
girdle	ceinture *f*	seNtēr
gloves	gants *m/pl.*	gäN
handkerchief	mouchoir *m*	mooshô·är
hat	chapeau *m*	shäpō
– straw hat	chapeau *m* de paille	shäpō də pä'ē
jacket *(lady's)*	veste *f*	vest
jacket *(man's)*	veston *m*	vestôN
knee socks	mi-bas *m/pl.*	mē-bä
leather coat	manteau *m* de cuir	mäNtō də kē·ēr
leather jacket	blouson *m* en cuir	bloozôN äN kē·ēr
lingerie	lingerie *f*	leNzherē
night shirt	chemise *f* de nuit	shemēz də nē·ē
nightie	chemise *f* de nuit	shemēz də nē·ē
pajamas	pyjama *m*	pēzhämä
panties	slip *m*	slēp
pants, trousers	pantalon *m*	päNtälôN
pants suit	costume *m*	kôstēm
parka	anorak *m*	änôräk
petticoat	jupon *m*	zhēpôN
raincoat	imperméable *m*	eNpermā·äb'əl
scarf	écharpe *f*	āshärp
shirt	chemise *f*	shemēz

– drip-dry	– sans repassage	– säN repäsäzh
– short-sleeved	– à manches courtes	– ä mäNsh ko͞ort
shorts	short *m*	shôrt
ski pants	pantalon *m* de ski	päNtälôN də skē
skirt	jupe *f*	zhēp
slacks	pantalon *m*	päNtälôN
slip	jupon *m*	zhēpôN
socks	chaussettes *f/pl.*	shôset
sport shirt	chemise *f* de sport	shemēz də spôr
sportswear	vêtements *m/pl.* de sport	vātmäN də spôr
stockings	bas *m/pl.*	bä
stole	étole *f*	ātôl
suède coat	manteau *m* de chamois	mäNtō də shämô·ä
suède jacket	blouson *m* de chamois	blo͞ozôN də shä-mô·ä
suit *(lady's)*	tailleur *m*	täyār
suit *(man's)*	costume *m*	kôstēm
summer dress	robe *f* d'été	rôb dātā
suspenders	jarretelles *f/pl.*	zhärtel
sweatshirt	sweatshirt *m*	so͞o·etshārt
sweater	pullover *m*	pēlōvār
swimsuit	maillot *m* de bain	mäyō də beN
tie	cravate *f*	krävät
tights	collants *m/pl.*	kôläN
track suit	survêtement *m*	sērvātmäN
trousers	pantalon *m*	päNtälôN
two-piece	tailleur *m*, deux-pièces	täyār, dā-pyās
underpants	caleçon *m*	kälsôN
undershirt *(men's)*	gilet *m* du corps	zhēlā dē kôr
– *women's*	chemise *f*	shəmēz
underwear	sous-vêtements *m/pl.*	so͞o-vātmäN
vest	gilet *m*	zhēlā
windbreaker	anorak *m*	änôräk

Dry Goods

accessories	accessoires *m/pl.*	äksesô·är
belt	ceinture *f*	seNtēr
braces	bretelles *f/pl.*	bretel
buckle	boucle *f*	bo͞ok'əl
button	bouton *m*	bo͞otôN
buttonhole thread	fil *m* pour boutonnières	fēl po͞or bo͞otônyār
darning cotton	coton *m* à repriser	kôtôN ä reprēzā
darning wool	laine *f* à repriser	len ä reprēzā
dress-shield	dessous *m* de bras	dəso͞o də brä
dry goods	mercerie *f*	mārserē
elastic	élastique *m*	āläsτēk
garters	jarretelles *f/pl.*	zhärtel
hooks and eyes	crochets *m/pl.*	krôshā
lining	doublure *f*	do͞oblēr
needle	aiguille *f*	āgē'ē
– sewing needle	aiguille *f* à coudre	āgē'ē ä ko͞od(ər)
panty hose	collant *m*	kôläN
pin	épingle *f*	āpeNg'əl
ribbon	ruban *m*	rēbäN
safety pin	épingle *f* de sûreté	āpeNg'əl də sērtā
scissors	ciseaux *m/pl.*	sēzō
silk thread	soie *f* à coudre	sô·ä ä ko͞od(ər)
snap	bouton-pression *m*	bo͞otôN-presyôN
suspenders	bretelles *f/pl.*	brətel
synthetic thread	fil *m* polyester	fēl pôlyestār
tape	ruban *m*	rēbäN
tape measure	centimètre *m*	säNtēmāt(ər)
thimble	dé *m*	dā
thread	fil *m* (à coudre)	fēl ä ko͞od(ər)
wool	laine *f*	len
zipper	fermeture *f* éclair	fārmetēr āklār

Fabrics

cloth	drap *m*	drä
corduroy	velours *m* côtelé	velo͞or kōtlā
cotton	coton *m*	kôtôN
fabric	tissu *m*; étoffe *f*	tēsē, ātôf

– checked	– quadrillé	– kädrēyā
– patterned, printed	– imprimé	– eNprēmā
– solid color	– uni	– *e*nē
– striped	– rayé	– rāyā
flannel	flanelle *f*	flänel
jersey	jersey *m*	zhersē
linen	toile *f*	tô·äl
material	tissu *m*; matière *f*	tēs*ē*; mätyār
nylon	nylon *m*	nēlôN
silk	soie *f* naturelle	sô·ä nät*ē*rel
– artificial silk	soie *f* artificielle	sô·ä ärtēfēsyel
synthetic fibre	fibre *f* synthétique	fēb(ər) seNtātēk
velvet	velours *m*	vel$\overline{oo}$r
wool	laine *f*	len
– pure wool	– pure laine	– p*ē*r len
– pure virgin wool	– pure laine vierge	– p*ē*r len vyārzh
worsted	laine *f* peignée	len penyā

Cleaning, Alterations, Repairs

I'd like to have this *dress (suit)* cleaned.
Je voudrais faire nettoyer *cette robe (ce costume)*.
zhə v$\overline{oo}$drā fār netô·äyā set rôb (sə kôst*ē*m)

I'd like to have these things laundered.
Je voudrais faire laver ce linge.
zhə v$\overline{oo}$drā fār lävā sə leNzh

Would you please *press this (take out this stain)*?
Pouvez-vous *me repasser ceci (enlever cette tache)*?
p$\overline{oo}$vā-v$\overline{oo}$ mə repäsā səsē (äNlevā set täsh)

Could you *darn this (sew on this button)*?
Pouvez-vous *repriser ceci (recoudre ce bouton)*?
p$\overline{oo}$vā-v$\overline{oo}$ reprēzā səsē (rek$\overline{oo}$d(ər) sə b$\overline{oo}$tôN)

Would you mend this run for me?
Vous pourriez me faire un remaillage?
v$\overline{oo}$ p$\overline{oo}$rē·ä mə fār eN remäyäzh

Could you *lengthen (shorten)* this?
Pouvez-vous *le (la) rallonger (raccourcir)* un peu?
p$\overline{oo}$vā-v$\overline{oo}$ lə (lä) rälôNzhā (räk$\overline{oo}$rsēr) eN p*ā*

Optician

Can you fix these glasses?
Pouvez-vous réparer ces lunettes?
po͞ovā-vo͞o rāpärā sā lenet

Can you replace these lenses?
Pouvez-vous remplacer ces verres?
po͞ovā-vo͞o räNpläsā sā vār

I'm *near-sighted (far-sighted).*
Je suis *myope (presbyte).*
zhə sē·ē mē·ôp (presbēt)

binoculars	jumelles *f/pl.*	zhēmel
compass	boussole *f*	bo͞osôl
contact lenses	verres *m/pl.* de contact	vār də kôNtäkt
eyeglass case	étui *m* à lunettes	ātē·ē ä lēnet
frame	monture *f*	môNtēr
glasses	lunettes *f/pl.*	lēnet
magnifying glass	loupe *f*	lo͞op
spectacles	lunettes *f/pl.*	lēnet
sunglasses	lunettes *f/pl.* de soleil	lēnet də sôlā'ē

Stationery

ball point pen	stylo *m* à bille	stēlō ä bē'ē
– cartridge	mine *f*; cartouche *f*	mēn; kärto͞osh
carbon paper	papier *m* carbone	päpyā kärbôn
crayons	crayons *m/pl.* de couleur	krāyôN də ko͞olār
envelope	enveloppe *f*	äNvelôp
eraser	gomme *f*	gôm
fountain pen	stylo *m*	stēlō
glue	colle *f*	kôl
ink	encre *f*	äNk(ər)
pad	bloc *m*	blôk
– scratch pad	bloc-notes *m*	blôk nôt
– sketch pad	bloc *m* à dessin	blôk ä deseN
paper	papier *m*	päpyā
– typewriter paper	papier *m* machine (à écrire)	– päpyā mäshēn (ä ākrēr)
– wrapping paper	papier *m* d'emballage	päpyā däNbäläzh
– writing paper	papier *m* à lettre	päpyā ä let(ər)
pencil	crayon *m*	krāyôN

Shoes

I take a size . . .
J'ai la pointure . . .
zhā lä pô·eNtēr . . .

I'd like a pair of . . .
Je désire une paire de . . .
zhə dāzēr ēn pār də . . .

beach sandals	sandales *f/pl.*	säNdäl
bedroom slippers	pantoufles *f/pl.*	päNtōōf'əl
boots	bottes *f/pl.*	bôt
ladies' shoes	chaussures *f/pl.* pour dames	shôsēr pōōr däm
loafers	mocassins *m/pl.*	môkäseN
rubber boots	bottes *f/pl.* de caoutchouc	bôt də kä·ôtshōō
sandals	sandales *f/pl.*	säNdäl
sneakers, gym shoes	chaussures *f/pl.* de gymnastique	shôsēr də zhēmnästēk
walking shoes	souliers *m/pl.* de marche	sōōlyā də märsh

They're too *tight (wide).*
Ils sont trop *étroits (trop larges).*
ēl sôN trōpātrô·ä (trō lärzh)

They pinch here.
Ils serrent ici.
ēl sār ēsē

Could you fix these shoes for me?
Voudriez-vous me réparer ces souliers?
vōōdrē·āvōō mə rāpärā sā sōōlyā

crêpe sole	semelle *f* de crépe	semel də krāp
heel	talon *m*	tälôN
– flat	– plat	– plä
– high	– haut	– ō
in-sole	semelle *f* intérieure	semel eNtārē·ār
leather	cuir *m*	kē·ēr
leather sole	semelle *f* de cuir	semel də kē·ēr
rubber sole	semelle *f* de caoutchouc	semel də kä·ôtshōō
shoe horn	chausse-pied *m*	shôs-pyā
shoe laces	lacets *m/pl.*	läsā
shoe polish	cirage *m*	sēräzh
sole *(noun)*	semelle *f*	semel
sole *(verb)*	ressemeler	resemәlā
suede	daim *m*	deN

Cigar Store

A pack of ... *cigarettes (tobacco)*, please.
Un paquet de *cigarettes (tabac)*, s'il vous plaît.
eN päkā də sēgäret (täbä), sēl vo͞o plā

Do you have American cigarettes?
Avez-vous des cigarettes américaines?
ävā-vo͞o dā sēgäret ämārēken

A dozen cigars, please.
Douze cigares, s'il vous plaît.
do͞oz sēgär, sēl vo͞o plā

Would you please refill my lighter?
Voudriez-vous me remplir le briquet, s'il vous plaît.
vo͞odrē·ā-vo͞o mə räNplēr lə brēkā, sēl vo͞o plā

A box of matches, please.
Une boîte d'allumettes, s. v. p.
ēn bô·ät dälēmet, sēl vo͞o plā

Could I please have a light?
Avez-vous du feu, s'il vous plaît?
ävā-vo͞o dē fā, sēl vo͞o plā

cigar	cigare *m*	sēgär
cigarette	cigarette *f*	sēgäret
– filtered	– à bout filtre	– ä bo͞o fēlt(ər)
– unfiltered	– sans filtre	– säN fēlt(ər)
flint	pierre *f* à briquet	pyār ä brēkā
lighter	briquet *m*	brēkā
– gas lighter	briquet *m* à gaz	brēkā ä gäz
lighter fluid	essence *f* à briquet	esäNs ä brēkā
matches	allumettes *f/pl.*	älēmet
pipe	pipe *f*	pēp
pipe cleaner	cure-pipe *f*	kēr-pēp
tobacco	tabac *m*	täbä

Toiletries

after shave	lotion *f* après rasage	lôsyôN äprā räzäzh
barette	barrette *f*	bäret
bath salts	sels *m/pl.* pour le bain	sel po͞or lə beN
bobby pins	pinces *f/pl.* à cheveux	peNs ä shevā
brush	brosse *f*	brôs
clothes brush	brosse *f* à habits	brôs ä äbē
comb	peigne *m*	pen(yə)
compact	poudrier *m*	po͞odrēyā

cream	crème *f* (de beauté)	krām (də bōtā)
curler	bigoudi *m*, rouleau *m*	bēgo͞odē, ro͞olō
deodorant	déodorant *m*	dā·ōdôräN
dye	teinture *f*	teNtēr
emery board	lime *f* à ongles en carton	lēm ä oNg'əl äN kärtôN
eye liner	crayon *m* (à paupières)	krāyôN (ä pôpyār)
eye shadow	ombre *f* à paupières	ôNbrä pôpyār
eyebrow pencil	crayon *m* à sourcils	krāyôN ä so͞orsē
face cream	crème *f* (pour le visage)	krām (po͞or lə vēzäzh)
hair conditioner	sèche-cheveux *m*	sāsh-shevā
hair net	filet *m*	fēlā
hair spray	vaporisateur *m*	väpôrēzätār
hair tonic	lotion *f* capillaire	lôsyôN käpēlār
hairbrush	brosse *f* à cheveux	brôs ä shevā
hairpin	épingle *f* à cheveux	āpeNg'əl ä shevā
lipstick	rouge *m* à lèvres	ro͞ozh ä lāv(ər)
mascara	rimmel *m*	rēmel
mirror	miroir *m*, glace *f*	mērô·är, gläs
mouthwash	eau *f* dentifrice	ō däNtēfrēs
nail file	lime *f* à ongles	lēm ä ôNg'əl
nail polish	vernis *m* à ongles	vārnē ä ôNg'əl
nail polish remover	dissolvant *m*	dēsôlväN
nail scissors	ciseaux *m/pl.* à ongles	sēzō ä ôNg'əl
orange stick	cure-ongles *m*	kēr-ôNg'əl
perfume	parfum *m*	pärfeN
powder	poudre *f*	po͞od(ər)
powder puff	houppette *f*	o͞opet
prophylactic	préservatif *m*	prāzervätēf
razor	rasoir *m* (mécanique)	räzô·är (mākänēk)
– electric shaver	rasoir *m* électrique	räzô·är ālektrēk
– safety razor	rasoir *m* de sûreté	räzô·är də sērtā
– straight razor	rasoir *m*	räzô·är
razor blades	lames *f/pl.* de rasoir	läm də räzô·är
rouge	rouge *m*	ro͞ozh
sanitary napkins	serviettes *f/pl.* hygiéniques	servyet ēzhē·ānēk
scissors	ciseaux *m/pl.*	sēzō
shampoo	shampooing *m*	shäNpô·eN
shaving brush	blaireau *m*	blārō

shaving cream	crème *f* à raser	krām ä räzā
shaving foam	mousse *f* à raser	mo͞os ä räzā
shaving soap	savon *m* à barbe	sävôN ä bärb
soap	savon *m*	sävôN
sponge	éponge *f*	āpôNzh
sun tan cream	crème *f* solaire	krām sôlār
– sun tan lotion	lotion *f* solaire	lôsyôN sôlār
– sun tan oil	huile *f* solaire	ē·ēl sôlār
tampons	tampons *m/pl.*	täNpôN
tissues	mouchoirs *m/pl.* en papier	mo͞oshô·är äN päpyā
toilet articles, toiletries	articles *m/pl.* de toilette	ärtēk'əl də tô·älet
toilet kit	nécessaire *m* de toilette	nāsesār də tô·älet
toilet paper	papier *m* hygiénique	päpyā ēzhē·ānēk
wash cloth	gant *m* de toilette	gäN də tô·älet
tooth brush	brosse *f* à dents	brôs ä däN
tooth paste	dentifrice *m*	däNtēfrēs
tooth powder	poudre *f* dentifrice	po͞od(ər) däNtēfrēs
towel	serviette *f*	servyet
– bath towel	serviette *f* de bain	servyet də beN
tweezers	pincettes *f/pl.*	peNset

Watchmaker

Can you fix this *watch (clock)*?
Pouvez-vous réparer cette montre?
po͞ovā-vo͞o rāpärā set môNt(ər)

How much will the repair cost?
Combien va coûter la réparation?
kôNbyeN vä ko͞otā lä rāpäräsyôN

It's running *fast (slow)*.
Elle *avance (retarde)*.
el äväNs (retärd)

alarm clock	réveil *m*	rāvā'ē
crystal	verre *m*	vār
clock	montre *f*	môNt(ər)
face	cadran *m*	kädräN
hand	aiguille *f*	āgē'ē
pocket watch	montre *f* de poche	môNt(ər) də pôsh

spring	ressort *m*	resôr
stop watch	chronomètre *m*	krônōmāt(ər)
watch	montre *f*	môNt(ər)
watch band	bracelet *m* (pour montre)	bräslā (po͞or môNt(ər)
wrist watch	montre-bracelet *f*	môNt(ər)-bräslā

Sundries

ash tray	cendrier *m*	säNdrēyā
bag	sac *m*	säk
ball	balle *f*	bäl
basket	corbeille *f*, panier *m*	kôrbā'ē, pänyā
battery	batterie *f*	bätərē
beach bag	sac *m* de camping	säk də käNpēng
bottle opener	décapsuleur *m*	dākäpsēlār
briefcase	portefeuille *m*; serviette *f*	pôrtfā'ē; servyet
camp stove	réchaud *m* à alcool	rāshō ä älkôl
can opener	ouvre-boîte *m*	o͞ov(ər)-bô·ät
candle	bougie *f*	bo͞ozhē
– beeswax	cire *f* d'abeille	sēr däbā'ē
candlestick	bougeoir *m*	bo͞ozhô·är
candy	bonbons *m/pl.*	bôNbôN
canned goods	conserves *f/pl.*	kôNsārv
cassette	cassette *f*	käset
ceramics	céramique *f*	sārämēk
china	porcelaine *f*	pôrsəlen
corkscrew	tire-bouchon *m*	tēr-bo͞oshôN
detergent	détergent *m*	dāterzhäN
– dishwashing detergent	détergent *m* à vaisselle	dāterzhäN ä vāsel
doll	poupée *f*	po͞opā
figurine	figure *f*	fēgēr
flashlight	flash *m*	fläsh
hammock	hamac *m*	ämäk
handbag	sac *m* à main	säk ä meN
handicrafts	objets *m/pl.* artisanaux	ôbzhā ärtēzänō
handkerchief	mouchoir *m*	mo͞oshô·är
jackknife	couteau *m* de poche	ko͞otō də pôsh

leash	laisse *f*	lās
mat	soucoupe *f*	so͞oko͞op
paper napkins	serviettes *f/pl.* en papier	servyet äN päpyā
phonograph record	disque *m*	dēsk
picture	image *f*	ēmäzh
plastic bag	sac *m* en plastique	säk äN plästēk
playing cards	cartes *f/pl.* à jouer	kärt ä zho͞o·ā
pocket knife	couteau *m* de poche	ko͞otō də pôsh
purse	porte-monnaie *m*	pôrt-mônā
recording tape	bande *f* magnétique	bäNd mänyātēk
rope	corde *f*	kôrd
rucksack	sac *m* à dos	säk ā dō
Scotch tape	ruban *m* adhésif, scotch	rēbäN ädāzēf, skôtsh
sled	luge *f*	lēzh
spot remover	détachant *m*	dātäshäN
string	ficelle *f*	fēsel
stuffed animal	animal *m* en peluche	änēmäl äN pelēsh
suitcase	valise *f*	välēz
tape recorder	magnétophone *m*	mänyātōfôn
thermometer	thermomètre *m*	termōmāt(ər)
thermos bottle	thermos *f*	termôs
toy	jouets *m/pl.*	zho͞o·ā
umbrella	parapluie *m*	päräplē'ē
vase	vase *m*	väz
video cassette	cassette-vidéo *f*	käset vēdā·ō
wallet	portefeuille *m*	pôrtfā'ē
washing line	corde *f* à linge	kôrd ä leNzh
wood carving	sculpture *f* sur bois	skēlptēr sēr bô·ä

AT THE POST OFFICE

> *The activities of European post offices are far broader in scope than they are in the United States. In addition to all the usual mail services, the post office is also the telegraph and telephone company, and provides full banking services, including checking and savings accounts. They will also hold mail for travelers. Simply tell your correspondents to write you* "poste restante" (pôst restäNt) *in the city of your destination.*

Post Office

Where is the post office?
Où est le bureau de poste?
o͞oā lə bērō də pôst

Where is there a mail box?
Où y a-t-il une boîte aux lettres?
o͞oyätēl ēn bô·ät ō let(ər)

How much does this *letter (card)* cost?
C'est combien pour cette *lettre (carte)?*
sā kôNbyeN po͞or set let(ər) (kärt)

– to the United States.
– pour les États-Unis.
– po͞or lāzātäzēnē

– to Canada.
– pour le Canada.
– po͞or lə känädä

What's the postage on ...
Le port, c'est combien pour ...
lə pôr, sā kôNbyeN po͞or

Five ... stamps please.
Cinq timbres à ..., s'il vous plaît.
seNk teNb(ər)-pôst ä ..., sēl vo͞o plā

this air mail letter ...	cette lettre par avion ...	set let(ər) pär ävyôN
this letter abroad	cette lettre pour l'étranger ...	set let(ər) po͞or lāträNzhä
this local letter	cette lettre locale	set let(ər) lôkäl
this parcel	ce colis ...	sə kôlē
this picture post card ...	cette carte postale illustrée ...	set kärt pôstäl ēlēstrā
this post card	cette carte postale	set kärt pôstäl
this printed matter ..	cet imprimé ...	set eNprēmā
this registered letter ...	cette lettre recommandée ...	set let(ər) rekômäNdā
this small parcel	ce petit colis ...	sə pətē kôlē
this special delivery letter	cette lettre exprès	set let(ər) eksprā

Do you have any special issues?
Vous avez aussi des timbres de collection?
vo͞ozävā ôsē dā teNb(ər) də kôleksyôN

Two of each, please.
Deux de chaque, s'il vous plaît.
dā də shäk, sēl vo͞o plā

This set of stamps, please.
Cette série de timbres-poste, s'il vous plaît.
set sārē də teNb(ər)-pôst, sēl vo͞o plā

I'd like to send this letter *by registered mail (special delivery)*.
Cette lettre *recommandée (par exprès)*, s'il vous plaît.
set let(ər) rekômäNdā (pär eksprā), sēl vo͞o plā

A *postal transfer (money order)*, please.
Un *mandat-poste (mandat-carte)*, s'il vous plaît.
eN mäNdä-pôst (mäNdä-kärt), sēl vo͞o plā

How long does it take for a *letter (package)* to get to . . .?
Combien de temps met *une lettre (un colis)* pour . . .?
kôNbyen də täN metēn let(ər) (eN kôlē) po͞or

Is there any mail here for me?
Y a-t-il du courrier pour moi?
ēyätēl dē ko͞oryā po͞or mô·ä

My name ist . . .
Je m'appelle . . .
zhə mäpel . . .

Where can I *mail (pick up)* a package?
Où est le guichet *d'enregistrement (de remise)* des colis postaux?
o͞o ā lə gēshā däNrezhēstrəmäN (də remēz) dā kôlē pôstō

Do I need a customs declaration?
Je dois faire une déclaration de douane?
zhə dô·ä fār ēn dāklärä syôN də do͞o·än

***Sign here, please.**
Signez ici, s'il vous plaît.
sēnyā ēsē, sēl vo͞o plā

I'd like to have my mail forwarded.
J'aimerais faire suivre mon courrier.
zhāmerā fār sē·ēv(ər) môN ko͞oryā

This is my new address.
Voici ma nouvelle adresse.
vô·äsē mä no͞ovel ädres

You can pay bills at the post office simply by transferring the money to your creditor's postal account or having a money order delivered to him by mail. Of course, the French Post Offices can help jou send money to the United States, or almost any other country in the world. Inquire at the "mandats" *window.*

Telegrams · Telephone

A telegram form, please.
Une formule de télégramme, s. v. p.
ēn fôrmēl də tālāgräm, sēl vo͞o plā

I'd like to send ...
Je voudrais envoyer ...
zhə vo͞odrā äNvô·äyā

a telegram	un télégramme	eN tālāgräm
a night letter	un télégramme-lettre	eN tālāgräm-let(ər)

How much do ten words to ... cost?
Combien coûtent dix mots pour ...?
kôNbyeN ko͞ot dē mō po͞or ...

When will it arrive at ...?
Quand sera-t-il *à (en)* ...?
käN sərätēl ä (äN) ...

Will the wire get to ... today?
Le télégramme arrivera encore aujourd'hui *à (en)* ...?
lə tālāgräm ärēvərä äNkôr ōzho͞ordē·ē ä (äN) ...

In most European countries it is wise to place long distance calls at the post office, as many hotels make sizable surcharges for use of the phone.

Where is the nearest phone booth?
Où est la cabine téléphonique la plus proche?
o͞o ā lä käbēn tālāfōnēk lä plē prôsh

Where can I make a phone call?
Où est-ce que je peux téléphoner?
o͞o eske zhə pā tālāfōnā

The phone book, please.
L'annuaire (du téléphone), s. v. p.
länē·är dē tālāfôn, sēl vo͞o plā

What's the area code for ...?
Quel est l'indicatif pour...?
kel ā leNdēkätēf po͞or ...

Can I direct dial to ...?
Je peux faire un numéro interurbain automatique?
zhə pā fār eN nēmārō eNterērbeN ôtōmätēk

You can direct dial the United States from almost any telephone in Europe. The country code for the U.S. and Canada is 001, followed, of course by the area code and the subscriber's number. You will need operator assistance for person-to-person or collect calls.

A long distance call to . . . please.
Une communication *interurbaine (or: internationale)* pour . . . s'il vous plaît.
ēn kômēnēkäsôN eNterērben (eNternäsyônal) pōōr . . ., sēl vōō plā

How long will that take?
Quelle sera la durée d'attente?
kel serä lä dērā dätäNt

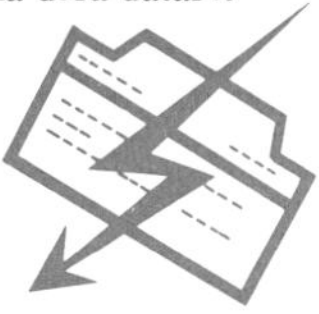

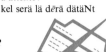

Can I have some coins for the pay phone?
Avez-vous des jetons pour le taxiphone?
ävā-vōō dā zhetôN pōōr lə täksēfôn

How much does a *local call (call to . . .)* cost?
Combien coûte une *communication urbaine (communication pour . . .)*?
kôNbyeN kōōt ēn kômēnēkäsyôN ērben (kômēnēkäsyôN pōōr)

What time does the night rate begin?
Le tarif de nuit, c'est à partir de quelle heure?
lə tärēf də nē·ē, sātä pärtēr də kelār

***Your call is ready in booth four.**
Votre communication: cabine quatre.
vôt(ər) kômēnēkäsyôN käbēn kät(ər)

***What's your number?**
Quel est votre numéro?
kel ā vôt(ər) nēmārō

Please connect me with . . .
Passez-moi . . ., s'il vous plaît.
päsā-mô·ä . . ., sēl vōō plā

There's no answer at that number.
Le correspondant ne répond pas.
lə kôrespôNdäN nə rāpôN pä

The line is *busy (out of order)*.
La ligne est *occupée (en dérangement)*.
lā lēn(yə) ātôkēpā (äN däräNzhmäN)

Wrong number!
C'est un faux numéro.
sāteN fō nēmārō

May I speak to *Mr. (Mrs., Miss)* . . .?
Je voudrais parler à *Monsieur (Madame, Mademoiselle)* . . .?
zhə vōōdrā pärlā ä məsyā (mädäm, mädəmô·äzel) . . .

Speaking!
Allô (oui)?
älō (ōō·ē)

This is . . . speaking.
C'est . . .
sā . . .

Who is this?
Qui est à l'appareil?
kē ātäläpärā'ē

Please hold the line.
Ne quittez pas!
nə kētā pä

Would you please cancel that call.
Veuillez annuler la communication.
vāyā änēlā lä kômēnēkäsyôN

Code Alphabet

A	= Anatole	änätôl	**N**	= Nicolas	nēkôlä
B	= Berthe	bārt	**O**	= Oscar	ôskär
C	= César	sāzär	**P**	= Paul	pôl
D	= Désiré	dāzērā	**Q**	= Québec	kābek
E	= Emile	āmēl	**R**	= Robert	rôbār
F	= François	fräNsô·ä	**S**	= Suzanne	sēzän
G	= Gaston	gästôN	**T**	= Théodore	tā·ōdôr
H	= Henri	äNrē	**U**	= Ursule	ērsēl
I	= Isidore	ēsēdôr	**V**	= Victor	vēktôr
J	= Jean	zhäN	**W**	= Wagon	o͞o·ägôN
K	= Kléber	klābār	**X**	= Xavier	gzävyā
L	= Louis	lo͞o·ē	**Y**	= Yvonne	ēvôn
M	= Marie	märē	**Z**	= Zoé	zō·ā

address	adresse *f*	ädres
addressee	destinataire *m*	destēnätār
air mail	poste *f* aérienne	pôst ä·ārē·en
area code	indicatif *m*	eNdēkätēf
c.o.d.	remboursement *m*	räNbo͞orsmäN
coin changer	changeur *m* de monnaie automatique	shäNzhār də mônā ôtōmätēk
collect call	communication *f* payable à l'arrivée	kômēnēkäsyôN pāyäb'əl älärēvā
counter	guichet *m*	gēshā
customs declaration	déclaration *f* de douane	dākläräsyôN də do͞o·än
destination	lieu *m* de destination	lēyā də destēnäsyôN
dial *(noun)*	cadran *m*	kädräN
dial *(verb)*	composer le numéro	kôNpōzā lə nēmārō
direct dialing	automatique *m*	ôtōmätēk
general delivery	poste *f* restante	pôst restäNt
information	renseignement *m*	räNsen(yə)mäN
insured mail	courrier *m* avec valeur déclarée	ko͞oryā ävek välār dāklärā
letter	lettre *f*	let(ər)
local call	communication *f* urbaine	kômēnēkäsyôN ērben

long distance call	communication *f* interurbaine	kôm*ē*nēkäsyôN eNter*ē*rben
mail box	boîte *f* aux lettres	bô·ät ō let(ər)
mail man	facteur *m*	fäkt*ār*
operator	téléphoniste *m/f*	tālāfōnēst
package, parcel	colis *m*	kôlē
package card	bulletin *m* d'expédition	b*ē*lteN dekspādē-syôN
person to person call	communication *f* avec avis d'appel	kôm*ē*nēkäsyôN ävek ävē däpel
picture postcard	carte *f* postale illustrée	kärt pôstäl ēl*ē*strā
post card	carte *f* postale	kärt pôstäl
post office box	boîte *f* postale	bô·ät pôstäl
postage	port *m*	pôr
postal clerk	employé *m* des postes	äNplô·äyā dā pôst
postal savings book	livret *m* de caisse d'épargne postale	lēvrā də kes dāpärn(ye) pôstäl
postman	facteur *m*	fäkt*ār*
printed matter	imprimé *m*	eNprēmā
pushbutton telephone	téléphone *m* à touches	tālāfôn ä to͞osh
receipt	quittance *f*	kētäNs
register	recommajder	rekômäNdā
registered letter	lettre *f* recommandée	let(ər) rekômäNdā
registered parcel with declared value	colis *m* avec valeur déclarée	kôlē ävek väl*ār* dāklärā
return postage	port *m* de retour	pôr də reto͞or
sender	expéditeur *m*	ekspādēt*ār*
small parcel	petit colis *m*	pətē kôlē
special delivery	exprès *m*	eksprā
special issue stamp	timbre *m* d'émission spéciale	teNb(ər) dāmēsyôN spāsyäl
stamp *(noun)*	timbre-poste *m*	teNb(ər)-pôst
stamp *(verb)*	affranchir	äfräNshēr
stamp machine	machine *f* à affranchir	mäshēn ä äfräNshēr
telegram	télégramme *m*	tālāgräm
telephone	téléphone *m*	tālāfôn
unstamped	non affranchi	nôN äfräNshē
value declaration	valeur *f* déclarée	väl*ār* dāklärā

BANK, CURRENCY EXCHANGE

French Franc (FF) – FF 1 = 100 c *(centimes)*

Where can I change some money?
Où est-ce que je peux changer de l'argent?
o͞o eske zhə p*ā* shäNzhā də lärzhäN

Where ist the bank?
Où est la banque?
o͞o ā lä bäNk

I need a hundred dollars in . . .
Je voudrais changer cents dollars en . . .
zhə vo͞odrā shäNzhā säN dôlär äN . . .

How much will I get for. . .?
Je touche combien pour . . .?
zhə to͞osh kôNbyeN po͞or . . .

What's the rate of exchange?
Quel est le cours?
kel ā lə ko͞or

Can you change . . . into . . . for me?
Pouvez-vous me changer . . . en . . .?
po͞ovā-vo͞o mə shäNzhā . . . äN . . .

Could I have some change please?
Donnez-moi aussi de la monnaie, s'il vous plaît.
dônā-mô·ä ôsē də lä mônā, sēl vo͞o plā

Can you change this?
Pouvez-vous changer?
po͞ovā-vo͞o shäNzhā

I'd like to cash this *check (traveller's cheque)*.
Je voudrais encaisser ce *chèque (chèque de voyage)*.
zhə vo͞odrā äNkesā sə shek (shek də vô·äyäzh)

Has some money arrived for me?
Y a-t-il eu un versement à mon compte?
ēyätēl *ē* eN versmäN ä môN kôNt

amount	montant *m*	môNtäN
bank	banque *f*	bäNk
bank account	compte *m* bancaire	kôNt bäNkār
bank charges	frais *m/pl.* bancaires	frā bäNkār
bank note	billet *m* de banque	bēyā də bäNk
bank transfer	virement *m* bancaire	vērmäN bäNkār
bill	billet *m* de banque	bēyā də bäNk
bond	obligation *f*	ôblēgäsyôN
branch manager	directeur *m* de banque	dērekt*ā*r də bäNk

cash ***(adj.)***	comptant	kôNtâN
cash ***(noun)***	espèces *f/pl.*	espās
check	chèque *m*	shek
coin	pièce *f* de monnaie	pyās də mônā
credit	crédit *m*	krādē
– take out a loan	prendre un crédit	präNdreN krādē
credit card	carte *f* de crédit	kärt də krādē
currency	monnaie *f*	mônā
daily rate	cours *m* du jour	ko͞or dē zho͞or
deposit	versement *m*	versmäN
foreign currency	devises *f/pl.*	dəvēz
form	formulaire *m*	fôrmēlār
letter of credit	lettre *f* de crédit	let(ər) də krādē
money	argent *m*	ärzhäN
Canadian dollars	dollars *m/pl.* canadiens	dôlär känädyeN
French francs	francs français *m/pl.*	fräN fräNsā
Swiss Francs	francs *m/pl.* suisses	fräN sē·ēs
American dollars	dollars *m/pl.* américains	dôlär ämārēkeN
money exchange	change *m*	shäNzh
mortgage	hypothèque *f*	ēpōtäk
pay out	payer; verser	pāyā; versā
payment	paiement *m*	pāmäN
rate of exchange	cours *m* du change	ko͞or dē shäNzh
receipt	quittance *f*	kētäNs
savings bank	caisse *f* d'épargne	kes dāpärn(yə)
savings book	livret *m* d'épargne	lēvrā dāpärn(yə)
security	valeur *f*	välär
share of stock	coupon *m* d'action	ko͞opôN däksyôN
signature	signature *f*	sēnyätēr
stock	action *f*	äksyôN
telegraphic	télégraphique	tālāgräfēk
teller	caissier *m*	kesyā
transfer	virement *m*	vērmäN
traveller's cheque	chèque *m* de voyage	shek də vô·äyäzh
withdraw	résilier	rāzēlyā

AT THE POLICE STATION

Reporting

I'd like to report ...
Je voudrais déposer une plainte au sujet ...
zhə vo͞odrā dāpōzā ēn pleNt ō sēzhā ...

an accident	d'un accident	denäksēdäN
a blackmail attempt	d'un chantage	deN shäNtäzh
a hold up	d'une agression	dēn ägresyôN
a kidnapping	d'un enlèvement	denäNlāvmäN
a loss	d'une perte	dēn pārt
a murder	d'un meurtre	deN mǟrt(ər)
a theft	d'un vol	deN vôl

My ... has been stolen.
On m'a volé ...
ôN mä vôlā ...

I lost my ...
J'ai perdu ...
zhā perdē ...

bag	le sac	lə säk
billfold	le portefeuille	lə pôrtfǟ'ē
bracelet	le bracelet	lə bräslā
briefcase	le portefeuille, la serviette	lə pôrtfǟ'ē, la servyät
camera	l'appareil photographique	läpärā'ē fōtōgräfēk
car key	les clés de voiture	lā klā də vô·ätēr
handbag	le sac à main	lə säk ä meN
jewelry	les bijoux	lā bēzho͞o
key	la clé	lä klā
money	l'argent	lärzhäN
necklace	la chaîne	lä shen
purse	le porte-monnaie	lə pôrt-mônā
ring	la bague	lä bäg
suitcase	la valise	lä välēz
umbrella	le parapluie	lə päräplē'ē
wallet	le portefeuille	lə pôrtfǟ'ē
watch	la montre	lä môNt(ər)
– wrist watch	la montre-bracelet	lä môNt(ər)-bräslā

I have nothing to do with *it (this business).*
Je n'ai rien à voir *là-dedans (dans cette affaire).*
zhə nārē·eN ä vô·är lä-dədäN (däN set äfār)

I'm innocent.
Je suis innocent.
zhə sē̆·ē ēnôsäN

I didn't do it.
Je n'ai pas fait cela.
zhə nā pä fā səlä

How long do I have to stay here?
Combien de temps dois-je rester ici?
kôNbyeN də täN dô·äzh restā ēsē

This man is *bothering (following)* me.
Cet homme *m'importune (me poursuit).*
setôm meNpôrtēn (mə poorsē̆·ē)

arrest	arrêter	ärātā
attorney	avocat *m*	ävōkä
confiscate	confisquer	kôNfēskā
court	tribunal *m*	trēbēnäl
crime	crime *m*	krēm
criminal	criminel *m*	krēmēnel
criminal investigation division	police *f* judiciaire	pôlēs zhēdēsyār
custody	détention *f*	dātäNsyóN
– pre-trial custody	détention *f* préventive	dātäNsyôN präväNtēv
drugs	drogues *f/pl.*	dróg
guilt	culpabilité *f*	kēlpäbēlētā
hold-up	agression *f*	ägresyôN
judge	juge *m*	zhēzh
lawyer	avocat *m*	ävōkä
narcotics	stupéfiants *m/pl.*	stēpāfē·äN
police	police *f*	pólēs
police car	voiture *f* de police	vô·ätēr də pôlēs
police station	commissariat *m* de police	kômēsärē·ä də pôlēs
prison	prison *f*	prēzôN
smuggling	contrebande *f*	kôNtrəbäNd
thief	voleur *m*	vôlār
verdict	jugement *m*	zhēzhmäN

BEAUTY SHOP / BARBER SHOP

At the Beauty Shop

May I make an appointment for Saturday?
Je voudrais un rendez-vous pour samedi.
zhə vo͞odrā eN räNdā-vo͞o po͞or sämdē

Would you put me down for a permanent wave?
Vous pouvez me prendre pour une permanente?
vo͞o po͞ovā mə präNd(ər) po͞or *ē*n pārmänäNt

For tomorrow?
Pour demain?
po͞or dəmeN

Will I have to wait?
Faut-il attendre?
fôtēl ätäNd(ər)

Will it take long?
Cela mettra combien de temps?
səlä meträ kôNbyeN də täN

Wash and set, please.
Faites-moi un shampoing et une mise en plis.
fāt-mô·ä eN shäNpô·eN ā *ē*n mēz äN plē

I'd like a *permanent (set)*, please.
Je voudrais *une permanente (une mise en plis)*.
zhə vo͞odrā *ē*n pārmänäNt (*ē*n mēz eN plē)

Please set my hair for the evening.
Faites-moi une coiffure du soir, s'il vous plaît.
fāt-mô·ä *ē*n kô·äf*ē*r d*ē* sô·är, sēl vo͞o plā

Please *dye (rinse)* my hair . . .
Une teinture (Un rinçage), s'il vous plaît.
*ē*n teNt*ē*r (eN reNsäzh), sēl vo͞o plā

Please cut my hair a little shorter.
Coupez-moi les cheveux un peu plus court, s'il vous plaît.
ko͞opā-mô·ä lā shev*ā* eN p*ā* pl*ē* ko͞or, sēl vo͞o plā

Just trim it, please.
Coupez-moi juste les pointes, s'il vous plaît.
ko͞opā-mô·ä zh*ē*st lā pô·eNt, sēl vo͞o plā

Please cut it wet.
Coupez-moi les cheveux mouillés.
ko͞opā-mô·ä lā shev*ā* mo͞oyā

Please pin it up.
Relevez-moi les cheveux, s'il vous plaît.
rəlevā-mô·ä lā shev*ā*, sēl vo͞o plā

Please tease it a little on the *top (sides)*.

Crêpez-moi un peu les cheveux *en haut (sur les côtés)*.
krāpā-mô·ä eN pā lā shevā äN ō (sēr lā kôtā)

It's a little too hot under the drier.

Le séchoir est trop chaud.
lə sāshô·är ā trō shō

No *setting lotion (hair spray)*, please.

Pas de *fixateur (laque)*, s'il vous plaît.
päd fēksätār (läk), sēl vo͞o plā

Could you give me a *manicure (pedicure)*?

Pourriez-vous me faire la *manucure (pédicure)*?
po͞orē·ā-vo͞o mə fār lä mänēkēr (pādēkēr)

Please file my nails *round (to a point)*.

Limez les ongles *ronds (pointus)*, s'il vous plaît.
lēmā lāzôNg'əl rôN (pô·eNtē), sēl vo͞o plā

Just polish them, please.

Faites-les seulement briller,
s'il vous plaît.
fāt-lā sālmäN brēyā,
sēl vo͞o plā

***With (Without)* nail polish.**

Avec (Sans) vernis.
ävek (säN) vārnē

Please *tweeze (shave)* my eyebrows.

Épilez (Rasez-moi) les sourcils, s'il vous plaît.
āpēlā (räzā-mô·ä) lā so͞orsē, sēl vo͞o plā

A *facial mask (face massage)*, please.

Un masque facial (Un massage facial), s'il vous plaît.
eN mäsk fāsyäl (eN mäsäzh fāsyäl), sēl vo͞o plā

Would you please put this *hairpiece (wig)* on for me?

Mettez-moi *ce postiche (cette perruque)*, s'il vous plaît.
metā-mô·ä sə pôstēsh (set perēk), sēl vo͞o plā

Yes, thank you, that's just fine.

Oui, merci, c'est bien.
o͞o·ē, mersē, sā byeN

Very nice!

Très bien!
trā byeN

At the Barber Shop

(Shave and) A haircut, please.
Une coupe de cheveux (et la barbe), s'il vous plaît.
*ē*n ko͞op də shv*ā* (ā lä bärb), sēl vo͞o plā

Not too short, please.
Pas trop courts, s'il vous plaît.
pä trō ko͞or, sēl vo͞o plā

(Very) Short, please.
(Très) Courts, s'il vous plaît.
(trā) ko͞or, sēl vo͞o plā

– at the back.	**– on top.**	**– in front.**	**– on the sides.**
– derrière.	– en haut.	– devant.	– sur les côtés.
– deryār	– äN ō	– dəväN	– s*ē*r lā kôtā

A razor cut, please.
Une coupe au rasoir, s'il vous plaît.
*ē*n ko͞op ō räzô·är, sēl vo͞o plā

***With (Without)* part, please.**
Avec (Sans) raie, s'il vous plaît.
ävek (säN) rā, sēl vo͞o plā

Part on the *left (right)*, please.
La raie *à gauche (à droite)*, s'il vous plaît.
lä rā ä gôsh (ä drô·ät), sēl vo͞o plā

A shampoo too, please!
Lavez-moi aussi les cheveux, s'il vous plaît.
lävā-mô·ä ôsē lā shv*ā*, sēl vo͞o plā

Scalp massage, please.
Un massage de la tête, s'il vous plaît.
eN mäsäzh dəlä tāt, sēl vo͞o plā

Would you trim my *beard (moustache)*, please?
Taillez-moi *la barbe (les moustaches)*, s'il vous plaît.
täyā-mô·ä lä bärb (lā mo͞ostäsh), sēl vo͞o plā

Just a shave, please.
Rien que la barbe, s'il vous plaît.
rē·eN ke lä bärb, sēl vo͞o plā

***Some hair tonic (A little brilliantine)*, please.**
Avec de la lotion (Un peu de brillantine), s'il vous plaît.
ävek dəlä lôsyôN (eN p*ā* də brēyäNtēn), sēl vo͞o plā

Please leave it dry.
Ne les mouillez pas, s'il vous plaît.
nə lā mo͞oyā pä, sēl vo͞o plā

Yes, thank you, that's just great.
Oui, merci, c'est parfait.
o͞o·ē, mersē, sā pärfā

barber	coiffeur *m* (pour hommes)	kô·äf*ā*r (po͞or ôm)
beard	barbe *f*	bärb
beauty parlor	salon *m* de beauté	sälôN də bōtā
brilliantine	brillantine *f*	brēyäNtēn
cold wave	permanente *f* à froid	pārmänäNt ä frô·ä
comb *(noun)*	peigne *m*	pen(yə)
comb *(verb)*	peigner	penyā
curls	boucles *f/pl.*	bo͞ok'əl
cut	couper	ko͞opā
dandruff	pellicules *f/pl.*	pelēk*ē*l
do *s.o.'s* hair	coiffer	kô·äfā
dye	teindre	teNd(ər)
hair	cheveux *m/pl.*	shv*ā*
– dry hair	– secs	– sek
– greasy hair	– gras	– grä
haircut	coupe *f* de cheveux	ko͞op də shv*ā*
hair-do	coiffure *f*	kô·äf*ē*r
hairdresser	coiffeur *m*	kô·äf*ā*r
hair drier	séchoir *m*	sāshô·är
hair loss	chute *f* des cheveux	sh*ē*t dā shv*ā*
hair style	coiffure *f*	kô·äf*ē*r
hairpiece	postiche *m*	pôstēsh
manicure	manucure *f*	män*ē*k*ē*r
moustache	moustaches *f/pl.*	mo͞ostäsh
part	raie *f*	rā
pedicure	pédicure *f*	pādēk*ē*r
permanent wave	permanente *f*	pārmänäNt
scalp massage	massage *m* de la tête	mäsäzh dəlä tāt
set	mettre en plis	metreN plē
shave	faire la barbe	fār lä bärb
sideburns	favoris *m/pl.*	fävôrē
strand	mèche *f*	māsh
tease	crêper	krāpā
tint	colorer	kôlôrā
toupé	postiche *m*	pôstēsh
wash	laver	lävā
wig	perruque *f*	per*ē*k
wisp	mèche *f*	māsh

HEALTH

Pharmacy

Where is the next pharmacy?
Où est la pharmacie la plus proche?
o͞o ā lä färmäsē lä plē̆ prôsh

Which pharmacy has night duty?
Quelle pharmacie assure le service de nuit?
kel färmäsē äsēr lə servēs də nē̆·ē

I'd like this medicine, please.
Ce médicament, s'il vous plaît.
sə mādēkämäN, sēl vo͞o plā

I'd like ...
Je voudrais ...
zhə vo͞odrā ...

Please give me something for ...
Je vous prie de me donner quelque chose contre ...
zhə vo͞o prē də mə dônā kelke shōz kôNt(ər) ...

Do I need a prescription for this medicine?
Ce remède est délivré sur ordonnance?
sə remād ā dālēvrā sēr ôrdônäNs

Can you order this medicine for me?
Pouvez-vous me procurer ce médicament?
po͞ovā-vo͞o mə prōkērā sə mādēkämäN

When can I pick it up?
Je peux l'avoir quand?
zhə pā lävô·är käN

Can I wait for it?
Puis-je attendre?
pē·ēzhätäNd(ər)

for external use	usage externe	ēzäzh ekstārn
for internal use	usage interne	ēzäzh eNtārn
before meals	avant le repas	äväN lə repä
after meals	après le repas	äprā lə repä
three times a day	trois fois par jour	trô·ä fô·ä pär zho͞or
as prescribed	comme prescrit	kôm preskrē
on an empty stomach	à jeun	ä zhān

Medication and Bandages

absorbent cotton	coton *m* hydrophile	kôtôN ēdrōfēl
lace bandage	pansement *m* élastique	päNsmäN äläsṫēk
adhesive bandage	sparadrap *m*	spärädrä
alcohol	alcool *m*	älkôl
ampule	ampoule *f*	äNpo͞ol
antidote	contrepoison *m*	kôNtrəpô·äzôN
boric acid ointment	acide *m* borique	äsēd bôrēk
burn ointment	pommade *f* contre les brûlures	pômäd kôNt(ər) lā brə̄lēr
camomile tea	infusion *f* camomille *f*	eNfə̄zyôN kämō-mē'ē
castor oil	huile *f* de ricin	ə̄·ēl də rēseN
cardiovascular drug	remède *m* pour la circulation	remād po͞or lä sērkə̄läsyôN
charcoal pills	poudre *f* de charbon	po͞od(ər) de shär-bôN
contraceptive pills	pilules *f/pl.* contraceptives	pēlə̄l kôNträseptēv
corn plaster	pansement *m* pour les cors	päNsmäN po͞or lā kôr
cotton swabs	cotons-tiges *m/pl.*	kôtôN-tēzh
cough medicine (-syrup)	remède *m* (sirop *m*) contre la toux	remād (sērō) kôNt(ər) lä to͞o
dextrose	glucose *m*	glə̄kōz
diaphoretic	sudorifique *m*	sə̄dôrēfēk
digestive tablets	comprimés *m/pl.* pour la digestion	kôNprēmā po͞or lä dēzhestyôN
digestive tonic	gouttes *f/pl.* pour la digestion	go͞ot po͞or lä dēzhestyôN
disinfectant	désinfectant *m*	dāzeNfektäN
diuretic	diurétique *m*	dē·ə̄rātēk
drops	gouttes *f/pl.*	go͞ot
ear drops	gouttes *f/pl.* pour les oreilles	go͞ot po͞or lāzôrā'ē
elastic bandage	bande *f* élastique	bäNd äläsṫēk
elastic stocking	bas *m* élastique	bä äläsṫēk
emetic	vomitif *m*	vômētēf
enema	lavement *m*	lävmäN

eye drops/ointment	gouttes *f/pl.*/pommade *f* pour les yeux	go͞ot/pômäd po͞or lāzy*ā*
fever cure	fébrifuge *m*	fābrēf*ē*zh
first-aid kit	pansements *m/pl.*	päNsmäN
gargle	gargarisme *m*	gärgärēsm
gauze bandage	bandage *m* de gaze	bäNdäzh də gäz
glycerine	glycérine *f*	glēsārēn
hydrogen peroxide	eau *f* oxygénée	ō ôksēzhānā
injection	injection *f*	eNzheksyôN
insect repellent	remède *m* contre les piqûres d'insectes	remād kôNt(ər) lā pēk*ē*r deNsekt
iodine	teinture *f* d'iode	teNt*ē*r dyōd
laxative	purgatif *m*	p*ē*rgätēf
liniment	liniment *m*; friction *f*	lēnēmäN; frēksyôN
medicine, remedy	remède *m*	remād
mouthwash	eau *f* dentifrice	ō däNtēfrēs
ointment	pommade *f*	pômäd
pain pills	comprimés *m/pl.* contre la douleur	kôNprēmā kôNt(ər) lä do͞ol*ā*r
peppermint	menthe *f*	mäNt
pill	pilule *f*; comprimé *m*	pēl*ē*l; kôNprēmā
powder	poudre *f*	po͞od(ər)
prophylactics	préservatifs *m/pl.*	prāzervätēf
quinine	quinine *f*	kēnēn
salve	pommade *f*; onguent *m*	pômäd; ôNgäN
sanitary napkins	serviettes *f/pl.* hygiéniques	servyet ēzhē·ānēk
sleeping pills	somnifère *m*	somnēfār
styptic pencil	bâton *m* hémostatique	bätôN āmôstätēk
suppository	suppositoire *m*	s*ē*pôzētô·är
talcum powder	poudre *f* de talc	po͞od(ər) də tälk
tincture	teinture *f*	teNt*ē*r
tonic	fortifiant *m*	fôrtēfē·äN
tranquilizer	calmant *m*	kälmäN
valerian drops	gouttes *f/pl.* de valériennes	go͞ot də välārē·en
vaseline	vaseline *f*	väzlēn
vitamin pills	comprimés *m/pl.* de vitamines	kôNprēmā də vētämēn
wound salve	pommade *f* cicatrisante	pômäd sēkätrēzäNt

The doctor is in

Quick, call a doctor!
Appelez d'urgence un médecin, s'il vous plaît.
äplā dērzhäNs eN mādəseN, sēl vo͞o plā

Is there a doctor in the house?
Y a-t-il un médecin dans la maison?
ēyätēl eN mādəseN däN lä māzôN

Can he come here?
Peut-il venir?
pātēl venēr

Where is there a doctor?
Où y a-t-il un médecin?
o͞o yätēl eN mādəseN

Please get a doctor!
Faites venir un médecin, s'il vous plaît.
fāt venēr eN mādəseN, sēl vo͞o plā

Where is there a hospital?
Où se trouve l'hôpital?
o͞o sə tro͞ov lôpētäl

When does the doctor have office hours?
Quand le médecin a-t-il ses consultations?
käN lə mādəseN ätēl sā kôNsēltäsyôN

Would you please come to the ...
Venez s'il vous plaît, *au (à la)* ...
venā sēl vo͞o plā, ō (älä) ...

I'm sick.
Je suis malade.
zhə sē·ē mäläd

***My husband (My wife, Our child)* is sick.**
Mon mari (Ma femme, Notre enfant) est malade.
môN märē (mä fäm, nôträNfäN) ā mäläd

doctor	médecin *m*	mādəseN
dermatologist	dermatologue *m*	dārmätōlôg
ear, nose and throat specialist	oto-rhino-laryngologiste *m*	ōtō-rēnō-läreNgōlōzhēst
eye doctor	oculiste *m*	ôkēlēst
general practitioner	médecin *m* de médecine générale	mādəseN də mādəsēn zhānāräl
gynecologist	gynécologue *m*	zhēnākōlôg
neurologist	neurologue *m*	nārōlôg
ophthalmologist	oculiste *m*	ôkēlēst
orthopedist	orthopédiste *m*	ôrtōpādēst
otolaryngologist	O.R.L. *m*	ō·ār·el
pediatrician	pédiatre *m*	pādē·ät(ər)
psychiatrist	psychiatre *m*	psēkyät(ər)

psychologist	psychologue *m*	psēkōlôg
specialist	spécialiste *m*	spāsyälēst
surgeon	chirurgien *m*	shērērzhē·eN
– plastic surgery	chirurgie *f* plastique	shērērzhē plästēk
urologist	urologue *m*	ērōlôg
doctor's office	cabinet *m* de consultation	käbēnā də kôNsēltäsyôN
office hours	(heures *f/pl.* des) consultations *f/pl.*	(ār dā) kôNsēltäsyôN
waiting room	salle *f* d'attente	säl dätäNt

I haven't felt well the last few days.
Depuis quelques jours je ne me sens pas bien.
depē·ē kelke zhoor zhə nə mə säN pä byeN

My *head (throat, stomach)* hurts.
J'ai mal *à la tête (au cou, au ventre)*
zhā mäl älä tāt (ō koo, ō väNt[ər])

It hurts here.
J'ai mal ici.
zhā mäl ēsē

I've got a *severe (sharp)* pain here.
J'ai *très (horriblement)* mal ici.
zhā trā (ôrēbləmäN) mäl ēsē

I've got a (high) fever.
J'ai *de la (beaucoup de)* fièvre.
zhā dəlä (bōkoo də) fē·äv(ər)

I've caught a cold.
J'ai pris froid.
zhā prē frô·ä

I can't handle the *heat (food)* here.
Je ne supporte pas *la chaleur (la nourriture)*.
zhə nə sēpôrt pä lä shälār

I must have done something to my stomach.
J'ai une indigestion, je suppose.
zhā ēn eNdēzhestyôN, zhə sēpōz

I ate ...
J'ai mangé ...
zhā mäNzhā ...

I threw up.
J'ai vomi.
zhä vômē

I feel sick.
J'ai mal au cœur.
zhā mäl ō kār

I have *no appetite (diarrhea)*.
Je n'ai pas d'appétit (J'ai la diarrhée.)
zhə nā pä däpātē (zhā lä dē·ärā)

I'm constipated.
Je suis constipé(e).
zhə sē·ē kôNstēpā

My eyes hurt.
J'ai mal aux yeux.
zhā mäl ōzy*ā*

I can't sleep.
Je ne peux pas dormir.
zhə nə p*ā* pä dôrmēr

I've got chills.
J'ai des frissons.
zhā dā frēsôN

I'm diabetic.
Je suis diabéthique.
zhə s*ē*·ē dē·äbātēk

I fell.
J'ai fait une chute.
zhā fā *ē*n sh*ē*t

... ***is (are)*** **swollen.**
... *est (sont)* enflé(*s*).
... ā (sôN) äNflā

I have an earache.
J'ai mal aux oreilles.
zhā mäl ōzôrā'ē

I feel nauseated.
J'ai mal au cœur.
zhā mäl ō k*ā*r

I can't move ...
Je ne peux pas bouger ...
zhə nə p*ā* pä boozhā ...

I'm expecting a baby.
J'attends un bébé.
zhätäN eN bābā

I sprained my ankle.
Je me suis foulé la cheville.
zhə mə s*ē*·ē foolā lä shevē'ē

Is it serious?
Est-ce grave?
es gräv

I'm feeling *a little (much)* better.
Je me sens *un peu (beaucoup)* mieux.
zhə mə säNseN p*ā* (bōkoo) my*ā*

Could you give me a prescription for ...?
Pouvez-vous me prescrire ...?
poovā-voo mə prāskrēr ...

I'd like to be vaccinated against ...
J'aimerais me faire vacciner contre *le (la)* ...
zhāmerā mə fār väksēnā kôNt(ər) lə (lä) ...

> *Suppositories are used frequently for various ailments, so don't be surprised if they are prescribed to you!*

The doctor will tell you:

Take your clothes off, please.
Déshabillez-vous, s'il vous plaît.
dāzäbēyā-vo͞o, sēl vo͞o plā

Does this hurt?
Cela vous fait mal ici?
səlä vo͞o fā mäl ēsē

Let me see your tongue.
Tirez la langue!
tērā lä läNg

What have you been eating?
Qu'avez-vous mangé?
kävā-vo͞o mäNzhā

Breathe deeply!
Respirez (Aspirez) profondément!
respērā (äspērā) prōfóNdāmäN

Open your mouth.
Ouvrez la bouche!
o͞ovrā lä bo͞osh

Cough.
Toussez!
to͞osā

How long have you been ill?
Depuis quand êtes-vous malade?
depē̆·ē käN āt-vo͞o mäläd

We'll have to do *a blood test (an urinalysis).*
Il faut faire une analyse *de sang (d'urine).*
ēl fō fār ēn änälēz də säN (dērēn)

You're going to need an operation.
Il faut vous faire opérer.
ēl fō vo͞o fār ōpārā

I'll have to refer you to . . .
Je vais vous envoyer chez . . .
zhə vā vo͞ozäNvô·äyā shā . . .

You must stop *drinking (smoking)!*
Il ne faut pas *boire d'alcool (fumer).*
ēl nə fō pä bô·är dälkôl (fēmā)

Spend the next few days in bed.
Restez quelques jours au lit!
restā kelke zho͞or ō lē

You'll have to stay *in bed (on a strict diet).*
Il faut *rester couché (observer un régime sévère).*
ēl fō restā ko͞oshā (ôbservā eN rāzhēm sāvār)

Take *two tablets (ten drops)* three times a day.
Prenez-en *deux comprimés (dix gouttes)* trois fois par jour.
prenāzäN dā kôNprēmā (dē go͞ot) trô·äfô·ä pär zho͞or

It's nothing serious.
Ce n'est rien de grave!
sə nā rē·eN də gräv

Come back and see me a week from now.
Revenez dans huit jours.
revənā däN ē·ē zho͞or

Parts of the Body and their Functions

abdomen	ventre *m*; bas-ventre *m*	väNt(ər), bä-väNt(ər)
ankle	jointure *f*; *(foot)* cheville *f*	zhô·eNtēr, shevē'ē
appendix	appendice *m*	äpäNdēs
arm	bras *m*	brä
armpit	aisselle *f*	āsel
artery	artère *f*	ärtār
back	dos *m*	dō
bile	bile *f*	bēl
bladder	vessie *f*	vesē
blood	sang *m*	säN
blood pressure	tension *f* artérielle	täNsyôN ärtārē·el
body	corps *m*	kôr
circulation	circulation *f*	sērkəläsyôN
bone	os *m*	ôs (*pl.*: ō)
bowel movement	selle *f*	sel
brain	cerveau *m*	sārvō
breast	poitrine *f*	pô·ätrēn
breathing	respiration *f*	respēräsyôN
buttocks	fesses *f/pl.*	fes
calf	mollet *m*	môlā
cheek	joue *f*	zhōō
chest	poitrine *f*	pô·ätrēn
chin	menton *m*	mäNtôN
collarbone	clavicule *f*	klävēkəl
digestion	digestion *f*	dēzhestyôN
disc	disque *m*	dēsk
ear	oreille *f*	ôrā'ē
eardrum	tympan *m*	teNpäN
elbow	coude *m*	kōōd
eye	œil *m* (*pl.* yeux)	*ā'ē* (*pl.* *yā*)
– eyeball	globe *m* oculaire	glôb ôkəlār
– eyelid	paupière *f*	pōpyār
face	visage *m*	vēzäzh
finger	doigt *m*	dô·ä
– thumb	pouce *m*	pōōs
– index finger	index *m*	eNdeks

– middle finger	médius *m*	mādyēs
– ring finger	annulaire *m*	änēlār
– pinkie	auriculaire *m*	ôrēkēlār
foot	pied *m*	pyā
forehead	front *m*	frôN
frontal sinus	sinus *m* frontal	sēnēs frôNtäl
gall bladder	vésicule *f* biliaire	vāzēkēl bēlyār
genital organs	organes *m/pl.* génitaux	ôrgän zhānētō
gland	glande *f*	gläNd
hair	cheveux *m/pl.*	shvā
hand	main *f*	meN
head	tête *f*	tāt
heart	cœur *m*	kār
heel	talon *m*	tälôN
hip	hanche *f*	äNsh
instep	cou-de-pied *m*	kōō-də-pyā
intestine	intestin *m*	eNtesteN
– large intestine	gros intestin *m*	grō eNtesteN
– small intestine	intestin grêle *m*	eNtesteN grāl
jaw	mâchoire *f*	mäshô·är
– upper jaw	mâchoire supérieure	mäshô·är sēpārē·ār
– lower jaw	mâchoire inférieure	mäshô·är eNfārē·ār
joint	articulation *f*	ärtēkēläsyôN
kidney	rein *m*	reN
knee	genou *m*	zhenōō
kneecap	rotule *f*	rôtēl
larynx	larynx *m*	lareNks
leg	jambe *f*	zhäNb
– thigh	cuisse *f*	kē·ēs
– lower leg	jambe *f*	zhäNb
limbs	membres *m/pl.*	mäNb(ər)
lip	lèvre *f*	lāv(ər)
liver	foie *f*	fô·ä
lung	poumon *m*	pōōmôN
male organ	verge *f*	vārzh
maxillary sinus	sinus *m*	sēnēs
menstruation	règles *f/pl.*	rāg'əl
metabolism	métabolisme *m*	mātäbōlēsm
mouth	bouche *f*	bōōsh
mucous membrane	muqueuse *f*	mēkāz
muscle	muscle *m*	mēsk'əl

nail	ongle *m*	ôNg'əl
neck	cou *m*; nuque *f*	ko͞o, nēk
– back of the neck	nuque *f*	nēk
– nape of the neck	nuque *f*	nēk
nerve	nerf *m*	nār
nerves	nerfs *m/pl.*	nār
nose	nez *m*	nā
palate	palais *m*	pälā
pancreas	pancréas *m*	päNkrā·äs
pelvis	bassin *m*, bas-ventre *m*	bäseN, bä-väNt(ər)
penis	pénis *m*	pānēs
pregnancy	grossesse *f*	grōses
respiration	respiration *f*	respērāsyôN
rib	côte *f*	kôt
shin	tibia *m*	tēbē·ä
shoulder	épaule *f*	āpôl
sinew	tendon *m*	täNdôN
skin	peau *f*	pō
skull	crâne *m*	krän
sole	plante *f* du pied	pläNt dē pyā
spinal cord	moelle *f* épinière	mô·äl āpēnyār
spine	épine *f* dorsale, colonne *f* vertébrale	āpēn dôrsäl, kôlôn vertābräl
spleen	rate *f*	rät
stomach	estomac *m*	estōmä
temple	tempe *f*	täNp
tendon	tendon *m*	täNdôN
thorax	thorax *m*	tôräks
throat	gorge *f*	gôrzh
toe	orteil *m*	ôrtā'ē
tongue	langue *f*	läNg
tonsils	amygdales *f/pl.*	ämēgdäl
tooth	dent *f*	däN
urin	urine *f*	ērēn
uterus	utérus *m*	ētārēs
vagina	vagin *m*	väzheN
vein	veine *f*	ven
wrist	poignet *m*	pô·änyā

What's wrong?

abscess	abcès *m*	äbsā
airsickness	mal *m* de l'air	mäl də lār
allergy	allergie *f*	älerzhē
anemia	anémie *f*	änāmē
appendicitis	appendicite *f*	äpäNdēsēt
arthritis	rhumatisme *m* articulaire	rēmätēsm ärtēkēlār
asthma	asthme *m*	äsm
attack	attaque *f*	ätäk
backache	mal *m* au dos	mäl ō dō
bleeding	hémorragie *f*	āmôräzhē
blood poisoning	septicémie *f*	septēsāmē
blood pressure	tension *f*	täNsyôN
– high	– haute	– ōt
– low	– basse	– bäs
boil	furoncle *m*	fērôNk'əl
breathing problem	troubles *m/pl.* respiratoires	tro͞ob'əl resperätô·är
bronchitis	bronchite *f*	brôNshēt
bruise	contusion *f*	kôNtēzyôN
burn	brûlure *f*	brēlēr
cancer	cancer *m*	käNsār
cardiac infarction	infarctus *m* du myocarde	eNfärktēs dē mē·ōkärd
chicken pox	varicelle *f*	värēsel
chills	frissons *m/pl.*	frēsôN
cholera	choléra *m*	kôlārä
circulatory problem	troubles *m/pl.* circulatoires	tro͞ob'əl sērkēlätô·är
cold	rhume *m*	rēm
colic	colique *f*	kôlēk
concussion	commotion *f* cérébrale	kômôsyôN sārābräl
conjunctivitis	conjonctivite *f*	kôNzhôNktēvēt
constipation	constipation *f*	kôNstēpäsyôN
cough	toux *f*	to͞o
cramp	crampe *f*	kräNp
cut	coupure *f*	ko͞opēr
diabetes	diabète *m*	dē·äbāt

diarrhea	diarrhée *f*	dē·ärā
diphtheria	diphthérie *f*	dēftärē
disease	maladie *f*	mälädē
– contagious	– contagieuse	– kôNtäzhē·*ā*z
dislocation	luxation *f*	l*ē*ksäsyôN
dizziness	vertige *m*	vārtēzh
dysentery	dysenterie *f*	dēzäNtərē
eye inflammation	inflammation *f* de l'œil	eNflämäsyôN də l*ā*'ē
fever	fièvre *f*	fē·āv(ər)
fit	attaque *f*	ätäk
flatulence	ballonnements *m/pl.*	bälôn·mäN
flu	grippe *f*	grēp
food poisoning	intoxication *f*	eNtôksēkäsyôN
	alimentaire	älēmäNtār
fracture	fracture *f*	fräkt*ē*r
frostbite	engelure *f*	äNzhel*ē*r
gall stones	calculs *m/pl.* biliaires	kälk*ē*l bēlyār
German measles	rubéole *f*	r*ē*bā·ôl
hemorrhage	hémorragie *f*	āmôräzhē
hay fever	rhume *m* des foins	r*ē*m dā fô·eN
heart attack	crise *f* cardiaque	krēz kärdē·äk
heart problems	troubles *m/pl.*	tro͞ob'əl
	cardiaques	kärdē·äk
heartburn	aigreurs *f/pl.* d'estomac	āgr*ā*r destōmä
hemorrhoids	hémorroïdes *f/pl.*	āmôrō·ēd
hoarseness	enrouement *m*	äNro͞omäN
hypertension	hypertension *f*	ēpārtäNsyôN
illness	maladie *f*	mälädē
indigestion	embarras *m* gastrique	äNbärä gästrēk
inflammation	inflammation *f*	eNflämäsyôN
influenza	grippe *f*	grēp
injury	blessure *f*	bles*ē*r
insomnia	insomnie *f*	eNsômnē
intestinal catarrh	entérite *f*	äNtārēt
jaundice	jaunisse *f*	zhōnēs
kidney stones	calculs *m/pl.* rénaux	kälk*ē*l rānō
leukemia	leucémie *f*	l*ā*sāmē
liver problem	maladie *f* du foie	mälädē d*ē* fô·ä
lockjaw	constriction *f* des	kôNstrēksyôN dā
	mâchoires	mäshô·är

lumbago	lumbago *m*	lôNbägō
measles	rougeole *f*	ro͞ozhôl
middle ear inflammation	otite *f*	ôtēt
mumps	oreillons *m/pl.*	ôrāyôN
nausea	nausées *f/pl.*	nōzā
nephritis	néphrite *f*	nāfrēt
neuralgia	névralgie *f*	nāvrälzhē
nosebleed	saignements *m/pl.* du nez	sān(yə)mäN dē nā
pain	douleurs *f/pl.*	do͞olār
paralysis	paralysie *f*	pärälēzē
passing out	évanouissement *m*	āväno͞o·ēsmäN
peptic ulcer	ulcère *m* d'estomac	ēlsār destōmä
piles	hémorroïdes *f/pl.*	āmôrō·ēd
pleurisy	pleurésie *f*	plārāzē
pneumonia	pneumonie *f*	pnāmōnē
poisoning	empoisonnement *m*	eNpô·äzônmäN
injury	blessure *f*	bläsēr
pulled tendon	déchirement *m* des tendons	dāshērmäN dā täNdôN
rash	éruption *f*	ārēpsyôN
rheumatism	rhumatisme *m*	rēmätēsm
scarlet fever	scarlatine *f*	skärlätēn
sciatica	sciatique *f*	sē·ätēk
seasickness	mal *m* de mer	mäl də mār
shock	choc *m* nerveux	shôk nervā
skin disease	maladie *f* de la peau	mälädē dəlä pō
skin lesion	égratignures *f/pl.*	āgrätēnyēr
smallpox	variole *f*	värē·ôl
sore throat	mal *m* de gorge	mäl də gôrzh
sprain	foulure *f*	fo͞olēr
stitch in the side	point *m* de côté	pô·eN də kôtā
stomach pains	maux *m/pl.* d'estomac	mō destōmä
stroke	apoplexie *f*	äpōpleksē
sunburn	coup *m* de soleil	ko͞o də sôlā'ē
sunstroke	insolation *f*	eNsōläsyôN
suppuration	suppuration *f*	sēpēräsyôN
swelling	enflure *f*	äNflēr
tetanus	tétanos *m*	tātänôs
tonsilitis	angine *f*	äNzhēn
tuberculosis	tuberculose *f*	tēbärkēlōz

tumor	enflure *f*; tumeur *f*	äNflēr; tēmār
typhoid fever	typhus *m*	tēfēs
ulcer	ulcère *m*	ēlsār
venereal disease	maladie *f* vénérienne	mälädē vānārē·en
vomiting	vomissement *m*	vômēsmäN
whooping cough	coqueluche *f*	kôklēsh
wound	plaie *f*	plā

In the Hospital

anesthetic	narcose *f*	närkōz
bed pan	bassin *m*	bäseN
blood count	hémogramme *m*	āmōgräm
blood test	prise *f* de sang	prēz də säN
blood transfusion	transfusion *f*	träNsfēzyôN
diagnosis	diagnostic *m*	dē·ägnôstēk
discharge	sortie *f* de clinique	sôrtē də klēnēk
doctor	médecin *m*	mādəseN
examination	examen *m*, analyse *f*	egzämeN, änälēz
examine	examiner	egzämēnā
hospital	hôpital *m*	ôpētäl
infusion	infusion *f*	eNfēzyôN
injection	injection *f*; piqûre *f*	eNzheksyôN; pēkēr
intensive care unit	service *m* de réanimation	servēs də rā·änēmäsyôN
medical director	médecin *m* chef	mādəseN shef
night nurse	infirmière *f* de nuit	eNfērmyār də nē·ē
nurse	infirmière *f*	eNfērmyār
operate on	opérer	ôpārā
operating room	salle *f* d'opération	säl dôpāräsyôN
operation	opération *f*	ôpāräsyôN
patient	malade *m*	mäläd
surgeon	chirurgien *m*	shērērzhē·eN
temperature	température *f*	täNpārätēr
temperature chart	courbe *f* de température	ko͞orb de täNpārätēr
visiting hours	heures *f/pl.* de visite	ār də vēzēt
ward	service *m*	servēs
x-ray *(noun)*	radiographie *f*	rädē·ōgräfē
x-ray *(verb)*	radiographier	rädē·ōgräfyā

Nurse, could you give me a *pain killer (sleeping pill)*.
Mademoiselle, donnez-moi *quelque chose contre la douleur (un somnifère)*.
mädəmô·äzel, dônā-mô·ä kelke shōz kôNt(ər) lä do͞olär (eN sômnēfär)

When can I get out of bed?
Quand est-ce que je pourrai me lever?
käNdeske zhə po͞orā mə levā

What's the diagnosis?
Quel est le diagnostic?
kel ā lə dē·ägnôstēk

At the Dentist's

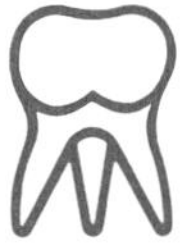

Where is there a dentist here?
Où y a-t-il un dentiste?
o͞o yätēl eN däNtēst

I've got a toothache.
J'ai mal aux dents.
zhā mäl ō däN

I'd like to make an appointment.
J'aimerais prendre rendez-vous.
zhāmerā präNd(ər) räNdā-vo͞o

This tooth hurts.
Cette dent me fait mal.
set däN mə fā mäl

– *up here (an upper tooth)*.
– *en haut (une dent du haut)*.
– äN ō (ēn däN dē ō)

– *down here (a lower tooth)*.
– *en bas (une dent du bas)*.
– äN bä (ēn däN dē bä)

I've lost a filling.
Un plombage est parti.
eN plôNbäzh ā pärtē

This tooth is loose.
La dent branle.
lä däN bräN'əl

. . . broke off.
. . . s'est cassée.
. . . sā käsā

Does this tooth have to be pulled?
Il faut arracher la dent?
ēl fōtäräshā lä däN

Can you do a temporary repair on this tooth?
Pouvez-vous soigner la dent provisoirement?
po͞ovā-vo͞o sô·änyā lä däN prōvēzō·är·mäN

Can you fix these dentures?
Pouvez-vous réparer cette prothèse?
po͞ovā-vo͞o rāpärā set prōtās

***Please don't *eat anything (smoke)* for two hours.**
Ne *mangez rien (fumez pas)* pendant deux heures, s'il vous plaît.
nə mäNzhä rē·eN (fēmā pä) päNdäN däzär, sēl vo͞o plā

When do you want me to come back?
Quand dois-je revenir?
käN dô·äzh rəvenēr

abscess	abcès *m*	äbsā
anesthesia	anesthésie *f*	änestāzē
– local	anesthésie *f* locale	änestāzē lôkäl
– general	anesthésie *f* générale	änestāzē zhānāräl
braces	appareil *m* (dentaire)	äpärā'ē (däNtār)
bridge	bridge *m*	brēdzh
cavities	carie *f*	kärē
crown	couronne *f*	ko͞orôn
cuspid	canine *f*	känēn
dental clinic	clinique *f* dentaire	klēnēk däNtār
dentist	dentiste *m*	däNtēst
denture	dentition *f*	däNtēsyôN
extract	arracher, extraire	äräshā, ekstrār
false tooth	fausse dent *f*	fōs däN
fill	plomber	plôNbā
filling	plombage *m*	plôNbäzh
gums	gencive *f*	zhäNsēv
incisor	incisive *f*	eNsēzēv
injection	injection *f*	eNzheksyôN
jaw	mâchoire *f*	mäshô·är
molar	molaire *f*	môlār
nerve	nerf *m*	nār
oral surgeon	chirurgien *m* dentiste	shērērzhē·eN däNtēst
orthodontist	orthodonto-stomato-logiste *m*	ôrtōdôNtō-stōmä-tōlōzhēst
plaster cast	plâtre *m*	plät(ə)r
plate	plaque *f*	pläk
root	racine *f*	räsēn
root canal work	traitement *m* de la racine	trātmäN dəlä räsēn
tartar	tartre *m*	tärt(ə)r
temporary filling	pansement *m*	päNsmäN
tooth	dent *f*	däN
tooth cervix	collet *m* d'une dent	kôlā dēn däN
toothache	mal *m* aux dents	mäl ō däN
wisdom tooth	dent *f* de sagesse	däN də säzhes

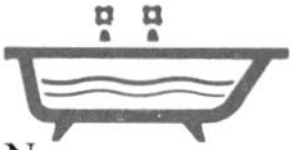

Taking a Cure

bath	bain *m*	beN
bath attendant	maître *m* nageur	māt(ər) näzhâr
convalescent home	maison *f* de convalescence	māzôN də kôNvälesäNs
cure	cure *f*	kēr
cure tax	taxe *f* de cure	täks də kēr
cure vacation	cure *f*	kēr
diet	régime *m*, diète *f*	rāzhēm, dē·āt
gymnastics	gymnastique *f*	zhēmnästēk
health resort	station *f* climatique	stäsyôN klēmätēk
hot spring	source *f* chaude	so͞ors shaud
inhale	faire des inhalations	fār dāzēnäläsyôN
massage *(noun)*	massage *m*	mäsäzh
massage *(verb)*	masser	mäsā
masseur	masseur *m*	mäsār
masseuse	masseuse *f*	mäsāz
medicinal spring	source *f* médicinale, thermes *f/pl.*	so͞ors mādēsēnäl, tārm
mineral bath	bain *m* thermal	beN tārmäl
mineral spring	source *f* thermale	so͞ors tārmäl
minerals	minéraux *m/pl.*	mēnārō
mud	boue *f* minérale	bo͞o mēnāräl
mud bath	bain *m* de boue	beN də bo͞o
mud pack	enveloppement *m* de boue	äNvelôpmäN də bo͞o
pump room	buvette *f*	bēvet
radiation therapy	traitement *m* par les rayons	trātmäN pär lā rāyôN
rest cure	cure *f* de repos	kēr də rəpō
sanatorium	sanatorium *m*	sänätôryôm
sauna	sauna *m*	sōnä
sea water	eau *f* de mer	ō də mār
short wave	onde *f* courte	ôNd ko͞ort
spa	station *f balnéaire (thermale)*	stäsyôN bälnā·ār (tārmäl)
steam bath	bain *m* de vapeur	beN də väpār
sunlamp	rayons *m/pl.* ultraviolets	rāyôN ēlträvē·ōlā
ultrasonics	écographie *f*	ākōgräfē

CONCERT, THEATRE, MOVIES

Most continental European theatres are repertory theatres, featuring a permanent company performing a different play, opera or operetta each evening.

At the Box Office

What's on tonight?
Qu'est-ce qu'on joue ce soir?
keskôN zho͞o sə sô·är

When does *the performance (the concert)* start?
À quelle heure commence *la représentation (le concert)?*
äkel*ā*r kômäNs lä repräzäNtäsyôN (le kôNsār)

Where can we get tickets?
Où est-ce qu'on prend les billets?
o͞o eskôN präN lā bēyā

Are there any discounts for . . . .?
Il y a une réduction pour . . .?
ēlyä *ē*n rād*ē*ksyôN po͞or . . .

Many European theatres and concert halls provide discount tickets for the disabled, for students and senior citizens.
If you're a student, be sure to get an international student identity card (ISIC) before leaving home. It entitles you to many reductions.

Are there still tickets available for *this (tomorrow)* evening?
Y a-t-il encore des billets pour *ce soir (demain soir)?*
ēyätēl äNkôr dā bēyā po͞or sə sô·är (demeN sô·är)

One ticket in the *third (tenth)* row, please.
Une place au *troisième (dixième)* rang, s'il vous plaît.
*ē*n pläs ō trô·äzyām (dēzyām) räN, sēl vo͞o plā

Two seats in the third row, first balcony, please.
Deux places au premier balcon, troisième rang, s'il vous plaît.
d*ā* pläs ō prəmyā bälkôN, trô·äzyām räN, sēl vo͞o plā

– in the middle.
– au milieu.
– ō mēlēy*ā*

– on the side.
– sur le côté.
– s*ē*r lə kôtā

accompanist	accompagnateur *m*	äkôNpänyät*ā*r
act	acte *m*	äkt
actor	acteur *m*	äkt*ā*r
actress	actrice *f*	äktrēs
advance ticket sales	location *f*	lôkäsyôN
alto	alto *m*	ältō
applause	applaudissements *m/pl.*	äplôdēsmäN
aria	aria *f*	ärē·ä
ballet	ballet *m*	bälā
balcony	balcon *m*	bälkôN
band	orchestre *m*	ôrkest(ər)
baritone	baryton *m*	bärētôN
bass	basse *f*	bäs
box office	caisse *f*; vente *f* de billets	kes; väNt də bēyā
chamber music	musique *f* de chambre	m*ē*zēk də shäNb(ər)
check room	vestiaire *m*	vestyār
chorus	chœur *m*	k*ā*r
coat check	ticket *m* de vestiaire	tēkā də vestyār
comedy	comédie *f*	kômädē
composer	compositeur *m*	kôNpōzēt*ā*r
concert	concert *m*	kôNsār
concert hall	salle *f* de concert	säl də kôNsār
conductor	chef *m* d'orchestre	shef dôrkest(ər)
contralto	contralto *m*	kôNträltō
costumes	costumes *m/pl.*	kôst*ē*m
costume designer	costumier *m*	kôst*ē*myā
curtain	rideau *m*	rēdō
curtain time	lever *m* de rideau	ləvā də rēdō
dancer	danseur *m*, danseuse *f*	däNs*ā*r, däNs*ā*z
director	metteur *m* en scène	met*ā*r äN sān
drama	drame *m*	drām
duett	duo *m*	d*ē*·ō
final curtain	fin *f*	feN
grand piano	piano *m* à queue	pē·änō ä k*ā*
intermission	entracte *m*	äNträkt
legitimate theatre	théâtre *m*	tā·ät(ər)
libretto	livret *m*	lēvrā
lobby	foyer *m*	fô·äyā
music	musique *f*	m*ē*zēk

musical	musical *m*	mēzēkäl
musician	musicien *m*	mēzēsyeN
opera	opéra *m*	ōpärä
opera glasses	jumelles *f/pl.* de théâtre	zhēmel də tä·ät(ər)
operetta	opérette *f*	ōpäret
orchestra	orchestre *m*	ôrkest(ər)
orchestra seats	fauteuils *m/pl.* d'orchestre	fôtā'ē dôrkest(ər)
overture	ouverture *f*	o͞ovärtēr
part/role	rôle *m*	rôl
– leading role	premier rôle *m*	prəmyā rôl
performance	représentation *f*	rəprāzäNtäsyôN
pianist	pianiste *m*	pē·änēst
piano recital	récital *m* de piano	rāsētäl də pē·änō
piece of music	morceau *m* de musique	môrsō də mēzēk
play	pièce *f* (de théâtre)	pyās (də tä·ät(ər))
producer	producteur *m*	prōdēktār
production	production *f*	prōdēksyôN
program	programme *m*	prōgrâm
scenery/settings	décors *m/pl.*	dākôr
set designer	décorateur *m*	dākôrātār
singer	chanteur *m*; cantatrice *f*	shäNtār; käNtätrēs
singing	chant *m*	shäN
soloist	soliste *m*	sōlēst
song	chanson *f*	shäNsôN
– folk song	chanson *f* populaire	shäNsôN pôpēlār
song recital	récital *m* de chant	rāsētäl də shäN
soprano	soprano *m*	sôpränō
stage	scène *f*	sān
stage director	metteur *m* en scène	metār äN sān
symphony concert	concert *m* symphonique	kôNsār seNfōnēk
tenor	ténor *m*	tānôr
theatre	théâtre *m*	tä·ät(ər)
theatre schedule	affiche *f* de théâtre	äfēsh də tä·ät(ər)
ticket	billet *m*	bēyā
ticket sales	vente *f* de billets	väNt də bēyā
tragedy	tragédie *f*	träzhādē
violin recital	récital *m* de violon	rāsētäl də vē·ōlôN
work	œuvre *f*	āv(ər)

At the Movies

What's on tonight at the movies?
Qu'est-ce qu'on joue au cinéma ce soir?
keskôN zho͞o ō sēnāmä sə sô·är

What time does *the box office open (the film start)*?
À quelle heure commence *la location (le film)*?
äkelār kômäNs lä lôkäsyôN (lə fēlm)

How long is the picture?
Combien de temps dure le film?
kôNbyeN də täN dēr lə fēlm

audience	spectateurs *m/pl.*, public *m*	spektätār, pēblēk
auditorium	salle *f* de spectacle	säl də spektäk'əl
cartoon	dessin *m* animé	deseN änēmā
cinema	cinéma *m*	sēnāmä
color film	film *m* en couleurs	fēlm äN ko͞olār
documentary	(film *m*) documentaire *m*	(fēlm) dôkēmäNtār
dubbed	synchronisé	seNkrōnēzā
dubbing	synchronisation *f*	seNkrônēzäsyôN
educational film	(film *m*) documentaire	(fēlm) dôkēmäNtār
feature film	long métrage *m*	lôN māträzh
film	film *m*	fēlm
film actor	acteur *m* de cinéma	äktār də sēnāmä
film festival	festival *m* du film	festēväl dē fēlm
film screening	écran *m*	ākräN
motion picture theatre	cinéma *m*	sēnāmä
movie	film *m*	fēlm
movie house	cinéma *m*	sēnāmä
newsreel	actualités *f/pl.* de la semaine	äktē·älētā dəlä smen
preview	prochains films *m/pl.*	prôshen fēlm
screen	écran *m*	ākräN
screenplay	scénario *m*	sānärē·ō
short subject	court métrage *m*	ko͞or māträzh
subtitled	sous-titré	so͞o-tēträ
thriller	film *m* policier	fēlm pôlēsyā
usher	ouvreuse *f*	o͞ovrāz

PASTIMES

Fun and Games

Where is there . . .?
Où y a-t-il ici . . .?
o͞o yätēl ēsē . . .

a bar	un bar	eN bär
a discotheque	une discothèque	ēn dēskōtāk
an ice skating rink	une pâtinoire	ēn pätēnô·är
a miniature golf course	un minigolf	eN mēnē-gôlf
a night club	une boîte de nuit	ēn bô·ät də nē·ē
a pool hall	un billard	eN bēyär
a riding stable	une école d'équitation	ēn ākôl dākētä-syôN
a sailing school	une école de yachting	ēn ākôl də yôtēng
a tennis court	un court de tennis	eN ko͞or də tenēs

I'd like to. . .
J'aimerais . . .
zhāmerā . . .

play badminton	jouer au volant	zho͞o·ā ō vôläN
play miniature golf	jouer au mini-golf	zho͞o·ā ō mēnē-gôlf
play ping pong	jouer au ping-pong	zho͞o·ā ō pēn(yə)-pôNg
watch the fashion show	aller voir le défilé de mode	älā vô·är lə dāfēlā də môd

Do you have television?
Vous avez la télévision?
vo͞ozävā lä tālāvēzyôN

Can I listen to the radio here?
Je peux écouter la radio ici?
zhə pāzāko͞otā lä rädē·ō ēsē

What station is that?
Quelle station est-ce?
kel stäsyôN es

What's on today?
Quel est le programme aujourd'hui?
kel ā lə prōgräm ōzho͞ordē·ē

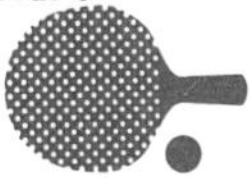

Do you play *chess (ping pong)?*
Jouez-vous *aux échecs (au ping-pong)?*
zho͞o·ā·vo͞o ōzāshek (ō pēn(yə)-pôNg)

amusement	distraction *f*	dēsträksyôN
beauty contest	concours *m* de beauté	kôNko͞or də bōtā
bowling alley	piste *f* de bowling	pēst də bo͞olēng
card game	jeu *m* de cartes	zhā də kärt
– cut	couper	ko͞opā
– deal	donner	dônā
– shuffle	battre	bät(ər)
– ace	as *m*	äs
– jack	valet *m*	välā
– queen	dame *f*	däm
– king	roi *m*	rô·ä
– clubs	trèfle *m*	trāf'əl
– diamonds	carreau *m*	kärō
– hearts	cœur *m*	k*ā*r
– spades	pique *m*	pēk
– joker	joker *m*	zhōkār
– trick	levée *f*	levā
– trump	atout *m*	äto͞o
checkers	(jeu *m* de) dames	(zh*ā* də) däm
chess	échecs *m/pl.*	āshek
– board	échiquier *m*	āshēkyā
– chessman	pièce *f*	pyās
– square	case *f*	käz
– bishop	fou *m*	fo͞o
– castle	tour *f*	to͞or
– king	roi *m*	rô·ä
– knight	cavalier *m*	kävälyā
– pawn	pion *m*	pyôN
– queen	reine *f*	ren
– rook	tour *f*	to͞or
chip	jeton *m*	zhetôN
circus	cirque *m*	sērk
club	club *m*	kl*ē*b
country fair	fête *f* populaire	fāt pôp*ē*lār
dice	dé *m*	dā
– shoot dice	jouer aux dés	zho͞o·ā ō dā
gambling casino	casino *m*	käzēnō
gambling game	jeu *m* de hazard	zh*ā* də äzär
– banker	banquier *m*	bäNkyā
– bet	miser (sur)	mēzā (s*ē*r)
– draw	faire un coup	fār eN ko͞o

– move	coup *m*	kōō
– piece	pion *m*	pyôN
– play	jouer	zhōō·ā
– stake	mise *f*	mēz
magazine	revue *f*, magazine *m*	revē, mägäzēn
– fashion magazine	journal *m* de modes	zhōōrnäl də môd
– glossy	illustré *m*	ēlēstrā
newspaper	journal *m*	zhōōrnäl
party games	jeux *m/pl.* de société	zhā də sôsē·ātā
pastime	passe-temps *m*	päs-täN
ping pong	ping-pong *m*	pēn(yə)-pôNg
radio	radio *f*	rädē·ō
– FM	modulations *f/pl.* de fréquence	môdēläsyôN də fräkäNs
– long wave	grandes ondes *f/pl.*	gräNdzôNd
– medium wave	ondes *f/pl.* moyennes	ôNd mô·äyen
– short wave	ondes *f/pl.* courtes	ôNd kōōrt
– radio play	pièce *f* radiophonique	pyās rädē·ōfōnēk
record	disque *m*	dēsk
record player	électrophone *m*	ālektrōfôn
recording tape	bande *f* magnétique	bäNd mänyātēk
table tennis	ping-pong *m*; tennis *m* de table	pēn(yə)-pôNg; tenēs də täb'əl
tape recorder	magnétophone *m*	mänyātōfôn
television	télévision *f*	tālāvēzyôN
– announcer	speaker *m*	spēkär
– breakdown	perturbation *f*	pertērbäsyôN
– news	informations *f/pl.*	eNfôrmäsyôN
– program	programme *m*	prōgräm
– program schedule	prochaines émissions	prôshen āmēsyôN
– turn off	éteindre	āteNd(ər)
– turn on	allumer	älēmā
– television play	jeu *m* télévisé	zhā tālāvēzā

Getting acquainted

Hope you don't mind if I talk to you.
Excusez-moi de vous adresser la parole.
ekskēzā-mô·ä də vo͞ozädresā lä pärôl

Mind if I join you?
Vous permettez que je m'asseye à côté de vous?
vo͞o pārmetā ke zhə mäsā ä kôtā də vo͞o

May I treat you to a *drink (coffee, tea)?*
Vous prenez *quelque chose (un café, un thé)?*
vo͞o prenā kelke shōz (eN käfā, eN tā)

You got something on for this evening?
Vous êtes déjà pris(e) ce soir?
vo͞ozāt dāzhä prē(z) sə sô·är

Shall we dance?
Vous voulez danser?
vo͞o vo͞olā däNsā

Is there a *discotheque (a dance hall)* here?
Y a-t-il ici *une discothèque (un dancing)?*
ēyätēl ēsē ēn dēskōtäk (eN däNsēng)

May I have the next dance?
(Voulez-vous m'accorder cette danse) Mademoiselle?
(vo͞olā-vo͞o mäkôrdā set däNs) mädəmô·äzel

We can chat undisturbed here.
Ici, nous pouvons bavarder sans être dérangés.
ēsē, no͞o po͞ovôN bävärdā säNzāt(ər) däräNzhā

May I invite you to a party?
Je voudrais vous inviter à une fête.
zhə vo͞odrā vo͞ozeNvētā ä ēn fāt

I'll be expecting you at . . .
Je vous attends *chez (à)* . . .
zhə vo͞ozätäN shā (ä) . . .

You look good in that dress.
Cette robe vous va très bien.
set rôb vo͞o vä trā byeN

When can you come visit me?
Quand est-ce que vous viendrez me voir?
käNdeske vo͞o vyeNdrā mə vô·är

When can we meet again?
Quand pouvons-nous nous revoir?
käN po͞ovôN-no͞o no͞o revô·är

May I give you a lift home?
Je peux vous raccompagner?
zhə pā vo͞o räkôNpänyā

Where do you live?
Où habitez-vous?
o͞o äbētā-vo͞o

Won't you come in for a minute?
Vous voulez entrer un moment?
vo͞o vo͞olā äNtrā eN mōmäN

May I walk part of the way with you?
Je peux vous accompagner un moment?
zhə pā vo͞ozäkôNpänyā eN mômäN

Thanks very much for a nice evening.
Merci beaucoup pour cette agréable soirée.
mersē bōko͞o po͞or set ägrā·äb'əl sô·ärā

accompany	accompagner	äkôNpänyā
dance *(noun)*	danse *f*	däNs
dance *(verb)*	danser	däNsā
dance hall	dancing *m*	däNsēng
dicotheque	discothèque *f*	dēskōtāk
enjoy oneself	s'amuser	sämēzā
expect somebody	attendre qn.	ätäNd(ər) kelkeN
flirting	flirt *m*	flārt
invite	inviter	eNvētā
kiss *(noun, only!)*	baiser *m*	bāzā
kiss *(verb)*	embrasser	äNbräsā
live	habiter	äbētā
love *(noun)*	amour *m*	ämo͞or
love *(verb)*	aimer	āmā
make love	flirter	flārtā
meet	(se) rencontrer, retrouver	(sə) räNkôNtrā, rətro͞ovā
meet again	se revoir	sə rəvô·är
party	fête *f*	fāt
take a walk	se promener	sə prômənā
visit	visiter	vēzētā
visit *(chat) (verb)*	causer	kôzā

On the Beach

Where can we go swimming here?
Où peut-on se baigner ici?
o͞o pātôN sə bānyā ēsē

Can we go swimming here?
On a le droit de se baigner ici?
ônä lə drô·ä də sə bānyā ēsē

Two tickets (with cabana), please.
Deux billets (avec cabine), s'il vous plaît.
d*ā* bēyā (ävek käbēn), sēl vo͞o plā

How far out can we swim?
Jusqu'où peut-on nager?
zh*ē*sko͞o p*ā*tôN näzhā

Can we swim *topless (nude)* here?
Nous pouvons-nous baigner *sans soutien-gorge (nus)?*
no͞o po͞ovôN-no͞o bānyā säN so͞otyeN-gôrzh (n*ē*)

How *deep (warm)* is the water?
Quelle est la *profondeur (température)* de l'eau?
kel ā lä prôfôNd*ā*r (täNpārätēr) dəlō

Is it dangerous for children?
Est-ce dangereux pour les enfants?
es däNzhār*ā* po͞or lāsäNfäN

***No swimming!**
Interdiction de se baigner!
(Baignade interdite)
eNterdēksyôN də sə bānyā
(bānyäd eNterdēt)

Is there an undertow here?
Y a-t-il des courants?
ēyätēl dā ko͞orâN

Where is the lifeguard?
Où est le maître-nageur?
o͞o ā lə māt(ər)-näzh*ā*r

A *deck chair (umbrella)*, please.
Une chaise-longue (Un parasol), s'il vous plaît.
*ē*n shāz-lông (eN päräsôl), sēl vo͞o plā

How much does ... cost?
Combien coûte ...?
kôNbyeN ko͞ot ...

I'd like to rent a *cabana (boat)*.
Je voudrais louer *une cabine (un bateau)*.
zhə vo͞odrā lo͞o·ā *ē*n käbēn (eN bätō)

Where *is (are)* ...?
Où *est (sont)* ...?
o͞o ā (sôN) ...

I'd like to go water skiing.
Je voudrais faire du ski nautique.
zhə vo͞odrā fār d*ē* skē nôtēk

Where can I go fishing?
Où peut-on pêcher à la ligne?
o͞o p*ā*tôN pāshā älä lēn(yə)

Would you be good enough to keep an eye on my gear.
Vous pourriez surveiller mes affaires, s'il vous plaît?
vo͞o po͞orē·ā s*ē*rvāyā māzäfār, sēl vo͞o plā

air mattress	matelas *m* pneumatique	mätlä pn*ā*mätēk
air temperature	température *f* de l'air	täNpärätēr də lār
bathing cap	bonnet *m* de bain	bônā də beN
bathing suit	maillot *m* de bain	mäyō də beN
– trunks	slip *m* de bain	slēp də beN
bathrobe	peignoir *m*	penyô·är
bay	baie *f*	bā

boat	bateau *m*	bätō
– dinghy	canot *m* pneumatique	känō pn*ā*mätēk
– motorboat	bateau *m* à moteur	bätō ä mōt*ā*r
– pedal boat	pédalo *m*	pādälō
– sailboat	voilier *m*	vô·älēyā
cabana	cabine *f* de bain	käbēn də beN
dive	plonger	plôNzhā
diving board	tremplin *m*	träNpleN
dune	dune *f*	d*ē*n
jellyfish	méduse *f*	mād*ē*z
locker room	vestiaire *m*	vestyār
non-swimmer	non-nageur *m*	nôN-näzh*ā*r
nude beach	plage *f* de nudistes (naturistes)	pläzh də n*ē*dēst (nät*ē*rēst)
saline content	teneur *f* en sel	ten*ā*r äN sel
sandy beach	plage *f* de sable	pläzh də säb'əl
scuba diving	plongée *f* sous-marine	plôNzhā so͞o-märēn
scuba equipment	équipment *m* de plongée sous-marine	ākēpmäN də plôNzhā so͞o-märēn
shells	coquillages *m/pl.*	kôkēyäzh
shower	douche *f*	do͞osh
swim	nager	näzhā
swimmer	nageur *m*	näzh*ā*r
swimming pier	passerelle *f*	päsərel
take a sunbath	prendre un bain de soleil	präNdreN beN də sôlā'ē
water	eau *f*	ō
water temperature	température *f* de l'eau	täNpārät*ē*r dəlō
wave	vague *f*	väg

Sports

What sports events do they have here?
Quelles manifestations sportives y a-t-il ici?
kel mänēfestäsyôN spôrtēv ēyätēl ēsē

Where's the *stadium (soccer field)?*
Où est *le stade (le terrain de football)?*
o͞o ā lə städ (lə tereN də fo͞otbôl)

***... is playing ... today.**
Aujourd'hui ... joue contre ...
ōzho͞ordē·ē ... zho͞o kôNt(ər)

I'd love to see the *game (race, fight)*.
J'aimerais bien voir *le jeu (la course, le combat)*.
zhāmrā byeN vô·är lə zhā (lä ko͞ors, lə kôNbä)

***When (Where)* is the soccer game?**
Quand (Où) le match de football a-t-il lieu?
käN (o͞o) lə mätsh də fo͞otbôl ätēl lēyā

Can you get us tickets for it?
Pourriez-vous nous procurer des *cartes (billets)*?
po͞orē·ā-vo͞o no͞o prôkērā dā kärt (bēyā)

Goal!
But!
bē(t)

What's the score?
Où en est le match?
o͞o änā lə mätsh

***The score is three to two for ...**
Le score est de trois à deux pour ...
lə skôr ā də trô·ä ä dā po͞or ...

Is there an *outdoor (indoor)* swimming pool here?
Y a-t-il une piscine *découverte (couverte)*?
ēyätēl ēn pēsēn dāko͞ovārt (ko͞ovārt)

What sports do you like to play?
Qu'est-ce que *vous faites (tu fais)* comme sport?
keske vo͞o fāt (tē fā) kôm spôr

I'm ...
Je suis ...
zhə sē·ē ...

I play ...
Je joue au ...
zhə zho͞o ō ...

I'm fond of ...
Je me passionne pour ...
zhə mə päsyôn po͞or ...

athlete	athlète *m/f*	ätlāt
auto racing	course *f* automobile	ko͞ors ôtōmōbēl
– race	course *f*	ko͞ors
– race car driver	coureur *m* automobile	ko͞orār ôtōmōbēl
– racing car	voiture *f* de course	vô·ätēr də ko͞ors
bicycling	cyclisme *m*	sēklēsm
– bicycle	bicyclette *f*	bēsēklet
– bicycle race	course *f* cycliste	ko͞ors sēklēst
– bicycle rider	cycliste *m*	sēklēst
– ride a bike	aller à bicyclette	älā ä bēsēklet
boat racing	régates *f/pl.*	rāgät
– racing boat	bateau *m* de course	bätō də ko͞ors
bowling	bowling *m*	bo͞olēng (bōlēng)

– bowling alley	piste *f* de bowling	pēst də bo͞olēng
boxing	(match *m* de) boxe *f*	(mätsh də) bôks
– box	boxer	bôksā
– boxer	boxeur *m*	bôksär
competition	compétition *f*	kôNpātēsyôN
– championship	championnat *m*	shäNpyônä
– defeat	défaite *f*	dāfāt
– draw	match *m* nul	mätsh nel
– free style	exercices *m/pl.* libres	eksersēs lēb(ər)
– game	jeu *m*	zhä
– goal	but *m*	be(t)
– half time	mi-temps *m*	mē-täN
– match	jeu *m*	zhä
– play	jouer	zho͞o·ā
– point	point *m*	pô·eN
– practice	entraînement *m*	äNtrānmäN
– result	résultat *m*	rāzeltä
– start	départ *m*	dāpär
– victory	victoire *f*	vēktô·är
– win	gagner	gänyā
dog races	course *f* de lévriers	ko͞ors də lāvrē·ā
fencing	escrime *f*	eskrēm
figure skating	patinage *m*	pätēnäzh
– skate	patiner	pätēnā
– skates	patins *m/pl.*	päteN
– skater	patineur *m*	pätēnär
fishing	pêche *f* à la ligne	pāsh älä lēn(yə)
– fishing rod	canne *f* à pêche	kän ä pāsh
– go fishing	pêcher à la ligne	pāshā älä lēn(yə)
– fishing license	permis *m* de pêche	permē də pāsh
golf	golf *m*	gôlf
gymnastics	gymnastique *f*	zhēmnästēk
– gymnast	gymnaste *m*	zhēmnäst
– gymnastics with apparatus	gymnastique *f* aux agrès	zhēmnästēk ōzägrā
– balance beam	poutre *f* horizontale	po͞otrôrēzôNtäl
– horizontal bar	barre *f* fixe	bär fēks
– parallel bars	barres *f/pl.* parallèles	bär pärälāl
– rings	anneaux *m/pl.*	änō
handball	handball *m*	äNdbôl
hockey	hockey *m*	ôkā

hunting	chasse *f*	shäs
– hunting license	permis *m* de chasse	permē də shäs
judo	judo *m*	zhēdō
marksmanship	tir *m*	tēr
– clay pigeon shooting	tir *m* au pigeon	tēr ō pēzhôN
– rifle range	(stand *m* de) tir *m*	(stäN də) tēr
– shoot	tirer	tērā
– target	cible *f*	sēb'əl
mountain climbing	alpinisme *m*	älpēnēsm
– mountain climber	alpiniste *m*	älpēnēst
ninepins	jeu *m* de quille	zhā də kē'ē
player	joueur *m*	zhoo·ār
referee	arbitre *m*	ärbēt(ər)
riding	hippisme *m*; équitation *f*	ēpēsm; ākētäsyôN
– horse	cheval *m*	shəväl
– horse race	course *f* de chevaux	koors də shəvō
– jumping	saut *m*	sō
– ride	monter à cheval	môNtā ä shəväl
– rider	cavalier *m*	kävälyā
– trotting race	course *f* de trot attelé	koors də trô ätəlā
rowing	aviron *m*	ävērôN
– scull	rame *f*	räm
– oarsman	rameur *m*	rämār
– coxswain	barreur *m*	bärār
sailing	voile *f*; yachting *m*	vô·äl; yôtēng
– sail *(noun)*	voile *f*	vô·äl
– sail *(verb)*	faire de la voile	fār dəlä vô·äl
– sailboat	voilier *m*	vô·älyā
skiing	ski *m*	skē
– ski *(noun)*	ski *m*	skē
– ski *(verb)*	faire du ski	fār dē skē
– ski binding	fixation *f*	fēksäsyôN
– ski jump	tremplin *m* (de saut)	träNpleN (də sō)
– ski lift	téléski *m*	tālāskē
– ski wax	fart *m*	färt
soccer	football; "foot"	footbôl; foot
– ball	ballon *m*	bälôN
– corner	corner *m*	kôrnār
– forward	avant *m*	äväN
– free kick	coup *m* franc	koo fräN

– fullback	arrière *m*	äryār
– kick a goal	marquer un but	märkā eN b*ē*(t)
– goal	but *m*	b*ē*(t)
– goalie	gardien *m* de but	gärdyeN də b*ē*(t)
– halfback	demi *m*, libero *m*	dəmē, lēbārō
– off-side	hors-jeu *m*	ôr-zh*ā*
– penalty kick	penalty *m*	pānältē
– play soccer	jouer au football	zhoo͞·ā ō foo͞tbôl
– player	joueur *m*	zhoo͞·*ā*r
– throw-in	touche *f*	too͞sh
sports	sport *m*	spôr
– athletic club	association *f* sportive	äsôsyäsyôN spôrtēv
– sports fan	passionné *m* de sport	päsyônā də spôr
swimming	natation *f*	nätäsyôN
– dive	plongeon *m*	plôNzhôN
– diving board	plongeoir *m*	plôNzhô·är
– swimmer	nageur *m*	näzh*ā*r
team	équipe *f*	ākēp
tennis	tennis *m*	tenēs
– singles/doubles	simple *m*/double *m*	sēNp'əl/doo͞b'əl
– play tennis	jouer au tennis	zhoo͞·ā ō tenēs
– tennis ball	balle *f* de tennis	bäl də tenēs
– tennis court	court *m* de tennis	koo͞r də tenēs
– badminton	badminton *m*, volant *m*	bädmēntôn, vôläN
tobogganing	luge *f*	l*ē*zh
– toboggan	luge *f*	l*ē*zh
track and field	athlétisme *m*	ätlātēsm
umpire	arbitre *m*	ärbēt(ər)
volleyball	volley-ball *m*	vôlā-bôl
wrestling	lutte *f*	l*ē*t
– wrestle	lutter	l*ē*tā
– wrestler	lutteur *m*	l*ē*t*ā*r

The most popular sport (especially for spectators) in France is soccer, called le football *or* le foot.
Another very popular sport is bicycle racing, le cyclisme, *which culminates in the gruelling* Tour de France *race. Sailing, tennis and skiing are also quite popular. Especially in the south of France, rugby enjoys enormous popularity.*

APPENDIX

Signs

À LOUER	ä lo͞o·ā	**to let**
À VENDRE	ä väNd(ər)	**for sale**
ARRÊT	ärā	**stop**
ARRIVÉE	ärēvā	**arrival**
ATTENTION	ätäNsyôN	**caution**
AVIS AU PUBLIC	ävē ō pēblēk	**public notices**
BUVETTE (BAR)	bēvet (bär)	**refreshments**
DAMES	däm	**ladies**
DANGER	däNzhā	**danger**
DANGER DE MORT	däNzhā də môr	**mortal danger**
DÉFENSE D'AFFICHER	dāfäNs däfēshā	**post no bills**
DÉFENSE DE FUMER	dāfäNs də fēmā	**no smoking**
DÉFENSE DE SE BAIGNER	dāfäNs də sə bānyā	**no swimming allowed**
DEUXIÈME ÉTAGE	dāzyām ātäzh	**third floor**
ENTRÉE	äNtrā	**entrance**
ENTRÉE INTERDITE	äNtrā eNterdēt	**no admittance**
ENTRÉE LIBRE	äNtrā lēb(ər)	**admission free**
ESCALIER ROULANT	eskälyā ro͞oläN	**escalator**
EXTINCTEUR	eksteNktār	**fire extinguisher**
FERMÉ	fārmā	**closed**
MESSIEURS	mesyā	**gentlemen**
NE PAS OUVRIR	nə päzo͞ovrēr	**do not open**
NE PAS SE PENCHER AU DEHORS	nə pä sə päNshä ō də·ôr	**do not lean out the window**
PEINTURE FRAÎCHE	peNtēr frāsh	**wet paint**
POUSSEZ	po͞osā	**push**
PREMIER ETAGE	prəmyār ātäzh	**second (!) floor**
PRIÈRE DE NE PAS TOUCHER	prēyār də nə pä to͞oshā	**do not touch**
PRIVÉ	prēvā	**private (road)**
SORTIE	sôrtē	**exit**
SORTIE DE SECOURS	sôrtē də səko͞or	**emergency exit**
TIREZ	tērā	**pull**

Abbreviations

A.C.F.	Automobile Club de France [ôtōmōbēl klēb də fräNs]	**French Automobile Association**
A.J.	Auberge de Jeunesse [ōbärzh də zhānes]	**youth hostel**
arr.	arrivée; arrondissement [ärēvā; ärôNdēsmäN]	**arrival; district**
bd.	boulevard [boolvär]	**boulevard**
B.P.	boîte postale [bô·ät pôstäl]	**post-office box**
c.-à-d.	c'est-à-dire [setädēr]	**that is**
C.C.P.	compte de chèques postaux [kôNt də shek pôstō]	**postal check account**
C.J.	camp de jeunesse [käN də zhānes]	**youth camp**
ct.	(du mois) courant [(dē mô·ä) kooräN]	**... instant**
C.U.	Cité Universitaire [sētā ēnēversētär]	**university camp**
dép.	départ [dāpär]	**departure**
dépt.	département [dāpärtmäN]	**department**
M.	Monsieur [məsyā]	**Mister**
Mlle	Mademoiselle [mädəmô·äzel]	**Miss**
MM	Messieurs [mesyā]	**Messieurs**
Mme	Madame [mädäm]	**Mistress**
O.R.T.F.	Office de la Radiotélévision française	**French Broadcasting Corporation**
P. et T.	Postes et Télécommunications [pôst ā tālākômēnēkäsyôN]	**Post and Telecommunication**
pl.	place [pläs]	**square**
R.E.R.	Réseau express régional [rāzō ekspres rāzhē·ônäl]	**system of suburban express trains**
R.N.	route nationale [root näsyônäl]	**Federal Highway**
S.A.M.U.	service d'aide médicale d'urgence [servēs dād mādēkäl dērzhäNs]	**life-saving-service**
S.N.C.F.	Société Nationale des Chemins de Fer Français	**French Railroad**
S.I.	syndicat d'initiative [seNdēkä dēnēsyätēv]	**tourist office**

Weights and Measures

1 millimeter	un millimètre (mm)	eN mēlēmāt(ər)
1 centimeter	un centimètre (cm)	eN säNtēmāt(ər)
1 decimeter	un décimètre (dm)	eN dāsēmāt(ər)
1 meter	un mètre (m) (=1.0936 yards)	eN māt(ər)
1 kilometer	un kilomètre (km) (=0.6214 miles)	eN kēlōmāt(ər)
1 inch	un pouce (=2.54 cm)	eN po͞os
1 foot	30.48 cm	
1 yard	0.914 m	
1 (statute) mile	une lieue (=1.609 km)	*ē*n lēy*ā*
1 nautical mile	un mille marin (=1.853 km)	eN mēl märeN
1 square foot	0.0929 m^2	
1 square yard	0.836 m^2	
1 square meter	un mètre carré (m^2) (=1.196 square yards)	eN māt(ər) kärā
1 square mile	2.59 kilomètres carrés (km^2)	kēlōmāt(ər) kärā
1 cubic foot	0.028 mètres cube (m^3)	mātrə k*ē*b
1 liter	un litre (l) (=2.113 pints)	eN lēt(ər)
1 pint	0.473 l	
1 quart	0.946 l	
1 gallon	3.785 l	
1 ounce	28.349 grammes (g)	gräm
1 pound	un demi kilo (une livre)	eN dəmē kēlō/ *ē*n lēv(ər)
1 hundredweight	un quintal (=45.359 kg)	eN keNtäl
1 ton	une tonne	*ē*n tôn
a piece (of . . .)	un morceau (de. . .)	eN môrsō (də . . .)
a pair (of . . .)	une paire (de . . .)	*ē*n pār (də . . .)
a dozen	une douzaine (de . . .)	*ē*n do͞ozen (də . . .)
a pack(et) (of . . .)	un paquet (de . . .)	eN päkā (də . . .)

Colors

beige	beige	bāzh
black	noir	nô·är
blonde	blond	blôN
blue	bleu	bl*ā*
– light blue	bleu clair	bl*ā* klār
– navy blue	bleu foncé	bl*ā* fôNsā
brown	brun	breN
– chestnut brown	châtain	shäteN
color	couleur *f*	ko͞ol*ā*r
– colored	coloré	kôlôrā
– colorful	multicolore	m*ē*ltēkôlôr
– solid-colored	uni	*ē*nē
gold	doré	dôrā
green	vert	vār
– dark green	vert foncé	vār fôNsā
– light green	vert clair	vār klār
gray	gris	grē
– ash gray	gris cendré	grē säNdrā
– dark gray	gris foncé	grē fôNsā
– pale gray	gris clair	grē klār
lavender/mauve	lavande/mauve	läväNd, mōv
orange	orange	ôräNzh
pink	rose	rōz
purple	pourpre	po͞orp(ər)
red	rouge	ro͞ozh
– bright red	rouge clair	ro͞ozh klār
– fire engine red	rouge vif	ro͞ozh vēf
– dark red/maroon	rouge foncé	ro͞ozh fôNsā
silver	argenté	ärzhäNtā
violet	violet	vē·ôlā
white	blanc (blanche)	bläN (bläNsh)
yellow	jaune	zhōn

BASIC FRENCH GRAMMAR RULES

I. The Article

1. There are two genders in French, masculine and feminine.

2. The **definite** article in the **masculine** singular is **le** [lə], e.g. *le livre* [lə lēv(ər)] the book.

3. The **definite** article in the **feminine** singular is **la** [lä], e.g. *la maison* [lä māzôN] the house.

4. The masculine and feminine **plural** is always **les** [lā], e.g. *les livres* [lā lēv(ər)] the books, *les maisons* [lā māzôN] the houses.

5. The **indefinite** article in the **masculine** singular is **un** [eN], e.g. *un cheval* [eN shəväl] a horse.

6. The **indefinite** article in the **feminine** singular is **une** [ēn], e.g. *une lettre* [ēn let(ər)] a letter.

7. Nouns expressing an indefinite amount or an indefinite number of items take the **partitive,** which is formed by the preposition **de** and the definite article, e.g. *du pain* [dē peN] bread, *de la viande* [də lä vē·äNd] meat, des *amis* [dāzämē] friends. There is no English equivalent for the partitive.

II. The Noun

1. As in English, the subject and object function of the noun is indicated by its place in the sentence.

2. The possessive case can be indicated by *de* [də] or *à* [ä].

3. *de* and *à* are combined with *le* and *les* in the following ways: *de le* becomes *du* [dē], *de les* becomes *des* [dā], *à le* becomes *au* [ō], *à les* becomes *aux* [ō].

III. The Adjective and Adverb

1. **Adjectives** agree in number and gender with the nouns they modify.

2. **Adverbs** are formed by adding **-ment** to the feminine form of the adjective.

3. The feminine form of the adjective is formed by adding *-e* to the masculine (*m*) form (if this does not already end in *-e*), e.g. *m grand* [gräN], *f grande* [gräNd] big; *m poli* [pôlē], *f polie* [pôlē] polite; but *m* and *f* sage [säzh] wise.

IV. Comparison

1. The **comparative** is formed by placing *plus* [plā̆] more, before the adjective or adverb, e.g. *beau* [bō] beautiful, *plus beau* [plā̆ bō] more beautiful; *rapidement* [räpēd·mäN] fast, *plus rapidement* [plā̆ räpēd·mäN] faster.

2. The following adjectives are irregular in the comparative: *bon* [bôN] good, *meilleur* [māyā̆r] better; *mauvais* [mōvā] bad, *pire* [pēr] worse; *petit* [pətē] little, small, *moindre* [mô·eNd(ər)] less, (*plus petit* [plā̆ pətē] smaller).

3. The following adverbs are irregular in the comparative: *bien* [byeN] well, *mieux* [myā̆] better; *mal* [mäl] badly, *pis* [pē] worse; *peu* [pā̆] little, *moins* [mô·eN] less; *beaucoup* [bōkōō] much, *plus* [plā̆] more.

4. "Than" after a comparative is *que*, e.g. *il est plus fort que moi* [ēlā plā̆ fôr kə mô·ä], he is stronger than I.

5. The **superlative** of adjectives and adverbs is formed by placing the definite article before the comparative, e.g. *le plus beau voyage* [lə plā̆ bō vô·äyäzh] the most beautiful trip; *le meilleur ami* [lə māyā̆rämē] the best friend; *le plus rapidement* [lə plā̆ räpēd·mäN] the fastest.

V. Formation of Plurals

1. As in English, the plural is generally formed by adding *s* to the singular noun, e.g. *le livre* [lə lēv(ər)] the book, *les livres* [lā lēv(ər)] the books.

2. Nouns ending in *s*, *x* and *z* do not change in the plural, e.g. *la souris* [lä sōōrē] the mouse, *les souris* [lā sōōrē] the mice; *la voix* [lä vô·ä] the voice, *les voix* [lā vô·ä] the voices.

3. Some nouns ending in *-ou* and all nouns ending in *au*, *eau*, *eu* and *œu* form the plural by adding *-x*, e.g. *le chou* [lə shōō] the cabbage, plural: *les choux* [lā shōō]; *le genou* [lə zhenōō] the knee, plural: *les genoux* [lā zhenōō]; *le cheveu* [lə shevā̆] the (strand of) hair, plural: *les cheveux* [lā shevā̆] hair; *le tableau* [lə täblō] the picture, plural: *les tableaux* [lā täblō].

4. Most nouns ending in *-al* and some nouns ending in *-ail* form the plural by *-aux*, e.g. *le cheval* [lə shəväl] the horse, plural: *les chevaux* [lā shəvō]; *le travail* [lə trävä·ē] work, plural: *les travaux* [lā trävō].

VI. Pronouns

Personal Pronouns

I. Subject Pronouns

je [zhə] I; *tu* [tē̆] you; *il* [ēl] he; *elle* [el] she; *nous* [no͞o] we; *vous* [vo͞o] you (*pl.*); *ils* [ēl] they (*m*); *elles* [el] they (*f*).

II. Direct and Indirect Object Pronouns

1. The **conjunctive** personal pronouns are:

Indirect Object			*Direct Object*		
me	[mə]	me	me	[mə]	me
te	[tə]	you	te	[tə]	you
lui	[lē̆·ē]	him, it	le	[lə]	him, it
lui	[lē̆·ē]	her, it	la	[lä]	her, it
se	[sə]	yourself, himself, herself, itself	se	[sə]	himself, herself, yourself, itself
nous	[no͞o]	us	nous	[no͞o]	us
vous	[vo͞o]	you [*pl.*]	vous	[vo͞o]	you [*pl.*]
leur	[lā̆r]	them	les	[lā]	them [*m*]
			les	[lā]	them [*f*]

In general, these personal pronouns precede the verb, e.g. *il me donne* [ēl mə dôn] he gives me.

2. The **disjunctive** personal pronouns are *moi* [mô·ä] me; *toi* [tô·ä] you; *lui* [lē̆·ē] him; *elle* [el] her; *nous* [no͞o] us; *vous* [vo͞o] you; *eux* [ā̆] them (*m*); *elles* [el] them (*f*), e.g. *Qui est venu? – Moi!* [kē ā vənē̆? – mô·ä!] Who has come? – I!

3. The **possessive** is formed by the preposition *de* [də] preceding the disjunctive personal pronoun, e.g. *Il se souvient de moi (vous)* [ēl sə so͞ovyeN də mô·ä (vo͞o)] He remembers me (you).

4. The **indirect object** is formed by the preposition *à* preceding the disjunctive personal pronoun, e.g. *à moi* [ä mô·ä] to me, *à eux* [ä ā̆] to them.

Possessive Pronouns

1. **adjective function** (preceding a noun):

Singular

masculine *mon* [môN] my; *ton* [tôN] your; *son* [sôN] his, feminine *ma* [mä] my; *ta* [tä] your; *sa* [sä] her; *notre* [nôt(ər)] our; *votre* [vôt(ər)] your; *leur* [lār] their.

Plural (masc. and fem.)

mes [mā] my; *tes* [tā] your; *ses* [sā] his, her; *nos* [nō] our; *vos* [vō] your; *leurs* [lār] their.

These pronouns agree with gender and number of the thing(s) possessed.

A noun in the third person singular can take *son*, *sa* or *ses* depending on the number and gender of the thing(s) possessed, e.g. *La famille prend ses repas au restaurant* [lä fämē·ē präN sā repä ō restôräN] The family has its meals at a restaurant.

A noun in the third person plural takes *leur(s)*, e.g. *Ces familles ont vendu leurs meubles* [sā fämē·ē ôN väNdē lār māb'əl] These families have sold their furniture.

The possessive pronoun "your" (polite form) is always *votre*, e.g. *Où prenez-vous votre petit déjeuner?* [o͞o prənā vo͞o vôt(ər) pətē dāzhānā] Where do you have breakfast?

2. **nominative function** (combined with an article):

le mien	[lə myeN],	*la mienne*	[lä myān]	mine (*m/f*)
le tien	[lə tyeN],	*la tienne*	[lä tyān]	yours (*m/f*)
le sien	[lə syeN],	*la sienne*	[lä syān]	his, hers, its
le nôtre	[lə nōt(ər)]	*la nôtre*	[lä nōt(ər)]	ours
le vôtre	[lə vōt(ər)],	*la vôtre*	[lä vōt(ər)]	yours (*pl.*)
le leur	[lə lār],	*la leur*	[lä lār]	theirs

The plural is formed by the addition of *-s*.

Demonstrative Pronouns

1. **adjective function** (preceding a noun)

ce [sə], *cet* [set], *cette* [set] this (*m/f*), *ces* [se] these (*m/f*)

Note: *cet* is the masculine singular before vowels and vowel sounds (*h*), e.g. *ce cheval* [sə shəväl] this horse, *cet homme* [setôm] this man, *cette femme* [set fäm] this woman, *ces enfants* [sezäNfäN] these children.

2. **nominative function** (standing alone)

celui-ci	[selē·ēsē],	*celle-ci*	[selsē]	this one here (*m/f*)
ceux-ci	[sāsē],	*celles-ci*	[selsē]	these here (*m/f*)
celui-là	[selē·ēlä],	*celle-là*	[sel-lä]	that one there (*m/f*)
ceux-là	[sālä],	*celles-là*	[sel-lä]	those over there (*m/f*)

celui, *celle* [selē·ē, sel] this, that
ceux, *celles* [sā, sel] these, those
ceci [sesē] this
cela [selä] that (informally: *ça*)

Relative Pronouns

qui	[kē]	who (persons), which, that (things)
dont	[dôN]	of whom, about whom (persons), of which, about which (things)
à qui	[äkē]	to whom
que	[kə]	whom (persons), which, that (things)

Interrogative Pronouns

1. **adjective function** (preceding a noun):

quel?	[kel],	*quelle?*	[kel]	what? which? (*m/f sing.*)
quels?	[kel],	*quelles?*	[kel]	what? which? (*m/f pl.*)

e.g. *quel livre?* [kelēv(ər)] which book?; *quelle fille?* [kel fē·ē] which girl?; *quels garçons?* [kel gärsôN] which boys?; *quelles villes?* [kel vēl] which cities?

2. **nominative function** (standing alone):

lequel?	[ləkel],	*laquelle?*	[läkel]	which one? (*m/f sing.*)
lesquels?	[lekel],	*lesquelles?*	[lekel]	which ones? (*m/f pl.*)

e.g. *lesquels de tes amis?* [lekel də tāzämē] which of your friends?

qui?	[kē]	who?	*de qui?*	[də kē]	of whom?
à qui?	[äkē]	to whom?	*qui?*	[kē]	whom? (as object)

qu'est-ce qui? [keskē] who?
qu'est-ce que? [keskə] or *que?* [kə] what?
de quoi? [də kô·ä] from what?
à quoi? [äkô·ä] what about?

VII. The Verb

A. The Auxiliary Verbs avoir and être

	Present	Imperfect	Past Definite	Future	Imperative
avoir	to have				
j'	ai	avais	eus	aurai	aie
tu	as	avais	eus	auras	ayons
il	a	avait	eut	aura	ayez
nous	avons	avions	eûmes	aurons	**Past**
vous	avez	aviez	eûtes	aurez	**Participle:**
ils	ont	avaient	eurent	auront	eu

	Present	Imperfect	Past Definite	Future	Imperative
être	to be				
je	suis	j'étais	fus	serai	sois
tu	es	étais	fus	seras	soyons
il	est	était	fut	sera	soyez
nous	sommes	étions	fûmes	serons	**Past**
vous	êtes	étiez	fûtes	serez	**Participle:**
ils	sont	étaient	furent	seront	été

B. The Regular Verbs

First Conjugation

	Present	Imperfect	Past Definite	Future	Imperative
blâmer	to blame				
je	blâme	blâmais	blâmai	blâmerai	blâme
tu	blâmes	blâmais	blâmas	blâmeras	blâmons
il	blâme	blâmait	blâma	blâmera	blâmez
nous	blâmons	blâmions	blâmâmes	blâmerons	**Past**
vous	blâmez	blâmiez	blâmâtes	blâmarez	**Participle:**
ils	blâment	blâmaient	blâmèrent	blâmeront	blâmé(e)

Second Conjugation

punir to punish

	Present	Imperfect	Past Definite	Future	Imperative
je	punis	punissais	punis	punirai	punis
tu	punis	punissais	punis	puniras	punissons
il	punit	punissait	punit	punira	punissez
nous	punissons	punissions	punîmes	punirons	**Past**
vous	punissez	punissiez	punîtes	punirez	**Participle:**
ils	punissent	punissaient	punirent	puniront	puni(e)

Third Conjugation

recevoir to receive

	Present	Imperfect	Past Definite	Future	Imperative
je	reçois	recevais	reçus	recevrai	reçois
tu	reçois	recevais	reçus	recevras	recevons
il	reçoit	recevait	reçut	recevra	recevez
nous	recevons	recevions	reçûmes	recevrons	**Past**
vous	recevez	receviez	reçûtes	recevrez	**Participle:**
ils	reçoivent	recevaient	reçurent	recevront	reçu(e)

Fourth Conjugation

	Present	Imperfect	Past Definite	Future	Imperative
vendre	to sell				
je	vends	vendais	vendis	vendrai	vends
tu	vends	vendais	vendis	vendras	vendons
il	vend	vendait	vendit	vendra	vendez
nous	vendons	vendions	vendîmes	vendrons	**Past**
vous	vendez	vendiez	vendîtes	vendrez	**Participle:**
ils	vendent	vendaient	vendirent	vendront	vendu(e)

THE FRENCH ALPHABET

A a [ä]	B b [bā]	C c [sā]	D d dā]	E e [ə]	F f [āf]	G g [zhā]
H h [äsh]	I i [ē]	J j [zhē]	K k [kä]	L l [el]	M m [ām]	N n [ān]
O o [ō, ô]	P p [pā]	Q q [kē̈]	R r [ār]	S s [es]	T t [tā]	
U u [ē̈]	V v [vā]	W w [do͞ob'əlvā]	X x [ēks]	Y y [ēgrāk]	Z z [zād]	

ENGLISH – FRENCH DICTIONARY

The translations are followed by phonetic transcriptions and page references, so that this dictionary serves as an index as well.

A

abbey abbaye *f* [äbā] 124
abdomen ventre *m* [väNt(ər)] 166 bas-ventre *m* [bäväNt(ər)] 166
above au-dessus de [ōdəsē də] 25
abscess abcès *m* [äbsā] 174
absorbent cotton coton *m* hydrophile [kôtôN ēdrōfēl] 160
accelerate accélérer [äkselārā] 51
accelerator accélérateur *m* [äkselerätār] 51
access road route *f* d'accès [ro͞ot däksā] 42
accessories accessoires *m/pl* [äksesô·är] 136
accident accident *m* [äksēdäN] 153
accommodations logis *m* [lôzhē] 90
accompanist accompagnateur *m* [äkôNpänyätār] 177
accompany accompagner [äkôNpänyā] 184
act acte *m* [äkt] 176
actor acteur *m* [äktār] 176
actress actrice *f* [äktrēs] 176
adapter plug fiche *f* intermédiaire [fēsh eNtermädyār] 90
address adresse *f* [ädres] 149
addressee destinataire *m* [destenätār] 149
admission entrée *f* [äNtrā] 118
admission free entrée libre [äNtrā lēb(ər)] 191
advance reservation réservation *f* [rāzerväsyôN] 95
advance ticket sales location *f* [lôkäsyôN] 177
after après [äprā] 159
after shave lotion *f* après rasage [lôsyôN äprā räzäzh] 140
afternoon après-midi *m* [äprāmēdē] 31; **in the ~** l'après-midi [läprāmēdē] 31; **this ~** cet après-midi [setäprā-mēdē] 31
against contre [kôNt(ər)] 164
age âge *m* [äzh 35]; **under ~** mineur [mēnār] 34
ago: a month ~ il y a un mois [ēlyä eN mô·ä] 32
air air *m* [är] 26; **~ conditioning** climatisation *f* [klēmätēzäsyôN] 75; **~ filter** filtre *m* d'air [fēlt(ər) där] 51; **~ jet** buse *f* d'aération [bēz dä·äräsyôN] 70; **~ mail** par avion [pär ävyôN] 145; **~ mattress** matelas *m* pneumatique [mätlä pnāmätēk] 185; **~ pump** pompe *f* à air [pôNpä är] 57; **~ sickness** mal *m* de l'air [mäl də lär] 169; **~ temperature** température *f* de l'air [täNpärätēr də lär] 185
aircraft avion *m* [ävyôN] 70
airline compagnie *f* aérienne [kôNpänyē ä·ärē·en] 70
airport aéroport *m* [ä·ärōpôr] 68; **~ service charge** taxe *f* d'aéroport [täks dä·ärōpôr] 68
alcohol alcool *m* [älkôl] 99
all tout [to͞o] 80
allergy allergie *f* [älerzhē] 169
alley ruelle *f* [rē·el]; allée *f* [älā] 120
allow-me? vous permettez? [vo͞o permetā] 20
almonds amandes *f/pl* [ämäNd] 110

alone seul, -e [sǝl] 14
already déjà [dezhä] 84
altar autel *m* [ôtel] 124
alter faire des retouches [fār dā retōōsh] 133
alto alto *m* [ältō] 177
amber ambre *m* jaune [äNb(ǝr) zhōn] 133
ambulance ambulance *f* [äNbēläNs] 48
American américain [āmārēkeN] 152; ~ **dollars** dollars américains [dôlär āmārēkeN] 152; ~ **plan** pension *f* complète [päNsyōN kôNplet] 83; ~ **studies** langue et littérature américaines [läNgā lētārātēr āmārēken] 39
amount montant *m* [môNtäN] 151
ampule ampoule *f* [äNpōōl] 160
amusement distraction *f* [dēsträksyôN] 181; ~ **park** parc *m* d'attractions [pärk däträksyôN] 120
anchor ancre *f* [äNk(ǝr)] 75
anchovies anchois *m/pl* [äNshô·ä] 102
anemia anémie *f* [änāmē] 169
anesthesia anesthésie *f* [änestāzē] 174; **general** ~ anesthésie *f* générale [änestāzē zhānāräl] 174; **local** ~ anesthésie *f* locale [änestāzē lôkäl] 174
anesthetic narcose *f* [närkōz] 172
ankle jointure *f* [zhô·eNtēr]; *(foot)* cheville *f* [shevē'ē] 166
announcer speaker *m* [spēkār] 182
annually tous les ans [tōō läzäN] 32
antidote contrepoison *m* [kôNt(rǝ-)pô·äzôN] 160
anti-freeze antigel *m* [äNtēzhel] 45
anyone quelqu'un [kelkeN] 85
anything quelque chose [kelke shōz] 80
apartment appartement *m* [äpärtǝ mäN] 81; **efficiency** ~ location *f* [lôkäsyôN] 82; ~ **building** immeuble *m* de studios [ēmāb'ǝl dǝ stēdē·ō] 90
appendicitis appendicite *f* [äpäNdēsēt] 169
appendix appendice *m* [äpäNdēs] 166
appetite appétit *m* [äpātē] 163
applause applaudissements *m/pl* [äplôdēsmäN] 177
apple pomme *f* [pôm] 110
appointment rendez-vous *m* [räNdāvōō] 155
apprentice apprenti *m* [äpräNtē] 36
approach *(plane)* approche *f* [äprôsh] 70
apricot abricot *m* [äbrēkō] 110
April avril *m* [ävrēl] 33
apron tablier *m* [täblēyā] 134
arch arc *m* [ärk] 124
archaeology archéologie *f* [ärkā·ōlōzhē] 39
architecture architecture *f* [ärshētektēr] 39
area région *f* [rāzhē·ôN] 120; ~ **code** indicatif *m* [eNdēkätēf] 149
aria aria *f* [ärē·ä] 177
arm bras *m* [brä] 166
armchair fauteuil *m* [fōtǝ'ē] 90
armpit aisselle *f* [äsel] 166
around *(time)* vers [vār] 31
arrest arrêter [ärātā] 154
arrival arrivée *f* [ärēvā] 60
arrive arriver [ärēvā] 34
art gallery galerie *f* [gälerē] 128
art history histoire *f* de l'art [ēstô·är dǝ lär] 39
artery artère *f* [ärtār] 166
arthritis rhumatisme *m* articulaire [rēmätēsm ärtēkēlär] 169
artichokes artichauts *m/pl* [ärtēshō] 107
articles objets *m/pl* [ôbzhā] 80
artist artiste *m* [ärtēst] 36

ash tray cendrier *m* [säNdrē·ā] 87
ashore: to go ~ descendre à terre [desäNdrä'tär] 72
asparagus asperge *f* [äspärzh] 107
asthma asthme *m* [äsme] 169
at *(time)* à [ä] 30; **~ night** la nuit [lä nē·ē] 94
athlete athlète *m/f* [ätlāt] 187
athletic club association *f* sportive [äsôsyäsyôN spôrtēv] 190
atmospheric pressure pression *f* atmosphérique [presyôN ätmôsfārēk] 26
attack attaque *f* [ätäk] 169
attend *(university)* étudier [ātēdyā] 38; *(school)* aller à [älā ä] 38
attendant pompiste *m* [pôNpēst] 45
attorney avocat *m* [ävōkä] 154
audience spectateurs *m/pl* [spektätār]; public *m* [pēblēk] 179
auditorium salle *f* de spectacle [säl də spektäk'əl] 179
August août *m* [o͞o(t)] 33
aunt tante *f* [täNt] 35
auto racing course *f* automobile [ko͞ors ôtōmōbēl] 187
autobiography autobiographie *f* [ôtōbē·ōgräfē] 130
automatic transmission changement *m* de vitesse automatique [shäNzh·mäN də vētes ôtōmätēk] 51
automobile club club *m* automobile [klēb ôtōmōbēl] 42
available *(seat)* libre [lēb(ər)] 68
avenue avenue *f* [ävənē] 120
axle essieu *m* [esyē] 51

B

baby bébé *m* [bābā] 164
back en arrière [äNäryār] 40; **from ... to ... and ~** de ... à ... et retour [də ... ä ... ā reto͞or] 73
back *(noun)* dos *m* [dō] 166; **~ seat** siège *m* arrière [syāzh äryār] 55; **~ wheel** roue *f* arrière [ro͞o äryār] 47
backache mal *m* au dos [mäl ō dō] 169
backfire raté *m* [rätā] 51
backwards dans le sens contraire de la marche [däN lə säNs kôNtrār dəlä märsh] 66
bacon lard *m* [lär] 100
bad: too ~! (quel) dommage! [(kel) dômäzh] 22
badminton badminton *m* [bädmēntôn]; volant *m* [vōläN] 190
bag sac *m* [säk] 126; **beach ~** sac *m* de camping [säk də käNpēng] 143; **plastic ~** sac *m* en plastique [säk äN plästēk] 144; **traveling ~** sac *m* de voyage [säk də vô·äyäzh] 64
baggage bagages *m/pl* [bägäzh] 63; **~ car** fourgon *m* [fo͞orgôN] 67; **~ check** bulletin *m* d'enregistrement [bēlteN däNrezhēstrəmäN] 84; **~ check area** enregistrement *m* des bagages [äNrezhēstrəmäN dā bägäzh] 63; **~ claim area** consigne *f* [kôNsēn(yə)] 63
baked cuit au four [kē·ē ō fo͞or] 100
baker boulanger *m* [bo͞oläNzhā] 36
bakery boulangerie *f* [bo͞oläNzhərē] 128
balance beam poutre *f* horizontale [po͞otrôrēzōNtäl] 188
balcony balcon *m* [bälkôN] 82; *(theatre)* rang *m* [räN] 176
ball balle *f* [bäl] 143; *(soccer)* ballon *m* [bälôN] 189; **~ bearings** roulement *m* à billes [ro͞olmäN ä bē'ē] 51; **~ point cartridge** mine *f* [mēn]; cartouche *f* [kärto͞osh] 138
ballet ballet *m* [bälā] 177
banana banane *f* [bänän] 110

band orchestre *m* [ôrkest(ər)] 177
bandage: adhesive ~ sparadrap *m* [spärädrä] 160; **lace ~** pansement *m* élastique [päNs·mäN ālästēk] 161
bandages pansement *m* [päNs·mäN] 48
bank banque *f* [bäNk] 151; **savings ~** caisse *f* d'épargne [kes dāpärn(yə)] 152; **~ account** compte *m* bancaire [kôNt bäNkār] 151; **~ charges** frais *m/pl* bancaires [frā bäNkār] 151; **~ note** billet *m* de banque [bēyā də bäNk] 151; **~ teller** employé *m* de banque [äNplô·äyā də bäNk] 36; **~ transfer** virement *m* bancaire [vērmäN bäNkār] 151
bank rivage *m* [rēväzh] 75
banker banquier *m* [bäNkyā] 181
baptism baptême *m* [bätām] 124
bar bar *m* [bär] 74
barber shop salon *m* de coiffure [sälôN də kô·äfēr] 74
barette barrette *f* [bäret] 140
barge chaland *m* [shäläN] 75
baritone baryton *m* [bärētôN] 177
barometer baromètre *m* [bärōmāt(ər)] 25
Baroque baroque [bärôk] 124
barrier barrière *f* [bäryār] 67
basement sous-sol *m* [so͞o-sôl] 90
bass basse *f* [bäs] 177
bath bain *m* [beN] 82; **~ attendant** maître *m* nageur [māt(ər) näzhār] 175; **~ salts** sels *m/pl* pour le bain [sel po͞or lə beN] 140; **mineral ~** bain *m* thermal [beN tārmäl] 175; **steam ~** bain *m* de vapeur [beN də väpār] 175; **take a ~** prendre un bain [präNdreN beN] 95
bathing cap bonnet *m* de bain [bônā də beN] 134
bathing suit maillot *m* de bain [mäyō də beN] 185
bathing trunks slip *m* de bain [slēp də beN] 185
bathrobe peignoir *m* [penyô·är] 185
bathroom salle *f* de bain [säl də beN] 90
battery batterie *f* [bätərē] 51
bay baie *f* [bā] 75
beach plage *f* [pläzh] 81; **private ~** plage *f* privée [pläzh prēvā] 92; **sandy ~** plage *f* de sable [pläzh də säb'əl] 186
beans haricots *m/pl* [ärēkō] 108; **butter ~** haricots *m/pl* beurre [ärēkō bār] 108; **French** (string) **~** haricots *m/pl* verts [ärēkō vār] 108
beard barbe *f* [bärb] 157
bearing coussinet *m* [ko͞osēnā] 51
beauty contest concours *m* de beauté [kôNko͞or də bōtā] 181
beauty parlor salon *m* de beauté [sälôN de bōtā] 158; institut *m* de beauté [eNstētē də bōtā] 128
bed lit *m* [lē] 90; **~ and two meals** demi-pension *f* [dəmē-päNsyôN] 90; **~ linen** draps *m/pl* de lit [drä də lē] 90; **~ rug** descente *f* de lit [desäNt də lē] 90; **day ~** canapé-lit *m* [känäpā-lē] 91
bedroom chambre *f* à coucher [shäNbrä ko͞oshā] 93
bedside table table *f* de nuit [täb'əl də nē·ē] 90
beef bœuf *m* [bāf] 105
beer bière *f* [byār] 111; **~ mug** chope *f* bière [shôp byār] 111; **dark ~** bière *f* brune [byār brēn] 111; **light ~** bière *f* blonde [byār blôNd] 111
beets betteraves *f/pl* rouges [betəräv ro͞ozh] 107
before *(time)* avant [āväN] 31
beige beige [bāzh] 194

bell cloche *f* [klôsh] 124; sonnette *f* [sônet] 88
below au-dessous de [ōdəsōō də] 25
belt ceinture *f* [seNtēr] 134
bet parier [pärē·ā]; miser (sur) [mēzā (sēr)] 181
beverage boisson *f* [bô·äsôN] 112; **alcoholic ~** boisson *f* alcoolique [bô·äsôN älkôlēk] 112; **non-alcoholic ~** boisson *f* non-alcoolique [bô·äsôN nôN-älkôlēk] 112
bicycle bicyclette *f* [bēsēklet] 41; **to go by ~** aller à bicyclette [älā ä bēsēklet] 42; **~ race** course *f* cycliste [kōōrs sēklēst] 187; **~ rider** cycliste *m* [sēklēst] 187
bicycling cyclisme *m* [sēklēsm] 187
big grand [gräN]
bike bicyclette *f* [bēsēklet] 187; **ride a ~** aller à bicyclette [älā ä bēsēklet] 187; **~ lane** piste *f* cyclable [pēst sēkläb'əl] 42
bikini bikini *m* [bēkēnē] 134
bile bile *f* [bēl] 166
bill billet *m* de banque [bēyā də bäNk] 151; note *f* [nôt] 90
billfold portefeuille *m* [pôrtfä'e] 153
binoculars jumelles *f/pl* [zhēmel] 138
biography biographie *f* [bē·ōgräfē] 130
biology biologie *f* [bē·ōlōzhē] 39
birthday anniversaire *m* [änēversār] 22; **happy ~!** bon anniversaire! [bônänēversār] 23
bishop fou *m* [fōō] 181
bitters bitter *m* [bētār] 112
black noir [nô·är] 194
black currants cassis *m/pl* [käsēs] 110
blackberries mûres *f/pl* [mēr] 110
blackmail attempt chantage *m* [shäNtäzh] 153
bladder vessie *f* [vesē] 166
blanket couverture *f* [kōōvertēr] 75
bleeding hémorragie *f* [āmôräzhē] 169
blinker clignotant *m* [klēnyôtäN] 51
blonde blond [blôN] 194
blood sang *m* [säN] 165; **~ count** hémogramme *m* [āmōgräm] 172; **~ poisoning** septicémie *f* [septēsāmē] 169; **~ pressure** tension *f* artérielle [täNsyôN ärtārē·el] 166; **~ test** analyse *f* de sang [änälēz də säN] 165; prise *f* de sang [prēz də säN] 172; **~ transfusion** transfusion *f* [träNsfēzyôN] 172
blouse chemisier *m* [shemēzyā] 134
blown *(fuse)* fondu [fôNdē] 55; sauté [sôtā] 88
blow-out crevaison *f* [krevāzôN] 47
blue bleu [blā] 194; **light ~** bleu clair [blā klār] 194; **navy ~** bleu foncé [blā fôNsā] 194; **~ jeans** blue-jeans *m/pl* [blōōdzēn] 134
blueberries airelles *f/pl* [ārel] 110
boar sanglier *m* [säNglēyā] 105
board bord *m* [bôr] 72; échiquier *m* [āshēkyā] 181
boarding house pension *f* [päNsyôN] 81
boarding school internat *m* [eNternä] 38
boat bateau *m* [bätō] 75; **pedal ~** pédalo *m* [pādälō] 186; **~ racing** régates *f/pl* [rāgät] 187; **~ trip** promenade *f* en bateau [prômenäd äN bätō] 120
body corps *m* [kôr] 166; *(car)* carosserie *f* [kärôsrē] 51; **~ and fender damage** dégâts *m/pl* matériels [dāgä mätārē·el] 49
boiled cuit [kē·ē]; bouilli [bōōyē] 100
bolt vis *f* [vēs] 57; **~ nut** écrou *m* [ākrōō] 57

bone os *m* [ôs] (*pl:* [ō]) 166
book livre *m* [lēv(ər)] 130; **children's ~** livre *m* pour enfants [lēv(ər) po͞or äNfäN] 130; **guide ~** guide *m* touristique [gēd to͞orēstēk] 130; **phrase ~** guide *m* de conversation [gēd də kôNverzäsyôN] 130; **poetry ~** recueil *m* de poésie [rekā'ē də pō·äzē] 130; **reference ~** ouvrage *m* de référence [o͞ovräzh də rāfāräNs] 130; **story ~** livre *m* de contes [lēv(ər) də kôNt] 130; **text ~** manuel *m* [mänē·el] 130
bookkeeper comptable *m* [kôNtäb'əl] 36
bookseller libraire *m* [lēbrār] 36
bookshop librairie *f* [lēbrārē] 128; **second-hand ~** librairie *f* d'occasion [lēbrārē dôkäzyôN] 129
booth cabine *f* [käbēn] 148
boots bottes *f/pl* [bôt] 139
border frontière *f* [frôNtyār] 79; **~ crossing** passage *m* de la frontière [päsäzh də lä frôNtyār] 80
born né [nā] 34
botanical gardens jardin *m* botanique [zhärdeN bôtänēk] 120
bother déranger [dāräNzhā] 16; importuner [eNpôrtēnā] 154
bottle bouteille *f* [bo͞otā'ē] 96; **~ opener** décapsuleur *m* [dākäpsēlār] 143
bouquet bouquet *m* de fleurs [bo͞okā də flār] 130
bow proue *f* [pro͞o] 75
bowel movement selle *f* [sel] 166
bowl terrine *f* [terēn] 97
bowling bowling *m* [bo͞olēng (bōlēng)] 187; **~ alley** piste *f* de bowling [pēst də bo͞olēng] 181
box *(verb)* boxer [bôksā] 188; *(noun)* boîte *f* [bô·ät] 126; **~ lunch** panier-repas *m* [pänyā-repä] 86; **~ office** caisse *f* [kes]; vente *f* de billets [väNt də bēyā] 177
boxer boxeur *m* [bôksār] 188
boxing (match *m* de) boxe *f* [(mätsh də) bôks] 188
boy garçon *m* [gärsôN] 35
bra soutien-gorge *m* [so͞otyeNgôrzh] 134
bracelet bracelet *m* [bräslā] 133
braces bretelles *m/pl* [bretel] 136; appareil *m* (dentaire) [äpärā'ē (däNtār)] 174
brain cerveau *m* [sārvō] 166
brake *(verb)* freiner [frānā] 43; *(noun)* frein *m* [freN] 51; **~ drum** tambour *m* de frein [täNbo͞or də freN] 51; **~ fluid** liquide *m* de freinage (de freins) [lēkēd də frenäzh (də freN)] 51 (45); **~ lights** feux *m/pl* de stop [fā də stôp] 51; **~ lining** garniture *f* de frein [gärnētēr də freN] 51; **~ pedal** pédale *f* de frein [pādäl də freN] 51
branch manager directeur *m* de banque [dērektār də bäNk] 151
brandy eau-de-vie *f* [ōdvē] 112; **apricot ~** liqueur *f* d'abricot [lēkār däbrēkō] 112; **cherry ~** liqueur *f* de cerises [lēkār də serēz] 112
brassière soutien-gorge *m* [so͞otyeNgôrzh] 134
bread pain *m* [peN] 98; **dark ~** pain *m* bis [peN bē(s)] 98; **white ~** pain *m* blanc [peN bläN] 98; **whole wheat ~** pain *m* complet [peN kôNplā] 98; **~ basket** corbeille *f* à pain [kôrbā'ē ä peN] 97
break off se casser [se käsā] 173
breakdown panne *f* [pän] 48
breakfast petit déjeuner *m* [pətē dāzhānā] 83; **eat ~** prendre son petit déjeuner [präNd(ər) sôN pətē dāzhānā] 90
breast poitrine *f* [pô·ätrēn] 166
breathe respirer [respērā] 165

breathing respiration *f* [respērä-syôN] 166; **~ problem** troubles *m/pl* respiratoires [tro͞ob'əl respē-rätô·är] 169
breeze brise *f* [brēz] 75
bricklayer maçon *m* [mäsôN] 36
bridge pont *m* [pôN] 42; bridge *m* [brēdzh] 174; passerelle *f* de manœuvre [päserel də mänāv(ər)] 75
briefcase portefeuille *m* [pôrtfā'ē], serviette *f* [servyet] 143
brilliantine brillantine *f* [brēyäNtēn] 157
bring apporter [äpôrtā] 20; **~ back** ramener [rämənā] 41
broiler poulet *m* de grain [po͞olā də greN] 105
broken cassé [käsā] 23
bronchitis bronchite *f* [brôNshēt] 169
broock broche *f* [brôsh] 133
broth consommé *m* [kôNsômā] 103; **chicken ~** potage *m* de volaille [pôtäzh də vôlä'ē] 103
brother frère *m* [frār] 35; **~-in-law** beau-frère *m* [bō-frār] 35
brown brun [breN] 194; **chestnut ~** châtain [shäteN] 194
bruise contusion *f* [kôNtēzyôN] 169
brush brosse *f* [brôs] 140; **clothes ~** brosse *f* à habits [brôs ä äbē] 140
Brussels sprouts chou *m* de Bruxelles [sho͞o də brēsel] 108
bucket seau *m* [sō] 90
buckle boucle *f* [bo͞ok'əl] 136
building édifice *m* [ädēfēs] 119
bulb ampoule *f* [äNpo͞ol] 51; **light ~** ampoule *f* (électrique) [äNpo͞ol (ālektrēk)] 92
bumper pare-chocs *m* [pär-shôk] 51
bungalow bungalow *m* [beNgälō] 81
buoy bouée *f* [bo͞o·ā] 75
Burgundy (vin *m* de) Bourgogne [(veN də) bo͞orgôn(yə)] 111
burn *(noun)* brûlure *f* [brēlēr] 169
burned out grillé [grēyā] 88
bus autobus *m* [ôtōbēs] 59; **~ stop** arrêt *m* d'autobus [ärā dôtōbēs] 59; **~ terminal** terminus *m* [termē-nēs] 59
business administration gestion *f* [zhestyôN] 39; **~ school** école *f* de commerce [ākôl də kômers] 38
busy occupé [ôkēpā] 148
butcher boucher *m* [bo͞oshā] 36
butter beurre *m* [bār] 98
buttocks fesses *f/pl* [fes] 166
button bouton *m* [bo͞otôN] 136
buttonhole thread fil *m* pour boutonnières [fēl po͞or bo͞otônyār] 136
buy acheter [äshtā] 126

C

cabaña cabine *f* [käbēn] 185
cabbage chou *m* [sho͞o] 108
cabin cabine *f* [käbēn] 73; **double ~** cabine *f* de deux personnes [käbēn də dā persôn] 73; **inside ~** cabine *f* intérieure [käbēn eNtärē·ār] 73; **outside ~** cabine *f* extérieure [käbēn ekstärē·ār] 73; **single ~** cabine *f* individuelle [käbēn eNdēvēdē·el] 73
cabinetmaker ébéniste *m* [ābānēst] 36
cable câble *m* [käb'əl] 51
cake gâteau *m* [gätō] 113
calf mollet *m* [môlā] 166
call *(verb)* faire venir [fār venēr] 123; appeler [äplā] 48; *(noun)* communication *f* [kômēnēkäsyôN] 148; **long distance ~** communication *f* interurbaine (internationale) [kômēnēkäsyôN eNterērben(eNter-

näsyônäl)] 148; **person to person ~** communication *f* avec avis d'appel [kômēnēkäsyôN ävek ävē däpel] 150; **make a phone ~** téléphoner [tälāfōnā] 147; **give** *(someone)* **a ~** téléphoner à [tälāfônā ä] 17
camera appareil *m* photographique [äpärä'ē fōtōgräfēk] 153
camomile tea infusion *f* camomille [eNfēzyôN kämōmē·ē] 160
camp camper [käNpā] 94; **~ bed** lit *m* pliant [lē plē·äN] 95; **~ site** terrain *m* de camping [tereN də käNpēng] 94; **~ stove** réchaud *m* à alcool [rāshō ä älkôl] 143
camping camping *m* [käNpēng] 95; **~ ID** carte *f* de l'A.C.C.F. [kärt dəlä sä·sä·ef] 95; **~ site** terrain *m* de camping [tereN də käNpēng] 81; **~ trailer** caravane *f* [käravän] 40
camshaft arbre *m* à cames [ärbräkäm] 51
can pouvoir [po͞ovô·är] 18
can opener ouvre-boîte *m* [o͞ov(ər) bô·ät] 143
canal canal *m* [känäl] 75
cancel annuler [änēlā] 69
cancellation fee taxe *f* d'annulation [täks dänēläsyôN] 69
cancer cancer *m* [käNsär] 169
candle bougie *f* [bo͞ozhē] 143
candlestick bougeoir *m* [bo͞ozhô·är] 143; chandelier *m* [shäNdelēyā] 124
candy bonbon *m* [bôNbôN]; chocolat *m* [shôkôlä] 113
canned goods conserves *f/pl* [kôNsärv] 143
cap casquette *f* [käsket] 134
capers câpres *f/pl* [käp(ər)] 100
capital capitale *f* [käpētäl] 120
captain capitaine *m* [käpēten] 75; **~'s table** table *f* du commandant [täb(əl) dē kômäNdäN] 75
car voiture *f* [vô·ätēr] 40; auto *f* [ôtō] 73; **~ door** portière *f* [pôrtyār] 52; **~ ferry** ferry-boat [ferē-bōt] 72; **~ key** clé *f* de la voiture [klā də lä vô·ätēr] 52; **~ repair service** service-entretien *m* [servēs-äNtrətyeN] 45; **go by ~** aller en voiture [älā äN vô·ätēr] 42
carafe carafe *f* [käräf] 97
caraway cumin *m* [kēmeN] 101
carburetor carburateur *m* [kärbērätār] 52; **~ jet** gicleur *m* [zhēklār] 52
card carte *f* [kärt] 145; **greeting ~** carte *f* de salutations [kärt də sälētäsyôN] 145; **greeting ~ telegram** télégramme *m* avec carte [tälägräm ävek kärt] 147; **post ~** carte *f* postale [kärt pôstäl] 145; **picture post ~** carte *f* postale illustrée [kärt pôstäl ēlēstrā] 145; **~ game** jeu *m* de cartes [zhā də kärt] 181
cardiac infarction infarctus *m* du myocarde [eNfärktēs dē mē·ōkärd 169
cardigan veste *f* de tricot [vest də] trēkō] 134
cardiovascular drug remède *m* pour la circulation [remād po͞or lä sērkēläsyôN] 160
careful! attention! [ätäNsyôN] 49
carp carpe *f* [kärp] 104
carpenter menuisier *m* [menē·ēzyā] 36
carpet tapis *m* [täpē] 90
carrot carotte *f* [kärôt] 107
cartoon dessin *m* animé [deseN änēmā] 179
cash (adj.) comptant [kôNtäN] 152
cassette cassette *f* [käset] 143
castle château *m* [shätō] 119;

(chess) tour *f* [tōōr] 181
castor oil huile *f* de ricin [ē·ēl də rēseN] 160
catalogue catalogue *m* [kätälôg] 130
category catégory *f* [kätägôrē] 90
cathedral cathédrale *f* [kätädräl] 124
cave caverne *f* [kävärn] 120
cavities cave *f* [käv] 174
ceiling plafond *m* [pläfôN] 90
celery céleri *m* [sälerē] 107
cellar cave *f* [käv] 90
cemetery cimetière *m* [sēmetyār] 120
center strip bande *f* médiane [bäNd mādē·än] 42
centimeter centimètre *m* [säNtēmāt(ər)] 193
ceramics céramique *f* [särämēk] 143
cereal céréales *f/pl* [sārā·äl] 98
certainly certainement [särten·mäN] 21; **~!** bien entendu! [byeN äNtäNdē] 20; **~ not** en aucun cas [äNōkeN kä] 21
chain chaîne *f* [shān] 52
chair chaise *f* [shāz] 90; **deck ~** chaise *f* longue [shāz·lôNg] 91
chamber music musique *f* de chambre [mēzēk də shäNb(ər)] 177
championship championnat *m* [shäNpyônä] 188
change *(noun)* monnaie *f* [mônā] 151; *(verb)* changer [shäNzhā] 46, 151; *(buses, trains)* changer de [shäNzhā də] 59; *(wind)* tourner [tōōrnā] 26
chapel chapelle *f* [shäpel] 124
charcoalpills poudre *f* de charbon [pōōd(ər) də shärbôN] 160
charge *(battery)* recharger [reshärzhā] 51
charter plane charter *m* [shärtār] 70
chassis chassis *m* de la voiture [shäsē də lä vô·ätēr] 52
chat bavarder [bävärdā] 183
chauffeur chauffeur *m* [shōfār] 41
check *(noun)* addition *f* [ädēsyôN] 115; chèque *m* [shek] 151; *(verb)* vérifier [vārēfē·ā] 45; **~ over** contrôler [kôNtrôlā] 52; **~ room** vestiaire *m* [vestyār] 177; **traveller's ~** chèque *m* de voyage [shek də vô·äyäzh] 127
checked quadrillé [kädrēyā] 137
checkers (jeu *m* de) dames [(zhā də) däm] 181
check-in déclaration *f* de séjour [dākläräsyôN də sāzhōōr] 90
check-out déclaration *f* de départ [dākläräsyôN də dāpär] 95
cheek joue *f* [zhōō] 166
cheers! à votre santé! [ä vôt(ər) säNtā] 99
cheese fromage *m* [frômäzh] 109; **blue ~** bleu *m* d'Auvergne [blā dōvārn(yə)] 109; **cottage ~** fromage *m* blanc [frômäzh bläN] 109; **cream ~** fromage *m* à pâte molle [frômäzh ä pät môl] 109; **Swiss ~** gruyère *m* [grēyār] 109; **~ spread** fromage *m* à tartiner [frômäzh ä tärtēnā] 109
chef chef cuisinier *m* [shef kē·ēzēnyā] 36
chemistry chimie *f* [shēmē] 39
cherries cerises *f/pl* [serēz] 110
chess échecs *m/pl* [āshek] 180
chessman pièce *f* [pyās] 181
chest poitrine *f* [pô·ätrēn] 166
chicken poule *f* [pōōl] 105; **~ breast** blanc *m* de poulet [bläN də pōōlā] 105; **~ pox** varicelle *f* [väresel] 169
child enfant *m* [äNfäN] 34
chills frissons *m/pl* [frēsôN] 164

chin menton *m* [mäNtôN] 166
china porcelaine *f* [pôrsəlen] 143
chip jeton *m* [zhetôN] 181
chisel ciseau *m* [sēzō] 57
chives civette *f* [sēvet] 101
chocolate chocolat *m* [shôkōlä] 113; **~ with ice cream** chocolat *m* glacé [shôkôlä gläsā] 113
choir chœur *m* [kār] 124
cholera choléra *m* [kôlārä] 169
chop côtelette *f* [kôtlet] 106
chorus chœur *m* [kār] 177
christening baptème *m* [bätām] 123
church église *f* [āglēz] 124; **Catholic ~** église *f* catholique [āglēz kätōlēk] 116; **Protestant ~** temple *m* [täNp'əl] 116
churchyard cimetière *m* [sēmetyār] 124
cider cidre *m* [sēd(ər)] 111
cigar cigare *m* [sēgär] 140
cigarette cigarette *f* [sēgäret] 140; **filtered ~** cigarette *f* à bout filtre [sēgäret ä bo͞o fēlt(ər)] 140; **unfiltered ~** cigarette *f* sans filtre [sēgäret säN fēlt(ər)] 140
cinema cinéma *m* [sēnāmä] 179
cinnamon cannelle *f* [känel] 101
circle traffic sens *m* giratoire [säNs zhērätô·är] 43
circulatory problem troubles *m/pl* circulatoires [tro͞ob'əl sērkēlätô·är] 169
circus cirque *m* [sērk] 181
city ville *f* [vēl] 120; **~ hall** hôtel *m* de ville [ôtel də vēl] 120
civil servant fonctionnaire *m* [fôNksyônār] 36
claim *(luggage)* retirer [retērā] 63; **~ check** bulletin *m* d'enregistrement [bēlteN däNrezhēstrəmäN] 63
class classe *f* [kläs] 73; **first ~** première classe *f* [prəmyār kläs] 73; **tourist ~** classe *f* touriste [kläs to͞orēst] 73
clean *(out)* nettoyer [netô·äyā] 47
clear *(sky)* dégagé [dāgäzhā] 26
clergyman prêtre *m* [prāt(ər)], curé *m* [kērā] 36
climate climat *m* [klēmä] 26
climb s'élever [sāləvā] 70
clock montre *f* [môNt(ər)] 31; **alarm ~** réveil *m* [rāvā'ē] 143; **it's... o'clock** il est ... heure(s) [ēlā ... ār] 30
close fermer [fermā] 18
closet placard *m* [pläkär] 91
cloth chiffon *m* [shēfôN] 57; drap *m* [drä] 136
clothes hanger cintre *m* [seNt(ər)] 87
cloud nuage *m* [nē·äzh] 26; **~ cover** nuages *m/pl* [nē·äzh] 26
cloudburst pluie *f* torrentielle [plē·ē tôräNsyel] 26
cloudy couvert [ko͞ovār] 26; **~ skies** nuages *m/pl.* [nē·äzh] 26
cloves clous *m/pl* de girofle [klo͞o də zhērôf'əl] 101
club club *m* [klēb] 181
clubs trèfle *m* [trāf'əl] 181
clutch embrayage *m* [äNbrāyäzh] 52; **~ pedal** pédale *f* d'embrayage [pādäl däNbrāyäzh] 52
coast côte *f* [kôt] 75
coastal road route *f* côtière [ro͞ot kôtyār] 43
coat manteau *m* [mäNtō] 134; **~ check** ticket *m* de vestiaire [tēkā də vestyār] 177
cobbler cordonnier *m* [kôrdônyā] 36
coconut coco *m* [kôkō] 110
cod cabillaud *m* [käbēyō]; morue *f* [môrē] 104
c.o.d. remboursement *m* [räNbo͞orsmäN] 149

coffee café *m* [käfā] 98; **black ~** café *m* noir [käfā nô·är] 98; **decaffeinated ~** café *m* décaféiné [käfā dākäfā·ēnā] 98; **~ with cream** café *m* au lait [käfā ō lā] 98; **~ with sugar** café *m* avec du sucre [käfā avek dē sēk(ər)] 98
cognac cognac *m* [kônyäk] 112
coin jeton *m* [zhetôN] 148; pièce *f* de monnaie [pyās də mônā] 152; **~ changer** changeur *m* de monnaie automatique [shäNzhār də mônā ôtōmätēk] 149
cold *(noun)* rhume *m* [rēm] 169; *(adj.)* froid [frô·ä] 25; **I'm ~** j'ai froid [zhā frô·ä] 25; **~ cuts** tranches *f/pl* de charcuterie [träNsh də shärkētərē] 98; assiette *f* anglaise [äsyet äNglāz] 102; **~ wave** permanente *f* à froid [pārmänäNt ä frô·ä] 158
colic colique *f* [kôlēk] 169
collarbone clavicule *f* [klävēkēl] 166
collect call communication *f* payable à l'arrivée [kômēnēkäsyôN pāyäb'əl älärēvā] 149
collision collision *f* [kôlēzyôN] 49
color couleur *f* [ko͞olār] 127; **~ of eye** couleur *f* des yeux [ko͞olār dāzyā] 79; **~ of hair** couleur *f* des cheveux [ko͞olār dā shevā] 79
colored coloré [kôlôrā] 194
colorful multicolore [mēltēkôlôr] 194
comb *(noun)* peigne *m* [pen(yə)] 140; *(verb)* peigner [penyā] 158
come venir [vənēr] 16; **~ in** *(train)* arriver [ärēvā] 61; **~ in!** entrez! [äNtrā] 16
comedy comédie *f* [kômādē] 177
communion communion *f* [kômēnyôN] 124
compact poudrier *m* [po͞odrēyā] 140
compartment compartiment *m* [kôNpärtēmäN] 67
compass boussole *f* [bo͞osôl] 138
competition compétition *f* [kôNpātēsyôN] 188
complaint réclamation *f* [rākläm äsyôN] 91; **register (make) a ~** faire une réclamation [fār ēn rākläm äsyôN] 23
composer compositeur *m* [kôNpōzētār] 177
compression compression *f* [kôNpresyôN] 52
concert concert [kôNsār] 177; **~ hall** salle *f* de concert [säl də kôNsār] 177
concierge concierge *m* [kôNsyārzh], portier *m* [pôrtyā] 91
concussion commotion *f* cérébrale [kômōsyôN sārābräl] 169
condenser condensateur *m* [kôNdäNsätār] 52
condolences condoléances *f/pl* [kôNdôlā·äNs] 23
conductor contrôleur *m* [kôNtrôlār] 67; chef *m* d'orchestre [shef dôrkest(ər)] 177
confectioner pâtissier *m* [pätēsyā] 36
confectionery pâtisserie *f* (fine) [pätēsərē (fēn)] 113
confesse se confesser [sə kôNfesā] 124
confession confession *f* [kôNfesyôN] 124
confiscate confisquer [kôNfēskā] 154
congratulations! mes félicitations! [mā felēsētäsyôN] 22
conjunctivitis conjonctivite *f* [kōNzhôNktēvēt] 169
connecting rod bielle *f* [byel] 52; **~ bearing** coussinet *m* de tête de bielle [ko͞osēnā də tāt də byel] 52
connection correspondance *f* [kô-

respôNdäNs] 61
constipated constipé [kôNstēpā] 163
constipation constipation *f* [kôNstēpäsyôN] 169
consulate consulat *m* [kôNsēlä] 78
contact contact *m* [kôNtäkt] 52; **~ lenses** verres *m/pl* de contact [vār də kôNtäkt] 138
contraceptive pills pilules *f/pl* contraceptives [pēlēl kôNträseptēv] 160
convalescent home maison *f* de convalescence [māzôN də kôNväleäNs] 175
convent couvent *m* [ko͞oväN] 124
cook *(verb)* préparer les repas [prāpärā lā repä] 95; *(noun)* cuisinier *m* [kē·ēzēnyā] 36
cookies petits gâteaux secs *m/pl* [pətē gätō sāk] 113
cooking utensils ustensiles *m/pl* de cuisine [ēstäNsēl də kē·ēzēn] 95
coolant fluide *m* réfrigérant [flē·ēd rāfrēzhäräN] 45
cordial cordial [kôrdyäl] 12
corduroy velours *m* côtelé [velo͞or kōtlā] 136
corkscrew tire-bouchon *m* [tērbo͞oshôN] 143
corn plaster pansement *m* pour les cors [päNsmäN po͞or lā kôr] 160
corner coin *m* [kô·eN] 120; *(sports)* corner *m* [kôrnār] 189
correct exact [egsäkt] 115
corridor corridor *m* [kôrēdôr]; couloir *m* [ko͞olô·är] 91
corset corselet *m* [kôrselā]; corset *m* [kôrsā] 134
cosmetic salon institut *m* de beauté [eNstētē də bōtā] 128
cost coûter [ko͞otā] 18; **how much does it ~?** combien dois-je payer? [kôNbyeN dô·äzh pāyā] 69
costume costume *m* [kôstēm] 177; **~ designer** costumier *m* [kôstēmyā] 177
cotton coton *m* [kôtôN] 136; **~ swabs** cotons-tiges *m/pl* [kôtôNtēzh] 160
couchette car, couchette sleeper voiture-couchette *f* [vô·ätēr-ko͞oshet] 64, 60
cough (verb) **tousser** [to͞osā] 165; *(noun)* toux *f* [to͞o] 169; **~ medicine** remède *m* (sirop *m*) contre la toux [remād (sērō) kôNt(ər) lä to͞o] 160
counter guichet *m* [gēshā] 149
country fair fête *f* populaire [fāt pôpēlār] 181
country road route *f* de campagne [ro͞ot də käNpän(yə)] 43
countryside paysage *m* [pā·ēzäzh] 120
course route *f* [ro͞ot] 75
court tribunal *m* [trēbēnäl] 154
courthouse palais *m* de Justice [pälā də zhēstēs] 120
cousin *(male)* cousin *m* [ko͞ozeN] 35; *(female)* cousine *f* [ko͞ozēn] 35
cover housse *f* d'édredon [ho͞os dādredôN] 90
covered market marché *m* couvert [märshā ko͞ovār] 120
coxswain barreur *m* [bärār] 189
cramp crampe *f* [kräNp] 169
cranberries airelles *f/pl* rouges [ārel ro͞ozh] 110
crankshaft vilebrequin *m* [vēlbrekeN] 52
crawfish écrevisse *f* [ākrevēs] 104
crayons crayons *m/pl* de couleur [krāyôN də ko͞olār] 138
cream crème *f* [krām] 141, 113; **face ~** crème *f* (pour le visage) [krām (po͞or lə vēzäzh)] 141; **whipped ~** Chantilly *f* [shäntēyē] 113

credit crédit *m* [krädē] 152; **~ card** carte *f* de crédit [kärt də krädē] 152; **letter of ~** lettre *f* de crédit [let(ər) də krädē] 152
creed profession *f* de foi [prôfesyôN də fô·ä] 124
crew équipage *m* [äkēpäzh] 70
crib lit *m* d'enfant [lē däNfäN] 83
crime crime *m* [krēm] 154
criminal criminel *m* [krēmēnel] 154; **~ investigation division** police *f* judiciaire [pôlēs zhēdēsyär] 154
cross croix *f* [krô·ä] 124; **~ road** route *f* secondaire [ro͞ot səgôNdär] 43
crossing traversée *f* [träversā] 72
crown couronne *f* [ko͞orôn] 174
crucifix crucifix *m* [krēsēfē] 124
cruet stand huilier *m* [ē·ēlēyā] 97
cruise croisière *f* [krô·äzyär] 75
crystal verre *m* [vär] 143
cucumber concombre *m* [kôNkôNb(ər)] 108
cufflinks boutons *m/pl* de manchette [bo͞otôN də mäNshet] 133
cup tasse *f* [täs] 96
cure cure *f* [kēr] 175; **~ tax** taxe *f* de cure [täks də kēr] 175; **~ vacation** cure *f* [kēr] 175; **rest ~** cure *f* de repos [kēr də rəpō] 175
curler bigoudi *m* [bēgo͞odē], rouleau *m* [ro͞olō] 141
curls boucles *f/pl* [bo͞ok'əl] 158
currency monnaie *f* [mônā] 152; **foreign ~** devises *f/pl.* [dəvēz] 152
curtain rideau *m* [rēdō] 91; **~ time** lever *m* du rideau [ləvā dē rēdō] 177; **final ~** fin *f* [feN] 177
curve virage *m* [vērāzh] 42
cuspid canine *f* [känēn] 174
custody détention *f* [dātäNsyôN] 154; **pre-trial ~** détention *f* préventive [dātäNsyôN präväNtēv] 154
customs douane *f* [do͞o·än] 80; **~ control** passage *m* de la douane [päsäzh də lä do͞o·än] 80; **~ declaration** déclaration *f* de douane [däkläräsyôN də do͞o·än] 146; **~ examination** contrôle *m* de douane [kôNtrôl də do͞o·än] 80; **~ office** bureau *m* de douane [bērō də do͞o·än] 80; **~ officer** douanier *m* [do͞o·änyā] 80
cut *(verb)* couper [ko͞opā] 155, 181; *(noun)* coupure *f* [ko͞opēr] 169
cutlery couvert *m* [ko͞ovār] 97
cylinder cylindre *m* [sēleNd(ər)] 52; **~ head** culasse *f* [kēläs] 52; **~ head gasket** joint *m* de culasse [zhô·eN də kēläs] 52
Canadian dollars dollars *m/pl* canadiens [dôlär känädyeN] 152
Catholic catholique [kätôlēk] 124; **Roman ~** catholique romain [kätôlek rômeN] 124
Christ Christ *m* [krēst] 124
Christian chrétien *m* [krātyeN] 124
Christianity christianisme *m* [krēstyänēsm] 124
Christmas Noël *m* [nō·el] 33; **merry ~!** joyeux Noël! [zhô·äyā nō·el] 23

D

daily tous les jours [to͞o lā zho͞or] 31; **~ rate** cours *m* du jour [ko͞or dē zho͞or] 152
dairy crèmerie *f* [krāmerē] 128
damage *(noun)* dommages *m/pl* [dômäzh] 49
dance *(verb)* danser [däNsā] 183; *(noun)* danse *f* [däNs] 183; **~ hall** dancing *m* [däNsēng] 183
dancer danseur *m* [däNsār]; danseuse *f* [däNsāz] 177
dandruff pellicules *f/pl* [pelēkēl] 158

dangerous dangereux [däNzhərā̆] 185
dark *(colour)* foncé [föNsā] 127
darn repriser [reprēzā] 137
darning cotton coton *m* à repriser [kôtôN ä reprēzā] 136
darning-wool laine *f* à repriser [len ä reprēzā] 136
date of birth date *f* de naissance [dät də nesäNs] 79
daughter fille *f* [fēˈē] 35
dawn aube *f* [ōb] 26
day jour *m* [zhōōr]; journée *f* [zhōōr-nā] 31; **New Year's Day** jour *m* de l'an [zhōōr də läN] 33; **~ room** salle *f* commune [säl kômēn] 95
dead-end street voie *f* sans issue [vô·ä säNzēsē̆] 120
deal donner [dônā] 181
dealership garage garage *m* concessionnaire [gäräzh kôNsesyô-när] 49
decanter carafe *f* [käräf] 97
December décembre *m* [dā-säNb(ər)] 33
deck pont *m* [pôN] 75; **boat ~** pont *m* des embarcations [pôN dāzäN-bärkäsyôN] 75; **fore ~** plage *f* avant [pläzh äväN] 75; **main ~** pont *m* principal [pôN preNsēpäl] 76; **poop ~** plage *f* arrière [pläzh äryär] 76; **promenade ~** pont-promenade *m* [pôN-prômenäd] 76; **saloon ~** pont *m* de première classe [pôN də prəmyär kläs] 76; **sun ~** sundeck *m* [sändek] 76; **upper ~** pont *m* supérieur [pôN sēpārē·ār] 76; **~ chair** transat(lantique) *m* [träNsät(läNtēk)] 76
declare déclarer [dāklärā] 80
deeply profondément [prôfôNdā-mäN] 165
defeat défaite *f* [dāfāt] 188
delicious délicieux [dālēsyā̆] 99
delivery truck camionette *f* [kämyô-net] 40
dental clinic clinique *f* dentaire [klē-nēk däNtār] 174
dentist dentiste *m, f* [däNtēst] 36
dentistry études *f/pl* dentaires [ātēd däNtār] 39
denture dentition *f* [däNtēsyôN] 174
deodorant déodorant *m* [dā·ōdô-räN] 141
depart partir [pärtēr] 67
departure départ *m* [dāpär] 67; sortie *f* [sôrtē] 79
deposit *(noun)* accompte *m* [äkôNt] 83; arrhes *f/pl* [är] 91; versement *m* [versmäN] 152; *(verb)* verser une caution [versā ēn kôsyôN] 41
dermatologist dermatologue *m* [dārmätōlôg] 162
destination lieu *m* de destination [lēyā̆ də destēnäsyôN] 149
detergent détergent *m* [dāterzhäN] 143; **dishwashing ~** détergent *m* à vaisselle [dāterzhäN ä vāsel] 143
detour déviation *f* [dāvē·äsyôN] 42
develop développer [dāvelôpā] 131
development développement *m* [dāvelôpmäN] 132
dew rosée *f* [rōzā] 26
dextrose glucose *m* [glēkōz] 160
diabetes diabète *m* [dē·äbāt] 170
diabetic diabéthique [dē·äbātēk] 164
diagnosis diagnostic *m* [dē·ägnôs-tēk] 172
dial *(noun)* cadran *m* [kädräN] 149; *(verb)* composer le numéro [kôN-pōzā lə nēmärō] 149
diamond brillant *m* [brēyäN] 133
diamonds carreau *m* [kärō] 181
diaphoretic sudorifique *m* [sēdôrē-fēk] 160
diaphragm diaphragme *m* [dē·ä-frägm] 132

diarrhea diarrhée *f* [dē·ärā] 170
dice dē *m* [dā] 181; **shoot ~** jouer aux dés [zhōō·ā ō dā] 181
dictionary dictionnaire *m* [dēksyônär] 130
diesel diesel *m* [dyezel] 45; **~ motor** moteur *m* diesel [môtär dyezel] 54; **~ nozzle** gicleur *m* diesel [zhēklär dyezel] 52
diet régime *m* [rāzhēm]; diète *f* [dē·ät] 175
differential différentiel *m* [dēfäräNsyel] 52
digestion digestion *f* [dēzhestyôN] 166
digestive tablets comprimés *m/pl* pour la digestion [kôNprēmā pōōr lä dēzhestyôN] 160
digestive tonic gouttes *f/pl* pour la digestion [gōōt pōōr lä dēzhestyôN] 160
dinghy canot *m* pneumatique [känō pnämätēk] 186
dining car wagon-restaurant *m* [vägôN restôräN] 60
dining room salle *f* à manger [sälä mäNzhā] 74
dinner dîner *m* [dēnā] 91
dip stick réglette-jauge *f* [rāgletzhôzh] 52
diphtheria diphthérie *f* [dēftārē] 170
dipped headlights feux *m/pl* de croisement [fā də krô·äz·mäN] 53
direct direct [dērekt] 68; **~ dial** faire un numéro interurbain automatique [fär eN nēmärō eNterērbeN ôtōmätēk] 147; **~ dialing** automatique *m* [ôtōmätēk] 149
direction direction *f* [dēreksyôN] 59; **~ sign** panneau *m* indicateur [pänō eNdēkätär] 42
director metteur *m* en scène [metär äN sān] 177
disc disque *m* [dēsk] 166; **~ brake** frein *m* à disques [freN ä dēsk] 51
discharge sortie *f* de clinique [sôrtē də klēnēk] 172
discotheque discothèque *f* [dēskôtāk] 180
discount réduction *f* [rādēksyôN] 176
disease maladie *f* [mälädē] 170; **contagious ~** maladie *f* contagieuse [mälädē kôNtäzhē·äz] 170
disembark débarquer [dābärkā] 76
disengage débrayer [dābräyā] 53
dish plat *m* [plä] 99
dishes vaisselle *f* [väsel] 95
disinfectant désinfectant *m* [dāzeNfektäN] 160
dislocation luxation *f* [lēksäsyôN] 170
distilled water eau *f* distillée [ō dēstēlā] 45
distributor distributeur *m* [dēstrēbētär] 52
district région *f* [rāzhē·ôN] 120
ditch fossé *m* [fôsā] 120
diuretic diurétique *m* [dē·ērātēk] 160
dive *(verb)* plonger [plôNzhā] 186; *(noun)* plongeon *m* [plôNzhôN] 190
diving board plongeoir *m* [plôNzhô·är] 190
divorced divorcé [dēvôrsā] 79
dizziness vertige *m* [värtēzh] 170
dock *(noun)* débarcadère *f* [dābärkädär] 76; *(verb)* aborder [äbôrdā] 76; faire escale [fär eskäl] 72
doctor médecin *m* [mādəseN] 36; *(in names)* monsieur *m* le Docteur [məsyā lə dôktär] 13; **doctor's office** cabinet *m* de consultation [käbēnā də kôNsēltäsyôN] 163
documentary (film *m)* documentaire *m* [(fēlm) dôkēmäNtär] 179
doll poupée *f* [pōōpā] 143

dome coupole *f* [kōōpôl] 125
door porte *f* [pôrt] 91; **~ handle** poignée *f* [pô·änyā] 91; **~ lock** serrure *f* de la portière [serēr də lä pôrtyār] 52
dormitory dortoir *m* [dôrtô·är] 95
doubles double *m* [dōōb'əl] 189
downtown area centre *m* (de la) ville [säNt(ər) (dəlä) vēl] 120
dozen douzaine *f* [dōōzān] 193
draft courant *m* d'air [kōōräN dār] 26
drain lavabo *m* [läväbō] 88
drama drame *m* [dräm] 177
drapery rideau *m* [rēdō] 91
draw *(verb)* faire un coup [fār eN kōō] 181; *(noun)* match *m* nul [mätsh nēl] 188
drawer tiroir *m* [tērô·är] 91
dress robe *f* [rôb] 134
dressing gown robe *f* de chambre [rôb də shäNb(ər)] 134
dressmaker tailleur *m* [täyār] 36
dress-shield dessous *m* de bras [dəsōō də brä] 136
drier séchoir *m* [sāshô·är] 156
drill foret *m* [fôrā] 57
drink *(verb)* boire [bô·är] 165; *(noun)* boisson *f* [bô·äsôN] 96
drinking water eau *f* potable [ō pôtäb'əl] 65
drip goutter [gōōtā] 88
drip-dry sans repassage [säN repäsäzh] 135
drive aller [älā] 42; rouler [rōōlā] 50
drive shaft arbre *m* moteur (de couche) [ärb(ər) môtār (də kōōsh)] 52
driver chauffeur *m* [shôfār] 36; conducteur *m* [kôNdēktār] 59
driver's licence permis *m* de conduire [permē də kôNdē·ēr] 42
driver's seat siège *m* du conducteur [syāzh dē kôNdēktār] 55
driveway entrée *f* [äNtrā] 42
driving instructor moniteur *m* d'auto-école [mônētār dôtō-äkôl] 36
drops gouttes *f/pl* [gōōt] 160; **ear ~** gouttes *f/pl* pour les oreilles [gōōt pōōr läzôrā·ē] 160; **eye ~** gouttes *f/pl* pour les yeux [gōōt pōōr läzyā] 161
druggist *(pharmacist)* pharmacien *m* [färmäsyeN] 36; *(drugstore owner)* droguiste *m* [drôgēst] 36
drugs drogues *f/pl* [drôg] 154
dry sécher [sāshā] 92; **~ cleaner's** nettoyage *m* à sec [netô·äyäzh ä sek] 128; **~ goods** mercerie *f* [mārserē] 136
dubbed synchronisé [seNkrōnēzā] 179
dubbing synchronisation *f* [seNkrônēzäsyôN] 179
duck canard *m* [känär] 105; **wild ~** canard *m* sauvage [känär sôväzh] 105
duet duo *m* [dē·ō] 177
dune dune *f* [dēn] 186
dusk crépuscule *m* [krāpēskēl] 26
duty droits *m/pl* de douane [drô·ä də dōō·än] 80; **pay ~** déclarer [dāklärā] 80; **in ~ free** en franchise [äN fräNshēz] 80; **export ~** droits *m/pl* de sortie [drô·ä də sôrtē] 80; **import ~** droits *m/pl* d'entrée [drô·ä däNtrā] 80
dye teinture *f* [teNtēr] 141
dynamo dynamo *f* [dēnämō] 52
dysentery dysenterie *f* [dēzäNtərē] 170

E

ear clips clips *m/pl* [klēp] 133
earache mal *m* aux oreilles [mäl ōzôrā·ē] 164

eardrum tympan *m* [teNpäN] 166
earlier plus tôt [plē tō] 32
early tôt [tō] 31
earrings boucles *f/pl* d'oreille [bo͞ok'əl dôrā·ē] 133
Easter Pâques *m* [päk] 33
economics économie *f* [ākônōmē] 39
economy class classe *f* économique [kläs ākônōmēk] 69
education *(subject)* pédagogie *f* [pādägōzhē] 39
eel anguille *f* [äNgē'ē] 104; **smoked ~** anguille *f* fumée [äNgē'ē fēmā] 102
egg œuf *m* [āf] 98; **hard-boiled ~** œuf *m* dur [āf dēr] 98; **soft-boiled ~** œuf *m* à la coque [āf älä kôk] 98; **ham and eggs** œufs *m/pl* au jambon [ā ō zhäNbôN] 98; **fried eggs** œufs *m/pl* sur le plat [ā sēr lə plä] 98; **scrambled eggs** œufs *m/pl* brouillés [ā bro͞oyā] 98; **~ cup** coquetier *m* [kôketyā] 97
eight huit [ē·ēt] 28
eighty quatre-vingts [kätrəveN] 28
elastic élastique *m* [ālästēk] 136; **~ bandage** bande *f* élastique [bäNd ālästēk] 160; **~ stocking** bas *m* élastique [bä ālästēk] 160
elbow coude *m* [ko͞od] 166
electric shaver rasoir *m* électrique [räzô·är ālektrēk] 141
electrician électricien *m* [ālektrēsyeN] 36
elevator ascenseur *m* [äsäNsār] 91
emerald émeraude *f* [āmerōd] 133
emergency: ~ brake signal *m* d'alarme [sēnyäl dälärm] 66; **~ chute** glissoire *f* de secours [glēsô·är də səko͞or] 70; **~ exit** sortie *f* de secours [sôrtē də səko͞or] 70; **~ landing** atterissage *m* forcé [äterēsäzh fôrsā] 70; **~ ward** poste *m* de secours [pôst də səko͞or] 49
emetic vomitif *m* [vômētēf] 160
enema lavement *m* [lävmäN] 160
engine réacteur *m* [rā·äktār] 71; *(railroad)* locomotive *f* [lōkōmōtēv] 67
engeneer *(scientific)* ingénieur *m* [eNzhānyār] 36; *(railroad)* mécanicien *m* [mākänēsyeN] 36
English anglais [äNglā] 24; *(subject)* langue *f* et littérature *f* anglaises [läNgā lētärätēr äNgläz] 39
enjoy oneself s'amuser [sämēzā] 184
enlargement agrandissement *m* [ägräNdēs·mäN] 131
enough assez [äsā] 46
entrance entrée *f* [äNtrā] 67
entry entrée *f* [äNtrā] 79; **~ visa** visa *m* d'entrée [vēzä däNtrā] 79
envelope enveloppe *f* [äNvelôp] 138
environs environs *m/pl* [äNvērôN] 120
eraser gomme *f* [gôm] 138
Eve; New Year's ~ Saint-Sylvestre *f* [seN sēlvest(ər)] 33
evening soir *m* [sô·är] 155; soirée *f* [sô·ärā] 16; **good ~!** bonsoir! [bôNsô·är] 12; **in the ~** le soir [lə sô·är] 31; **this ~** ce soir [sə sô·är] 31
every day tous les jours [to͞o lā zho͞or] 31
everything tout [to͞o] 83
exact exact [egzä(kt)] 30
exactly exactement [egzäktəmäN] 30
examination examen *m* [egzämeN]; analyse *f* [änälēz] 172
examine examiner [egzämēnā] 172
excavations fouilles *f/pl* [fo͞o'ē] 120
excess baggage bagages *m/pl* en excédent [bägäzh äN eksādäN] 68

exchange *(verb)* échanger [āshäNzhā] 127; **rate of ~** cours *m* de change [ko͞or də shäNzh] 152
excursion excursion *f* [ekskērsyôN] 72; **~ program** programme *m* d'excursion [prôgräm dekskērsyôN] 76; **land excursions** excursions *f/pl* (à terre) [ekskērsyôN (ä tār)] 76
excuse me! excusez-moi! [ekskēzāmô·ä] 22
excuse me? vous permettez? [vo͞o permetā] 20
exhaust échappement *m* [āshäp·mäN] 52
exhibition exposition *f* [ekspōzēsyôN] 119
exit sortie *f* [sôrtē] 42; **~ visa** visa *m* de sortie [vēzä də sôrtē] 79
expect attendre [ätäNd(ər)] 85
expensive cher [shār] 127
exposure exposition *f* [ekspōzēsyôN] 132; **~ meter** posemètre *m* [pōzmāt(ər)] 132
express train train *m* direct [treN dērekt]; express *m* [ekspres] 60
expressway autoroute *f* [ôtōro͞ot] 58
extend prolonger [prōlôNzhā] 79
extension cord rallonge *f* [rälôNzh] 91
external externe [ekstārn] 159
extra week semaine *f* supplémentaire [semen sēplāmäNtār] 91
extract arracher [äräshā]; extraire [ekstrār] 174
eye œil *m* (*pl* yeux) [ā'ē (*pl* yā)] 166; **~ doctor** oculiste *m* [ôkēlēst] 162; **~ inflammation** inflammation *f* de l'œil [eNflämäsyôN də lā'ē] 170; **~ liner** crayon *m* (à paupières) [krāyôN (ä pōpyār)] 141; **~ shadow** ombre *f* à paupières [ôNbrä pôpyār] 141
eyeball globe *m* oculaire [glôb ôkēlār] 166
eyebrows sourcils *m/pl* [so͞orsē] 156
eyebrow pencil crayon *m* à sourcils [krāyôN ä so͞orsē] 141
eyeglass case étui *m* à lunettes [ātē·ē ā lēnet] 138
eyelid paupière *f* [pōpyār] 166

F

fabric tissu *m* [tēsē], étoffe *f* [ātôf] 137
face visage *m* [vēzäzh] 166; *(of a clock)* cadran *m* [kädräN] 143; **~ massage** massage *m* facial [mäsäzh fäsyäl] 156
facial mask masque *m* facial [mäsk fäsyäl] 156
factory usine *f* [ēzēn] 120
fall *(verb)* faire une chute [fār ēn shēt] 164; *(barometer)* descendre [desäNd(ər)] 25; *(noun: season)* automne *m* [ôtôn] 33
falling rocks chute *f* de pierres [shēt də pyār] 42
false tooth fausse dent *f* [fōs däN] 174
family famille *f* [fäme·ē] 35
fan ventilateur *m* [väNtēlätār] 53; **~ belt** courroie *f* trapézoidale [ko͞orô·ä träpāzō·ēdäl] 53
far loin [lô·eN] 40
fare prix *m* du billet [prē dē bēyā] 62; **~ discount** tarif *m* réduit [tärēf rādē·ē] 67
farewell dinner dîner *m* d'adieux [dēnā dädyā] 76
farmer agriculteur *m* [ägrēkēltār] 36
farmhouse ferme *f* [fārm] 120
far-sighted presbyte [presbēt] 138
fashion boutique magasin *m* de haute couture [mägäzeN də ōt

kōōtēr] 128
fashion show défilé *m* de mode [dāfēlā də môd] 180
fast vite [vēt] 42; ~ **train** rapide *m* [räpēd] 60
fasten seat belts attacher les ceintures [ätäshā lā seNtēr] 70
fat gras [grä] 100
father père *m* [pār] 35
father-in-law beau-père *m* [bō-pār] 35
fatty gras [grä] 115
faucet robinet *m* [rôbēnā] 88
February février *m* [fāvrē·ā] 33
fee: rental ~ prix *m* de location [prē də lôkäsyôN] 95
fencing escrime *f* [eskrēm] 188
fender garde-boue *m* [gärd-bōō] 53
ferry, car ~, **train** ~ ferry-boat *m* [ferē-bōt] 76
fetch aller chercher [älā shārshā] 20
fever fièvre *f* [fē·āv(ər)] 170; ~ **cure** fébrifuge *m* [fābrēfēzh] 161
fiancé fiancé *m* [fē·äNsā] 14
fiancée fiancée *f* [fē·äNsā] 14
fibre fibre *f* [fēb(ər)] 137; **synthetic** ~ fibre *f* synthétique [fēb(ər) seNtātēk] 137
fight combat *m* [kôNbä] 187
figs figues *f/pl* [fēg] 110
figure skating patinage *m* [pätēnäzh] 188
figurine figure *f* [fēgēr] 143
file *(verb)* limer [lēmā] 156; *(noun)* lime *f* [lēm] 57
fill plomber [plôNbā] 174; ~ **her up** faites le plein [fāt lə pleN] 45; ~ **in** remplir [räNplēr] 78
filling plombage *m* [plôNbäzh] 174; **temporary** ~ pansement *m* [päNsmäN] 174
film *(noun)* rouleau *m* [rōōlō] 131; film *m* [fēlm] 179; pellicule *f* [pelēkēl] 132; *(verb)* filmer [fēlmā] 132; **cartridge** ~ film *m* à chassis [fēlm ä shäsē] 131; **color** ~ pellicule *f* en couleur [pelēkēl äN kōōlār] 132; **color negative** ~ pellicule *f* négative en couleurs [pelēkēl nāgätēv äN kōōlār] 132; **educational** ~ (film *m)* documentaire *m* [(fēlm) dôkēmäNtār] 179; **feature** ~ long métrage *m* [lôN māträzh] 179; **reversal** ~ film *m* inversible [fēlm eNversēb'əl] 132; **roll** ~ pellicule *f* [pelēkēl]; rouleau *m* [rōōlō] 132; **sixteen millimeter color** ~ film *m* en couleur seize millimètres [fēlm äN kōōlār sāz mēlēmāt(ər)] 131; **super eight color** ~ film *m* en couleur super huit [fēlm äN kōōlār sēpār ē·ēt] 131; **thirty five millimeter** ~ film *m* trente cinq millimètres [fēlm träNt seNk mēlēmāt(ər)] 131; **thirty-six exposure** ~ pellicule *f* de trente-six poses [pelēkēl də träNt-sē pōz] 131; **twenty exposure** ~ pellicule *f* de vingt poses [pelēkēl də veN pōz] 131; ~ **actor** acteur *m* de cinéma [äktār də sēnāmä] 179; ~ **festival** festival *m* du film [festēväl dē fēlm] 179; ~ **screen** écran *m* [ākräN] 179
fine bien [byeN] 12; *(weather)* beau [bō] 25
finger doigt *m* [dô·ä] 167; **index** ~ index *m* [eNdeks] 167; **middle** ~ médius *m* [mādyēs] 167; **ring** ~ annulaire *m* [änēlār] 167
fire department pompiers *m/pl* [pôNpyā] 49
fire extinguisher extincteur *m* [eksteNtār] 53
fireplace cheminée *f* [shemēnā] 91
first premier [prəmyā] 29; ~ **class** première classe *f* [prəmyār kläs] 64

first-aid kit pansements *m/pl* [päNs-mäN] 161
first-aid station poste *m* de secours [pôst də səkōōr] 121; infirmerie *f* [eNfērmərē] 60
fish *(noun)* poisson *f* [pô·äsôN] 104; *(verb)* pêcher à la ligne [pāshā älä lēn(yə)] 185; **~ market** poissonnerie *f* [pô·äsônrē] 128
fisherman pêcheur *m* [pāshār] 36
fishing pêche *f* à la ligne [pāsh älä lēn(yə)] 188; **~ license** permis *m* de pêche [permē də pāsh] 188; **~ rod** canne *f* à pêche [kän ä pāsh] 188; **~ trawler** bateau *m* de pêche [bätō də pāsh] 75; **go ~** pêcher à la ligne [pāshā älä lēn(yə)] 188
fit *(noun)* attaque *f* [ätäk] 170
five cinq [seNk] 28
fix faire [fār] 50; réparer [rāpärā] 138
flannel flanelle *f* [flänel] 137
flash flash *m* [fläsh] 132; **~ bulb** ampoule *f* flash [äNpōōl fläsh] 132; **~ cube** cube *m* flash [kēb fläsh] 132
flashing signal avertisseur *m* lumineux [ävertēsār lēmēnā] 54
flashlight flash *m* [fläsh] 143
flat plat [plä] 139
flatulence ballonnements *m/pl* [bälôn·mäN] 170
flight vol *m* [vôl] 68; **~ attendant** hôtesse *f* de l'air [ôtes də lär] 71
flint pierre *f* à briquet [pyār ä brēkā] 140
flirting flirt *m* [flārt] 184
float *(car)* flotteur *m* [flôtār] 53
floor étage *m* [ātäzh] 91; **first ~** premier étage *m* [prəmyer ātäzh] 82; **ground ~** rez-de-chaussée *m* [rādə-shôsā] 82; **second ~** deuxième étage *m* [dāzyāmātäzh] 82
flower fleur *f* [flār] 130; **~ pot** pot *m* de fleurs [pô də flār] 130
flu grippe *f* [grēp] 170
fly voler [vôlā] 71
flying time durée *f* de vol [dērā də vôl] 71
FM modulations *f/pl* de fréquence [môdēläsyôN də frākäNs] 182
fog brouillard *m* [brōōyär] 27
follow poursuivre [pōōrsē·ēv(ər)] 154
fond of passionné pour [päsyônā pōōr]
font fonts *m/pl* batismaux [fôN bätēzmō] 125
food nourriture *f* [nōōrētēr] 163; **diet ~** menus *m/pl* diététiques [menē dē·ātātēk] 96; **vegetarian ~** menus *m/pl* végétariens [menē vāzhātärē·eN] 96; **~ poisoning** intoxication *f* alimentaire [eNtôksēkäsyôN älēmäNtār] 170
foot pied *m* [pyā] 167; **by ~** à pied [ä pyā] 116; **~ brake** frein *m* à pied [freN ä pyā] 51
footpath trottoir *m* [trôtô·är] 42
forehead front *m* [frôN] 167
forester garde *m* forestier [gärd fôrestyā] 36
forgive pardonner [pärdônā] 22
fork fourchette *f* [fōōrshet] 97
form formulaire *m* [fôrmēlār] 78
fortress forteresse *f* [fôrtəres] 119
forward *(verb)* faire suivre [fār sē·ēv(ər)] 89; *(noun; sports)* avant *m* [äväN] 189
fountain fontaine *f* [fôNten]; jet *m* d'eau, [zhā dō] 121
four quatre [kät(ər)] 28
fracture fracture *f* [fräktēr] 170
frame monture *f* [môNtēr] 138
free libre [lēb(ər)] 44; **~ kick** coup *m* franc [kōō fräN] 189; **~ style** exercices *m/pl* libres [eksersēs lēb(ər)] 188; **~ wheel hub** moyeu

m à roue libre [mô·äyā ä ro͞o lēb(ər)] 53
freeway autoroute *f* [ôtôro͞ot] 58
freighter cargo *m* [kärgō] 77
French français [fräNsā] 24
fresco fresque *f* [fresk] 125
fresh frais [frā] 100
Friday vendredi *m* [väNdrədē] 33; **Good ~** vendredi *m* saint [väNdrədē seN] 33
fried sauté [sôtā] 100; **deep ~** frit [frē] 100
friend *(male)* ami *m* [ämē] 14; *(female)* amie *f* [ämē] 14
front: on the ~ of the train à l'avant du train [ä läväN dē treN] 66; **up ~** à l'avant [ä läväN] 65; **~ desk** réception *f* [räsepsyôN] 91; **~ door** porte *f* d'entrée [pôrt däNtrā] 91; **~ seat** siège *m* avant [syāzh äväN] 55; **~ passenger seat** siège *m* avant droit [syāzh äväN drô·ä] 55; **~ wheel** roue *f* avant [ro͞o äväN] 47
frontal sinus sinus *m* frontal [sēnēs frôNtäl] 167
frost gelée *f* [zhelā] 27
frostbite engelure *f* [äNzhelēr] 170
frozen dessert parfait *m* [pärfā] 109
fruit fruits *m/pl* [frē·ē] 110; **~ market** épicerie *f m* [āpēsərē]; marché *m* [märshā] 128
fuel: ~ injector pompe *f* à injection [pôNp ä eNzheksyôN] 53; **~ lines** conduite *f* d'essence [kôNdē·ēt desäNs] 53; **~ pump** pompe *f* d'essence [pôNp desäNs] 53
full coverage insurance assurance *f* tous risques [äsēräNs to͞o rēsk] 41
fullback arrière *m* [äryār] 190
funnel entonnoir *m* [äNtônô·är] 57
fur coat (manteau *m* de) fourrure *f* [(mäNtō də) fo͞orēr] 134
fur jacket veste *f* de fourrure [vest də fo͞orēr] 134
furrier pelleterie *f* [peletərē] 128
fuse fusible *m* [fēsēb'əl] 53

G

gall bladder vésicule *f* biliaire [vāzēkēl bēlyār] 167
gall stones calculs *m/pl* biliaires [kälkēl bēlyār] 170
gallery galerie *f* [gälerē] 119
gambling casino casino *f* [käzēnō] 181
gambling game jeu *m* de hazard [zhā də äzär] 181
game jeu *m* [zhā] 187; *(animals)* gibier *m* [zhēbyā] 105
gangway passerelle *f* [päserel] 76
garage garage *m* [gäräzh] 44
garden jardin *m* [zhärdeN] 121
gardener jardinier *m* [zhärdēnyā] 36
gargle gargarisme *m* [gärgärēsm] 161
garlic ail *m* [ä·ē] 101
garter belt porte-jarretelles *m* [pôrt-zhärtel] 134
garters jarretelles *f/pl* [zhärtel] 136
gas accélérateur *m* [äkselārätār] 53; **~ bottle** bouteille *f* de gaz [bo͞otā'ē də gäz] 94; **~ station** station *f* d'essence [stäsyôN desäNs] 45
gasket joint *m* [zhô·eN] 53
gasoline essence *f* [esäNs] 45; **~ can** jerrycan *m* [dzherēkän] 45
gate portail *m* [pôrtä'ē] 121; *(airport)* pont *m* d'embarquement [pôN däNbärkmäN] 71
gauze bandage bandage *m* de gaze [bäNdäzh də gäz] 161
gear affaires *f/pl* [äfār] 185; *(car)* vitesse *f* [vētes] 53; **put it in ~** passer en ... vitesse [päsā äN vētes] 53; **~ lever** levier *m* de change-

ment de vitesse [levyā də shäNzh-mäN də vētes] 53; ~ **oil** huile *f* de graissage [ē·ēl də gresäzh] 46
gear-box boîte *f* de vitesse [bô·ät də vētes] 53
gearshift changement *m* de vitesse [shäNzh·mäN də vētes] 53
general delivery poste *f* restante [pôst restäNt] 149
general practitioner médecin *m* de médecine générale [mādəseN də mādəsēn zhānāräl] 162
genital organs organes *m/pl* génitaux [ôrgän zhānētō] 167
gentlemen messieurs *m/pl* [mesyā] 65
geology géologie *f* [zhā·ōlōzhē] 39
german allemand [älmäN] 24; ~ **measles** rubéole *f* [rēbā·ôl] 170
get avoir [ävô·är] 18; ~ **in,** ~ **aboard** monter (en voiture) [môNtā (äN vô·ätēr)] 67; ~ **out,** ~ **off** descendre [desäNd(ər)] 117, 67; ~ **together again** se revoir [sə rəvô·är] 17
gin gin *m* [dzēn] 112
ginger gingembre *m* [zheN-zhäNb(ər)] 101
girdle ceinture *f* [seNtēr] 134
girl fille *f* [fē'ē] 35
give donner [dônā] 20
gladioli glaïeuls *m/pl* [gläyāl] 130
gland glande *f* [gläNd] 167
glass verre *m* [vār] 96; **water** ~ verre *m* à eau [vār ä ō] 97; **wine** ~ verre *m* à vin [vār ä veN] 97
glasses *(spectacles)* lunettes *f/pl* [lēnet] 138
glazier vitrier *m* [vētrēyā] 37
glossy *(adj.)* brillant [brēyäN] 132; *(noun)* illustré *m* [ēlēstrā] 182
gloves gants *m/pl* [gäN] 134
glue colle *f* [kôl] 138
glycerine glycérine *f* [glēsārēn] 161
go aller [älā] 19
goal but *m* [bē(t)] 187; **kick a** ~ marquer un but [märkā eN bē(t)] 190
goalie gardien *m* de but [gärdyeN də bē(t)] 190
God Dieu *m* [dyā] 125
gold *(noun)* or *m* [ôr] 133; *(adj.)* doré [dôrā] 194; ~ **plated** doré [dôrā] 133
golf golf *m* [gôlf] 188
good bien [byeN] 21
good-bye! au revoir! [ō revô·är] 17
goods marchandises *f/pl* [märshäNdēz] 70
goose oie *f* [ô·ä] 105; ~ **liver pâté** pâté *m* de foie gras [pätā də fô·ä grä] 102
gooseberries groseilles *f/pl* à maquereau [grôzā'ē ä mäkərō] 110
Gospel Evangile *m* [äväNzhēl] 125
Gothic gothique [gōtēk] 125
government office administration *f* [ädmēnēsträsyôN] 121
grammar school école *f* primaire [ākôl prēmār] 38
grand piano piano *m* à queue [pē·änō ä kā] 177
grandchild petit-fils *m* [pətē-fēs] 35
granddaughter petite-fille *f* [pətētfē'ē] 35
grandfather grand-père *m* [gräN-pār] 35
grandmother grand-mère *f* [gräN-mār] 35
grandparents grands-parents *m/pl* [gräN-päräN] 35
grandson petit-fils *m* [pətē-fēs] 35
grapefruit pamplemousse *f* [päN-pləmōōs] 110; ~ **juice** jus *m* de pamplemousse [zhē də päNpləmōōs] 112
grapes raisins *m/pl* [rāzeN] 110
grateful reconnaissant [rekônāsäN] 21
grave tombe *f* [tôNb] 121

gravy jus *m* de rôti [zhē de rôtē] 101
gray gris [grē] 194; **ash ~** gris cendré [grē säNdrā] 194; **dark ~** gris foncé [grē fôNsā] 194; **pale ~** gris clair [grē klār] 194
grease graisse *f* [gres] 53
greasy gras [grä] 158
great grand [gräN] 22
green vert [vār] 194; **dark ~** vert foncé [vār fôNsā] 194; **light ~** vert clair [vār klār] 194
grill room grill-room *m* [grēl-ro͞om] 91
grilled grillé [grēyā] 100
grocery store magasin *m* d'alimentation [mägäzeN dälēmäNtäsyôN] 94
group fare ticket billet *m* de groupe [bēyā də gro͞op] 62
grown up adulte [ädēlt] 34
guard garder [gärdā] 44
guarded gardé [gärdā] 44
guest house pension *f* [päNsyôN] 91
guide guide *m* [gēd] 121
guilt culpabilité *f* [kēlpäbēlētā] 154
gums gencive *f* [zhäNsēv] 174
gym shoes chaussures *f/pl* de gymnastique [shôsēr də zhēmnästēk] 139
gymnast gymnaste *m* [zhēmnäst] 188
gymnastics gymnastique *f* [zhēmnästēk] 188; **~ with apparatus** gymnastique *f* aux agrès [zhēmnästēk ōzägrā] 188
gynecologist gynécologue *m* [zhēnäkōlôg] 162

H

haberdashery mercerie *f* [märserē] 128
haddock aiglefin *m* [āgləfeN] 104
hail grêle *f* [grāl] 27
hair cheveux *m/pl* [shevā] 155; **~ conditioner** sèche-cheveux *m* [sāsh-shevā] 141; **~ drier** séchoir *m* [sāshô·är] 158; **~ loss** chute *f* des cheveux [shēt dā shevā] 158; **~ net** filet *m* [fēlā] 141; **~ spray** vaporisateur *m* [väpôrēzätār] 141; **~ style** coiffure *f* [kô·äfēr] 158; **~ tonic** lotion *f* capillaire [lôsyôN käpēlār] 141
hairbrush brosse *f* à cheveux [brôs ä shevā] 141
haircut coupe *f* de cheveux [ko͞op də shevā] 157
hair-do coiffure *f* [kô·äfēr] 158
hairdresser coiffeur *m* [kô·äfār] 158
hairpiece perruque *f* [perēk] 156
hairpin épingle *f* à cheveux [āpeNg'əl ä shevā] 141
half demi [dəmē] 30
half fare demi-place *f* [dəmē-pläs] 59
half time mi-temps *m* [mē-täN] 188
hall hall *m* d'hôtel [äl dôtel] 91
ham jambon *m* [zhäNbôN] 102
hammer marteau *m* [märtō] 57
hammock hamac *m* [ämäk] 144
hand main *f* [meN] 167; *(on clock)* aiguille *f* [āgē'ē] 143; **~ brake** frein *m* à main [freN ä meN] 51; **~ luggage** bagage *m* à main [bägäzh ä meN] 63
handbag sac *m* à main [säk ä meN] 144
handball handball *m* [äNdbôl] 188
handicrafts objets *m/pl* artisanaux [ôbzhā ärtēzänō] 144
handkerchief mouchoir *m* [mo͞oshô·är] 134
handle poignée *f* [pô·änyā] 53
happen se passer [sə päsā] 18
harbor port [pôr] 72; **~ police sta-**

tion police *f* du port [pôlēs dē pôr] 73
hard dur [dēr] 100
hare lièvre *m* [lē·äv(ər)] 106
hat chapeau *m* [shäpō] 134; **straw ~** chapeau *m* de paille [shäpō də pä'ē] 134
have avoir [ävô·är] 18; **we're going to ~** nous aurons [nōōzôrôN] 25; **~ to** devoir [dəvô·är] 41
hay fever rhume *m* des foins [rēm dā fô·eN] 170
hazel nuts noisette *f/pl* [nô·äzet] 110
head tête *f* [tāt] 167; **~ clerk** chef *m* de réception [shef də rāsepsyôN] 91
headlight phare *m* [fär] 53
head-on collision collision *f* de face [kôlēzyôN də fäs] 49
health resort station *f* climatique [stäsyôN klēmätēk] 175
heart attack crise *f* cardiaque [krēz kärdē·äk] 170
heart problems troubles *m/pl* cardiaques [trōōb'əl kärdē·äk] 170
heartburn aigreurs *f/pl* [āgrār] 170
hearts *(cards)* cœur *m* [kār] 181
heat canicule *f* [känēkēl] 27; chaleur *f* [shälār] 163
heating *(system)* chauffage *m* [shôfäzh] 54; **central ~** chauffage *m* central [shôfäzh säNträl] 90
heel talon *m* [tälôN] 139
height taille *f* [tä'ē] 79
helicopter hélicoptère *m* [ālēkôptār] 71
hello! salut! [sälē] 12; *(on answering phone)* allô! [älō] 12
helm gouvernail *m* [gōōvernä'ē] 76
helmsman pilote *m* [pēlôt] 76
help *(noun)* aide *f* [ād] 20; *(verb)* aider [ādā] 66; **mary I ~ you?** que désirez-vous? [ke dāzērā-vōō] 18
hemorrhage hémorragie *f* [āmôräzhē] 170
hemorrhoids hémorroïdes *f/pl* [āmôrô·ēd] 170
herbs fines herbes *f/pl* [fēnzārb] 101
here ici [ēsē] 14
herring hareng *m* [äräN] 104
hi! salut! [sälē] 12
high haut [ō] 139; **~ mass** grand-messe *f* [gräN mes] 123; **~ pressure** *(system)* anticyclone *m* [äNtēsēklôn] 27; **~ school** *(academic)* académie *f* [äkädāmē] 38; *(general)* lycée *m* [lēsā]; collège *m* [kôläzh] 38; **~ test** super *m* [sēpār] 45
high-rise building building *m* [bēldēng]; tour *f* [tōōr] 121
highway autoroute *f* [ôtōrōōt] 42; **~ patrol** police *f* routière [pôlēs rōōtyār] 42
hiking path sentier *m* de randonnée [säNtyā də räNdônā] 121
hill colline *f* [kôlēn] 121
hip hanche *f* [äNsh] 167
history histoire *f* [ēstô·är] 39
hitch-hike faire de l'auto-stop [fār də lôtōstôp] 43
hoarseness enrouement *m* [äNrōōmäN] 170
hockey hockey *m* [ôkā] 188
hold up agression *f* [ägresyôN] 153
honey miel *m* [myel] 98
hood capot *m* [käpō] 54
hooks and eyes crochets *m/pl* [krôshā] 136
horizontal bar barre *f* fixe [bär fēks] 188
horn avertisseur *m* sonore [ävertēsār sônôr] 54
horse cheval *m* [shəväl] 189; **~ cart** roulotte *f* [rōōlôt] 41; **~ race** course *f* de chevaux [kōōrs də shəvō] 189
horseradish raifort *m* [rāfôr] 101

hospital hôpital *m* [ôpētäl] 49
hostel: ~ father père *m* aubergiste [pār ōbārzhēst] 95; **~ mother** mère *f* aubergiste [mār ōbārzhēst] 95; **~ parents** parents *m/pl* aubergistes [päräN ōbārzhēst] 95
hot chaud [shō] 25; *(spicy)* épicé [āpēsā]; piquant [pēkäN] 100; **~ chocolate** chocolat *m* [shôkōlä] 98; **~ spring** source *f* chaude [so͞ors shōd] 175
hotel hôtel *m* [ôtel] 81; **beach ~** hôtel *m* de la plage [ôtel də lä pläzh] 91; **~ restaurant** restaurant *m* d'hôtel [restôräN dôtel] 91
hour heure *f* [ār] 31; **every ~** toutes les heures [to͞ot lāzār] 31; **half ~** demi-heure [dəmē-ār] 87; **quarter ~** quart *m* d'heure [kär dār] 87
hourly toutes les heures [to͞ot lāzār] 31
house maison *f* [māzôN] 91; **~ key** clé *f* de la maison [klä dəlä māzôN] 91; **~ number** numéro *m* de la maison [nēmārō dəlä māzôN] 121
how comment [kômäN] 18; **~ are you?** ça va? [sä vä] 12
hub moyeu *m* [mô·äyā] 54; **~ cap** enjoliveur *m* [äNzhôlēvār] 54
hundred cent [säN] 151
hundredweight quintal *m* [keNtäl] 193
hunting chasse *f* [shäs] 189; **~ license** permis *m* de chasse [permē də shäs] 189
hurt *(adj.)* blessé [blesā] 49
husband mari *m* [märē] 13
hydrogen peroxide eau *f* oxigénée [ō ôksēzhānā] 161
hypertension hypertension *f* [ēpärtäNsyôN] 170

I

ice glace *f* [gläs] 27
ice cream glace *f* [gläs] 109; **~ parlor** pâtisser glacier *m* [pätēsyā gläsyā] 113; **assorted ~** glace *f* panachée [gläs pänäshā] 113; **chocolate ~** glace *f* au chocolat [gläs ō shôkôlä] 113; **strawberry ~** glace *f* à la fraise [gläs älä frāz] 113; **vanilla ~** glace *f* à la vanille [gläs älä vänē'ē] 113
ice skating rink pâtinoire *f* [pätēnô·är] 180
icy road verglas *m* [verglä] 27
identity card carte *f* d'identité [kärt dēdäNtētā] 79
ignition allumage *m* [älēmäzh] 54; **~ cable** fil *m* d'allumage [fēl dälēmäzh] 54; **~ key** clé *f* de contact [klā də kôNtäkt] 54; **~ lock** serrure *f* de contact [serēr də kôNtäkt] 54; **~ system** installation *f* de l'allumage [eNstäläsyôN də lälēmäzh] 54
illness maladie *f* [mälädē] 170
inch pouce *m* [po͞os] 193
incisor incisive *f* [eNsēzēv] 174
included compris [kôNprē] 83
including inclus [eNklē] 41
indicator light lampe-témoin *f* [läNp-tāmô·eN] 53
indigestion embarras *m* gastrique [äNbärä gästrēk] 170
inflammation inflammation *f* [eNflämäsyôN] 170
influenza grippe *f* [grēp] 170
information renseignements *m/pl* [räNsen(yə)mäN] 65; information *f* [enfôrmäsyôN] 71; **~ office** bureau *m* de renseignements [bērō də räNsen(yə)mäN] 60
infusion infusion *f* [eNfēzyôN] 172
inhale faire des inhalations *f* [fār dā-

zēnäläsyôN] 175
injection piqûre *f* [pēkēr] 172
injured blessé [blesā] 48
injury blessure *f* [blesēr] 49
ink encre *f* [äNk(ər)] 138
inn auberge *f* [ōbārzh] 81
inner tube chambre *f* à air [shäNb(ər) ä är] 46
innocent innocent [ēnôsäN] 154
inquiry renseignement *m* [räNsen-(yə)mäN] 92
insect repelent remède *m* contre les piqûres d'insectes [remād kôNt(ər) lā pēkēr deNsekt] 161
inside (à) l'intérieur *m* [(ä) leNtā-rē·ār] 47
in-sole semelle *f* intérieure [semel eNtārē·ār] 139
insomnia insomnie *f* [eNsômnē] 170
inspection light lampe-témoin *f* [läNp-tāmô·eN] 57
insulation isolement *m* [ēzôlmäN] 54
insurance assurance *f* [äsēräNs] 49; **~ certificate** carte *f* d'assurance [kärt däsēräNs] 79
insured assuré; [äsērā] 49
intensive care unit service *m* de réanimation [servēs də rā·änēmä-syôN] 172
intermission entracte *m* [äNträkt] 177
internal interne [eNtārn] 159
interpreter interprète *m/f* [eNter-prät] 37
interrupt interrompre [eNte-rôNp(ər)] 61
interrupter interrupteur *m* [eNterēp-tār] 54
intersection croisement *m* [krô·äz-mäN] 42
intestinal catarrh entérite *f* [äNtārēt] 170
intestine intestin *m* [eNtesteN] 167
invitation invitation *f* [eNvētäsyôN] 16
invite inviter [eNvētā] 183
iodine teinture *f* d'iode [teNtēr dyōd] 161
iron *(verb)* repasser [repäsā] 95
Islam islamisme *m* [ēslämēsm] 125
island île *f* [ēl] 76

J

jack valet *m;* cric *m* [välā; krēk] 181; 47
jacket veste *f;* veston *m* [vest; ve-stôN] 134
jackknife couteau *m* de poche [ko͞otō də pôsh] 144
jam confiture *f* [kôNfētēr] 98
January janvier [zhäNvyā] 33
jar verre *m* [vār] 126
jaundice jaunisse *f* [zhōnēs] 170
jaw mâchoire *f* [mäshô·är] 167
jelly gélatine *f;* aspic *m;* gelée *f* [zhālätēn; äspek; zhelā] 101
jellyfish méduse *f* [mādēz] 186
jersey jersey *m* [zhersē] 137
jet turbo-réacteur *m* [tērbō rā·äktār] 71; **~ plane** avion *m* à réaction [ävyôN ä rā·äksyôN] 71
jetty môle *m* [môl] 76
Jew juif [zhē·ēf] 124
jewelry parure *f;* bijoux *m/pl* [pärēr; bēzho͞o] 133, 153; **costume ~** bijoux fantaisie [bēzho͞o fäNtāzē] 133
Jewish juif [zhē·ēf] 125
joint articulation *f* [ärtēkēläsyôN] 167
journalist journaliste *m* [zho͞ornä-lēst] 37
journey voyage *m* [vô·äyäzh] 43
judge juge *m* [zhēzh] 37
judo judo *m* [zhēdō] 188
juice jus *m* [zhē] 98; **grapefruit ~**

jus de pamplemousse [zhē də päNpləmo͞os] 112
juicy juteux [zhētā] 100
July juillet [zhē·ēyā] 33
June juin [zhē·eN] 33

K

key clé *f* [klā] 153
kidnapping enlèvement *m* [äNläv-mäN] 153
kidney rein *m* [reN] 167; **~ stones** calculs *m/pl* rénaux [kälkäl rānō] 170
kidneys rognons *m/pl* [rônyôN] 107
kilometer kilomètre *m* [kēlōmāt(ər)] 193
kind; what ~ of quel, ~le, ~ls, ~les [kel] 18
king roi *m* [rô·ä] 181
kiss *(noun)* baiser *m* [bāzā] 184; **kiss** *(verb)* embrasser [äNbräsā] 184
kitchen cuisine *f* [kē·ēzēn] 92
kitchenette coin *m* cuisine [kô·eN kē·ēzēn] 92
knee genou *m* [zheno͞o] 167; **~ socks** mi-bas *m/pl* [mē-bä] 134
kneecap rotule *f* [rôtēl] 167
knife couteau *m* [ko͞otō] 97; **pocket ~** couteau de poche [ko͞otō də pôsh] 144
knight *(cards)* cavalier *m* [kävälyā] 181
knocks *(moteur)* cogne [kôn(yə]) 54
knot nœud *m* [nā] 76

L

ladies dames *f/pl;* mesdames [däm; mādäm] 65, 13; **~ 'room** toilettes *f/pl* pour dames [tô·älät po͞or däm] 92
lake lac *m* [läk] 76
lamb agneau *m* [änyō] 105
lamp lampe *f* [läNp] 54; **reading ~** lampe *f* de chevet [läNp də shevā] 92
land *(noun)* terre *f;* pays *m* [tār; pā·ē] 76; **land** *(verb)* aborder, accoster [äbôrdā, äkôstā] 76; **land** *(plane)* atterrir [äterēr] 70
landing atterrissage *m* [äterēsäzh] 71; **~ gear** train *m* d'atterrissage [treN däterēsäzh] 71; **~ place** endroit *m* de débarquement [äN-drô·ä də dābärkmäN] 76; **~ stage** débarcadère *m* [dābärkädār] 76
landscape paysage *m* [pā·ēzäzh] 121
lane chaussée *f;* ruelle *f* [shôsā; rē·el] 42; 121
lap rug couverture *f* de laine [ko͞overtēr də lān] 76
lard saindoux *m* [seNdo͞o] 101
larynx larynx *m* [läreNks] 167
last dernier [dernyā] 59; **~ stop** terminus *m* [termēnēs] 121
late tard [tär] 17; **to be ~** (*train, bus*) avoir du retard [ävô·är dē retär] 61
later plus tard [plē tär] 32
launder (faire) laver [(fār) lävā] 87
laundromat laverie *f* automatique [lävrē ōtômätēk] 129
laundry linge *m* [leNzh] 92
laundry *(shop)* blanchisserie *f* [bläNshēsərē] 129
lavender lavande [läväNd] 194
law droit *m* [drô·ä] 39
lawyer avocat *m* [ävōkä] 37
laxative purgatif *m* [pērgätēf] 161
leak *(verb)* goutter [go͞otā] 52
lean maigre [māg(ər)] 100
leash laisse *f* [lās] 144
leather cuir *m* [kē·ēr] 126; **~ coat** manteau *m* de cuir [mäNtō də kē·ēr] 134; **~ jacket** blouson *m* en

cuir [bloōozôN äN kē·ēr] 134
leave partir; laisser [pärtē; läsā] 34; 44
lecture cours *m* [kōōr] 38
left à gauche [ä gōsh] 116
leg jambe *f;* gigot *m* [zhäNb; zhēgō] 167; 106
legitimate theatre théâtre *m* [tā·ät(ə)r)] 177
lemon citron *m* [setrôN] 101
lemonade limonade *f* [lēmônäd] 112
lend prêter [prātā] 48
lengthen rallonger [rälôNzhā] 137
lens *(opt.)* verre *m* [vār] 138
lens *(photogr.)* objectif *m* [ôbzhektēf] 132
letter lettre *f* [let(ə)r)] 34; **local ~** lettre *f* locale [let(ə)r) lôkäl] 145; **registered ~** lettre *f* recommandée [let(ə)r) rekômäNdā] 145
letter abroad lettre *f* pour l'étranger [let(ə)r) pōōr lāträNzhā] 145
leukemia leucémie *f* [lāsāmē] 170
librarian bibliothécaire *m* [bēblē·ôtākār] 37
library bibliothèque *f* [bēblē·ôtāk] 121
libretto livret *m* [lēvrā] 177
license plate plaque *f* d'immatriculation [pläk dēmätrēkēläsyôN] 54
life: ~ belt bouée *f* de sauvetage [bōō·ā də sōvtäzh] 76; **~ jacket** gilet *m* de sauvetage [zhēlā də sōvtäzh] 71
lifeboat canot *m* de sauvetage [känō də sōvtäzh] 75
lifeguard maître-nageur *m* [māt(ə)r) näzhār] 185
light, pale clair [klār] 127
light *(noun)* lumière *f* [lēmyār] 88; **~ bulb** ampoule *f* électrique [äNpōōl ālektrēk] 92
lighter briquet *m* [brēkā] 140; **~ fluid** essence *f* à briquet [esäNs ä brēkā] 140
lighthouse phare *m* [fär] 76
lighting system éclairage *m* [āklārāzh] 54
lightning éclair *m* [āklār] 27
lights éclairage *m* [āklārāzh] 92
like: I'd ~ je voudrais [zhə vōōdrā] 73
lilacs lilas *m* [lēlä] 130
limbs membres *m/pl* [mäNb(ə)r]) 167
linen toile *f* [tô·äl] 137
liniment liniment *m;* friction *f* [lēnēmäN; frēksyôN] 161
lining doublure *f* [dōōblēr] 136
lip lèvre *f* [läv(ə)r)] 167
lipstick rouge *m* à lèvres [rōōzh ä läv(ə)r)] 141
liqueur liqueur *f* [lēkār] 112
liter litre *m* [lēt(ə)r)] 45
little: a ~ un peu [eN pā] 24
live vivre; habiter [vēv(ə)r); äbētā] 119; 14
liver foie *m* [fô·ä] 106; **~ problem** maladie *f* du foie [mälädē dē fô·ä] 170
living room séjour *m* [sāzhōōr] 93
loafers mocassins *m/pl* [môkäseN] 139
loan prêter [prātā] 57
lobby vestibule *m;* hall *m* [vestēbäl; ôl] 92
lobster homard *m* [ômär] 104; **spiny ~** langouste *f* [läNgōōst] 105
local call communication *f* urbaine [kômēnēkäsyôN ērben] 149
located: is ~ se trouve [sə trōōv] 19
lock *(noun)* serrure *f* [serēr] 92
lock up fermer à clé [fermā ä klā] 92
locker room vestiaire *m* [vestyār] 186
lockjaw constriction des mâchoires [kôNstrēksyôN dā mäshô·är] 171
locksmith serrurier *m* [serēryā] 37
long long [lôN] 133; **~ wave** gran-

des ondes *f/pl* [gräNdzôNd] 182
look after prendre soin de [präNd(ər) sô·eN də] 48
look for chercher [shershā] 18
loosen desserrer [deserā] 55
lost perdu [perdē] 153; **~ and found office** bureau *m* des objets trouvés [bērō dāzôbzhā trōōvā] 121
loss perte *f* [pert] 153
lounge salle *f* de séjour [säl də sāzhōōr] 74
love *(noun)* amour *m* [ämōōr] 184
love *(verb)* aimer [āmā] 184
lovely charmant [shärmäN] 16
low bas, -se [bä, bäs] 169; **~ pressure** *(system)* basses pressions *f/pl* [bäs presyôN] 27
lubricant lubrifiant *m* [lēbrēfyäN] 54
lubrication lubrification *f* [lēbrēfēkäsyôN] 46
luck: Good ~ Bonne chance [bôn shäNs] 23
luggage bagages *m/pl* [bägäzh] 59; **~ car** fourgon *m* [fōōrgôN] 64; **~ locker** consigne *f* automatique [kôNsēn(yə) ōtōmätēk] 63; **~ rack** filet *m* [fēlā] 67
lumbago lumbago *m* [lôNbägō] 171
lunch déjeuner *m* [dāzhānā] 92
lung poumon *m* [pōōmôN] 167

M

mackerel maquereau *m* [mäkərō] 104
madam madame [mädäm] 13
magazine revue *f* [rəvē] 182; **fashion ~** journal *m* de modes [zhōōrnäl də môd] 182
maid femme *f* de chambre [fäm də shäNb(ər)] 87
maiden name nom *m* de jeune fille [nôN də zhān fē'ē] 79
mail *(verb)* expédier [ekspādē·ā] 34
mail *(noun)* courrier *m* [kōōryā] 85; **~ box** boîte *f* aux lettres [bô·ät ō let(ər)] 145; **~man** facteur *m* [fäktār] 37
main road route *f* principale [rōōt preNsēpäl] 43; **~ station** gare *f* centrale [gär säNträl] 60; **~ street** rue *f* principale [rē preNsēpäl] 43
major matière *f* principale [mätyār preNsēpäl] 38
male organ verge *f* [vārzh] 167
malt liquor bière *f* de malt [byār də mält] 111
manager gérant *m* [zhāräN] 23
manicure manucure *f* [mänēkēr] 156;
many: how ~ combien de [kôNbyeN də] 18
map carte *f;* plan *m* [kärt; pläN] 40, 130; **road ~** carte *f* routière [kärt rōōtyār] 130
march mars [märs] 33
marital status situation *f* de famille [sētē·äsyôN də fämē'ē] 79
mark signe *m* [sēn(yə)] 79
markmanship tir *m* [tēr] 189
maroon rouge foncé [rōōzh fôNsā] 194
marriage mariage *m* [märē·äzh] 22
married marié [märē·ā] 79
mascara rimmel *m* [rēmel] 141
mass messe *f* [mes] 125; **high ~** grand-messe *f* [gräNmes] 125
massage *(noun)* massage *m* [mäsäzh] 175
massage *(verb)* masser [mäsā] 175
mast mât *m* [mä] 76
mat dessous *m* de plat [desōō də plä] 144
matches allumettes *f/pl* [älēmet] 140
material tissu *m* [tēsē] 137
mathematics mathématiques *f/pl* [mätāmätēk] 39

mattress matelas *m* [mätlä] 90
maxillary sinus sinus *m* [sēnēs] 167
maximum speed vitesse *f* maximum [vētes mäksēmôm] 42
May mai [mā] 33
maybe peut-être [pātāt(ər)] 21
meal repas *m* [repä] 86
mean: means veut dire [vā dēr] 18
meanwhile entre-temps [äNtrətäN] 32
measles rougeole *f* [ro͞ozhôl] 171
meat viande *f* [vē·äNd] 105
mechanic mécanicien *m* [mākänē-syeN] 37
mechanical engineering construction *f* mécanique [kôNstrēksyôN mākänēk] 39
medical director médecin *m* chef [mādəsēN shef] 172
medicinal spring source *f* médicinale [so͞ors mādēsēnäl] 175
medicine remède *m* [remād] 161
medicine *(discipl.)* médecine *f* [mādəsēn] 39
medium *(done)* à point [ä pô·eN] 100
meet *(again)* se revoir [sə revô·är] 183
melon melon *m* [məlôN] 110
membership card carte *f* de membre [kärt də mäNb(ər)] 95
memorial monument *m* commémoratif [mônēmäN kômemôrätēf] 119
men's room toilettes *f/pl* pour messieurs [tô·älet po͞or mesyā] 92
menstruation règles *f/pl* [rāg'əl] 167
mention: don't ~ it il n'y a pas de quoi [ēlnyä pä də kô·ä] 21
meringue méringue *f* [māreNg] 113
metabolism métabolisme *m* [mātäbōlēsm] 167
metalworker métallurgiste *m* [mātälērzhēst] 37
meter mètre *m* [māt(ər)] 192
Methodist méthodiste *m* [mātôdēst] 124
middle milieu *m* [mēlēyā] 65; **~ ear inflammation** otite *f* [ôtēt] 171
midnight minuit *f* [mēnē·ē] 31
midwife sage-femme *f* [säzh-fäm] 37
mile lieue *f* [lēyā] 193; **nautical ~** mille *m* marin [mēl märeN] 193
mileage indicator compteur *m* kilométrique [kôNtār kēlōmātrēk] 54
military base base *f* militaire [bäz mēlētār] 121
milk lait *m* [lā] 114
millimeter millimètre *m* [mēlēmāt(ər)] 193
mine à moi [ä mô·ä] 80
miner mineur *m* [mēnār] 37
minerals minéraux *m/pl* [mēnārō] 175
miniature golf mini-golf *m* [mēnēgôlf] 180
ministry ministère *m* [mēnēstār] 121
minute minute *f* [mēnēt] 30
mirroir miroir *m* [mērô·är] 92
missing: is ~ il manque [ēl mäNk] 63
Miss mademoiselle *f* [mädəmô·äzel] 13
mist brouillard *m* [bro͞oyär] 27
molar molaire *f* [môlār] 174
mole môle *m* [môl] 76
moment instant *m* [eNstäN] 87; **at the ~** actuellement [äktē·elmäN] 32
monastery couvent *m* [ko͞oväN] 124
Monday lundi [leNdē] 33
money de l'argent *m* [də lärzhäN] 151; **~ exchange** bureau *m* de change [bērō də shäNzh] 60; **~ order** mandat-carte *m* [mäNdä kärt] 146
month mois *m* [mô·ä] 32
monument monument *m* [mônē-

mäN] 119
moon lune *f* [lēn] 27
moped cyclomoteur *m* [sēklōmôtār] 41
morning matin *m* [mäteN] 31; **good ~** bonjour [bôNzhōōr] 12; **this ~** ce matin [sə mäteN] 31
mortal danger danger *m* de mort [däNzhā də môr] 191
mortgage hypothèque *f* [ēpôtāk] 152
mosaic mosaïque *f* [môzä·ēk] 125
Moslem musulman [mēzēlmäN] 124
mosque mosquée *f* [môskā] 125
motel motel *m* [môtel] 81
mother mère *f* [mār] 35; **~-in-law** belle-mère *f* [bel-mār] 35
motion pictures cinéma *m* [sēnāmä] 121
motor moteur *m* [môtār] 54; **~ oil** huile *f* de moteur [ē·ēl də môtār] 46; **~ scooter** scooter *m* [skōōtār] 41
motorail service train *m* auto-couchettes [treN ôtō-kōōshet] 60
motorboat bateau *m* à moteur [bätō ä môtār] 75
motorcycle moto *f* [môtō] 41
mountain montagne *f* [môNtän(yə)] 122; **~ range** chaîne *f* de montagnes [shen də môNtän(yə)] 122; **~ climber** alpiniste *m* [älpēnēst] 189; **~ climbing** alpinisme *m* [älpēnēsm] 189
mousse mousse *f* [mōōs] 109
moustache moustaches *f/pl* [mōōstäsh] 157
mouth bouche *f* [bōōsh] 168
mouthwash eau *f* dentifrice [ō däNtēfrēs] 161
move *(verb)* bouger [bōōzhā] 164; **~ in** emménager [äNmānäzhā] 92; **~ out** déménager [dāmānäzhā] 92
move *(games)* coup *m* [kōō] 181
movie film *m* [fēlm] 179
movies cinéma *m* [sēnāmä] 179
Mr. monsieur [məsyā] 12
Mrs. madame [mädäm] 12
much: too ~ trop [trō] 127; **how ~** combien de [kôNbyeN də] 127
mucous membrane muqueuse *f* [mēkāz] 168
mud boue *f* minérale [bōō mēnāräl] 175; **~ pack** enveloppement de boue [äNvelôpmäN də bōō] 175
muggy lourd [lōōr] 25
mumps oreillons *m/pl* [ôrāyôN] 171
murder meurtre *m* [mārt(ər)] 153
Muscatel muscat *m* [mēskä] 111
muscle muscle *m* [mēsk'əl] 168
museum musée *m* [mēzā] 116
mushrooms champignons *m/pl* [shäNpēnyôN] 101
music musique *f* [mēzēk] 178
musician musicien *m* [mēzēsyeN] 178
mussels moules *f/pl* [mōōl] 104
mustard moutarde *f* [mōōtärd] 101; **~ jar** moutardier *m* [mōōtärdyā] 97
mutton mouton *m* [mōōtôN] 105
my ma, mon, mes [mä, môN, mā] 48

N

nail ongle *m* [ôNg'əl] 156; **~ file** lime *f* à ongles [lēm ä ôNg'əl] 141; **~ polish** vernis *m* à ongles [vernē ä ôNg'əl] 141; **~ polish remover** dissolvant *m* [dēsôlväN] 141; **~ scissors** ciseaux *m/pl* à ongles [sēzō ä ôNg'əl] 141
name nom *m* (de famille) [nôN (də fämē'ē)] 14 (79); **first ~** prénom *m* [prānôN] 79

napkin serviette *f* [servyet] 97
narcotics stupéfiants *m/pl* [stēpā-fē·äN] 154
narrow étroit [ātrô·ä] 127
national park parc *m* national [pärk näsyônäl] 121
nationality nationalité [näsyônälētā] 79; **~ plate** plaque *f* de nationalité [pläk də näsyônäletā] 79
nausea nausée *f/pl* [nōzā] 171; **nauseated: I feel ~** j'ai mal au cœur [zhā mäl ō kär] 164
nave nef *f* [nef] 125
nearby près d'ici [prā dēsē] 44
nearest prochain [prôsheN] 19
near-sighted myope [mē·ôp] 138
neck cou *m* [ko͞o] 168; **back of the ~** nuque *f* [nēk] 168; **nape of the ~** nuque *f* [nēk] 168
necklace châine *f* [shān] 133
need *(Verb)* avoir besoin de [avô·är bezô·eN də] 18
needle aiguille *f* [āgē·ē] 136; **sewing ~** aiguille *f* à coudre [āgē·ē ä ko͞od(ər)] 136
negative négatif *m* [nāgätēf] 131
nephew neveu *m* [nevā] 35
nephritis néphrite *f* [nāfrēt] 171
nerve(s) nerf(s) *m/pl* [nār] 168
neuralgia névralgie *f* [nāvrälzhē] 171
neurologist neurologue *m* [nārōlôg] 162
neutral *(gear)* point *m* mort [pô·eN môr] 53
never jamais [zhämā] 21
new nouveau, **~** elle [no͞ovō, no͞ovel] 50
news informations *f/pl* [eNfôrmä-syôN] 182; **~ dealer** marchand *m* de journaux [märshäN də zho͞or-nō] 129
newspaper journal *m* [zho͞ornäl] 86
next prochain [prôsheN] 32
nice agréable [ägrā·äb'əl] 184
niece nièce *f* [nē·äs] 35
night nuit *f* [nē·ē] 82; **all ~** toute la nuit [to͞ot lä nē·ē] 44; **at ~** la nuit [lä nē·ē] 31; **Good ~** Bonne nuit [bônē·ē] 17; **~** club boîte *f* de nuit [bô·ät də nē·ē] 180; **~ duty** service *m* de nuit [servēs də nē·ē] 159; **~ rate** tarif *m* de nuit [tärēf də nē·ē] 148; **~ shirt; nightie** chemise *f* de nuit [shemēz də nē·ē] 134
night's lodging nuitée *f* [nē·ētā] 92
nine neuf [nāf] 28
ninepins jeu *m* de quille [zhā də kē·ē] 189
no non [nôN] 21; **~ admittance** entrée interdite [äNtrā eNterdēt] 191
nobody personne [persôn] 49
non-swimmer non-nageur *m* [nôN-näzhār] 186
noodles nouilles *f/pl* [no͞o·ē] 103
noon midi *m* [mēdē] 31; **this ~** ce midi [sə mēdē] 32
nose né *m* [nā] 168
nosebleed saignements *m/pl* du nez [sān(yə)mäN dē nā] 171
notary notaire *m* [nôtār] 37
nothing rien *m* [rē·eN] 21
novel roman *m* [rômäN] 130; **detective ~** roman *m* policier [rômäN pôlēsyā] 130
November novembre [nôväNb(ər)] 33
now maintenant [meNtənäN] 32; **~ and then** de temps à autre [də täNzä ōt(ər)] 32
nude nu [nē] 185; **~ beach** plage *f* de nudistes [pläzh də nēdēst] 186
number numéro *m* [nēmārō] 64
nurse *m/f* infirmier, -ère [eNfērmyā, -ār] 37; **night ~** infirmière *f* de nuit [eNfērmyār də nē·ē] 172
nursery chambre *f* d'enfants [shäNb(ər) däNfäN] 93

nutmeg muscade *f* [mēskäd] 101
nuts noix *f/pl* [nô·ä] 110
nylon nylon *m* [nēlôN] 137

O

oarsman rameur *m* [rämār] 189
observatory observatoire *m* [obser-vätô·är] 121
occupation profession *f* [prôfe-syôN] 79
occupied occupé [ôkēpā] 66
ocean océan *m* [ôsā·äN] 77
October octobre [oktôb(ər)] 33
offer offrir [ôfrēr] 16
office bureau *m* [bērō] 74
office hours *(med.)* consultations *f/pl* [kôNsēltäsyôN] 162
officer officier *m* [ôfēsyā] 74; **deck ~** premier officier [prəmyā ôfē-syā] 74
off-side hors-jeu [ôr-zhā] 190
often: how ~ combien de fois [kôN-byeN də fô·ä] 72
oil huile *f* [ē·ēl] 45; **~ change** vi-dange *f* d'huile [vēdäNzh dē·ēl] 46; **~ level** niveau *m* d'huile [nēvō dē·ēl] 46; **~ filter** filtre *m* à huile [fēlt(ər) ä ē·ēl] 54; **~ pump** pompe *f* à huile [pôNp ä ē·ēl] 54
ointment pommade *f* [pômäd] 161; **boric acid ~** acide *m* borique [äsēd bôrēk] 160; **burn ~** pomma-de *f* contre les brulûres [pômäd kôNt(ər) lā brēlēr] 160
old: I'm... years ~ j'ai... ans [zhā... äN] 34
older plus âgé [plēzäzhā] 34
olives olives *f/pl* [ôlēv] 102
one un, une [eN, ēn] 78; **~ way street** sens *m* unique [säNs ēnēk] 58; **~ way ticket** (billet) aller [(bēyā) älā] 62
onion oignon *m* [ônyôN] 101
open *(adj.)* ouvert [o͞ovār] 44
open *(verb)* ouvrir [o͞ovrēr] 118; **Do not ~** Ne pas ouvrir [nə päzo͞o-vrēr] 191; **~ market** marché *m* [märshā] 122
opera opéra *m* [ôpärä] 178; **~ glas-ses** jumelles *f/pl* de théâtre [zhē-mel də tā·ät(ər)] 178
operate on opérer [opārā] 172
operating room salle *f* d'opération [säl dôpāräsäsyôN] 172
operation opération *f* [ôpäräsyôN] 172
operator téléphoniste *m/f* [tālāfô-nēst] 150
operetta opérette *f* [ōpäret] 178
ophthalmologist oculiste *m* [ôkē-lēst] 162
optician opticien *m* [ôptēsyeN] 37
oral surgeon chirurgien *m* dentiste [shērērzhē·eN däNtēst] 41
orange orange *f* [ôräNzh] 110; **~ juice** jus *m* d'orange *[zhē* dô-räNzh] 112; **~ stick** cure-ongles *m* [kēr-ôNg'əl] 141
orangeade orangeade *f* [ôräNzhäd] 112
orchestra orchestre *m* [ôrkest(ər)] 178; **~ seats** fauteuils *m/pl* d'or-chestre [fôtā·ē dôrkest(ər)] 178
orchid orchidée *f* [ôrkēdā] 130
order *(verb)* commander [kômäNdā] 115; **out of ~** ...ne marche pas [nə märsh pä] 23
organ orgue *m* [ôrg] 125
orthodontist (orthodonto-)stomato-logiste *m* [(ôrtōdôNtō-)stōmätōlō-zhēst] 174
orthopedist orthopédiste *m* [ôrtō-pādēst] 162
otolaryngolist O.R.L. *m* [ō-är-el] 162
ouverture ouverture *f* [o͞ovärtēr] 178
overpass pont *m* [pôN] 65
oysters huîtres *f/pl* [ē·ēt(ər)] 102

P

pack; packet (petit) paquet *m* [(pətē) päkā] 126
package colis *m* [kôlē] 150
pad bloc *m* [blôk] 138; **scratch ~** bloc-notes *m* [blôk nôt] 138; **sketch ~** bloc à dessin [blôk ä deseN] 138
pail seau *m* [sō] 92
pain mal *m;* douleurs *f/pl* [mäl; do͞olār] 163, 171; **~ killer** remède *m* contre la douleur [rəmād kôNt(ər) lä do͞olār] 173; **~ pills** comprimés *m/pl* contre la douleur [kôNprēmā kôNt(ər) lä do͞olār] 161
paint *(verb)* peindre [peNd(ər)] 119; **~ job** laque *m/f* [läk] 54
painter peintre *m* [peNt(ər)] 37
painting *(noun)* peinture *f* [peNtēr] 39
pair paire *f* [pār] 126
pajamas pyjama *m* [pēzhämä] 134
palace palais *m* [pälā] 119
palate palais *m* [pälā] 168
pale, light clair [klār] 127
pancreas pancréas *m* [päNkrā·äs] 168
panties slip *m* [slēp] 134
pants pantalon *m* [päNtälôN] 134; **~ suit** costume *m* [kôstēm] 134
paper papier *m* [päpyā] 132; **~-back** livre *m* de poche [lēv(ər) də pôsh] 130; **~ napkins** serviettes *f/pl* en papier [servyet äN päpyā] 144
papers papiers *m/pl* [päpyā] 78
paprika paprika *m* [päprēkä] 101
parallel bars barres *f/pl* parallèles [bär pärälāl] 188
paralysis paralysie *f* [pärälēzē] 171
parcel colis *m* [kôlē] 145; **small ~** petit colis *m* [pətē kôlē] 150
pardon: Beg your ~ pardon [pärdôN] 20; 22
parents parents *m/pl* [päräN] 35
park *(verb)* stationner [stäsyônā] 43
park *(noun)* parc *m* [pärk] 122
parka anorak *m* [änôräk] 134
parking: no ~ stationnement *m* interdit [stäsyônmäN eNterdē] 42; **~ disc** disque *m* bleu [dēsk blā] 42; **~ lights** feux *m/pl* de position [fā də pôzēsyôN] 53; **~ lot** parking *m* [pärkēng] 42; **~ meter** parcomètre *m* [pärkômāt(ər)] 42; **~ space** box *m* [bôks] 44
parsley persil *m* [persēl] 101
part *(stage)* rôle *m* [rôl] 178
part raie *f* [rā] 157
part of town quartier *m* [kärtyā] 122
partridge perdrix *f* [perdrē] 105
party fête *f* [fāt] 183; **~ games** jeux *m/pl* de société [zhā də sôsē·ātā] 182
pass *(mountain)* col *m* [kôl] 42
pass *(verb)* passer [päsā] 99
pass *(on the road)* dépasser; doubler [dāpäsā; do͞oblā] 43
passenger passager *m* [päsäzhā] 77; **~ car** voiture *f* particulière [vô·ätēr pärtēkēlyār] 40
passing: no ~ interdiction *f* de dépasser [eNterdēksyôN də dāpäsā] 42; **~ out** évanouissement *m* [āväno͞o·ēsmäN] 171
passport passeport *m* [päspôr] 78; **~ control** contrôle *m* des passeports [kôNtrôl dā päspôr] 79
pastime passe-temps *m* [pästäN] 182
pastor curé *m;* pasteur *m* [kērā; pästār] 125
pastry chef pâtissier *m* [pätēsyā] 37
patch réparer [rāpärā] 46
path chemin *m;* route *f* [shmeN; ro͞ot] 122; 19
patient malade *m* [mäläd] 172
patio cour *f* intérieure [ko͞or eN-

tārē·ǟr] 92
patterned imprimé [eNprēmā] 137
pawn *(chess)* pion *m* [pyôN] 181
pay *(verb)* payer [pāyā] 41; **I'd like to ~** l'addition, s.v.p. [lädēsyôN sēl vo͞o plā] 115; **~ out** payer; verser [pāyā; versā] 152
payment paiement *m* [pāmäN] 152
peas petits pois *m/pl* [pətē pô·ä] 108
peach pêche *f* [pāsh] 110
peanuts cacahouètes *f/pl* [kä-kä·o͞o·et] 110
pear poire *f* [pô·är] 110
pearles perles *f/pl* [pārl] 133
pedal pédale *f* [pādäl] 54
pedestrian piéton *m* [pyātôN] 122; **~ crossing** passage *m* clouté [pä-säzh klo͞otā] 122
pediatrician pédiatre *m* [pādē·ät(ər)] 162
pedicure pédicure *f* [pādēkē̄r] 156
pelvis bassin *m;* bas-ventre *m* [bä-seN; bäväNt(ər)] 168
pen: fountain ~ stylo *m* [stēlō] 138; **ballpoint ~** stylo *m* à bille [stēlō ä bēˈē] 138
penalty kick penalty *m* [pēnältē] 190
pencil crayon *m* [krāyôN] 138
pendant pendant *m* [päNdäN] 133
penis pénis *m* [pānēs] 168
pension pension *f* [päNsyôN] 81
people personnes *f/pl* [persôn] 41
pepper poivre *m* [pô·äv(ər)] 97; **~ mill** moulin *m* à poivre [mo͞oleN ä pô·äv(ər)] 97; **~ shaker** poivrier *m* [pô·ävrēyā] 97
peppermint menthe *f* [mäNt] 161
peppers poivrons *m/pl* [pô·ävrôN] 108
peptic ulcer ulcère *m* d'estomac [ēl-sār destōmä] 171
perch perche *f* [pārsh] 104
performance représentation *f* [re-prāzäNtäsyôN] 176
perfume parfum *m* [pärfeN] 141
perhaps peut-être [pǟtāt(ər)] 21
period époque *f* [āpôk] 119
permanent set permanente *f* [per-mänäNt] 155
personal personnel [persônel] 80
petticoat jupon *m* [zhēpôN] 134
pharmacist pharmacien *m* [färmā-syeN] 37
pharmacy pharmacie *f* [färmäsē] 159; 39
pheasant faisan *m* [fāzäN] 105
phone *(verb)* téléphoner à [tālāfônā ä] 78
phone *(noun)* téléphone *m* [tālāfôn] 147; **~ book** annuaire *m* [änē̄·är] 147; **~ booth** cabine *f* télépho-nique [käbēn tālāfônēk] 147; **~ call** coup *m* de téléphone [ko͞o də tālāfôn] 147; **pay ~** taxiphone *m* [täksēfôn] 148
photo shop magasin *m* de photo [mägäzeN də fōtō] 131
photographer photographe *m* [fōtō-gräf] 74
physics physique *f* [fēzēk] 39
pianist pianiste *m/f* [pē·änēst] 178
piano recital récital *m* de piano [rā-sētäl də pē·änō] 178
pick up venir chercher [vənēr sher-shā] 41
picture tableau *m;* image *f* [täblō; ēmäzh] 119; 144
picture film *m* [fēlm] 179
piece bout *m;* morceau *m* [bo͞o; môrsō] 57; 126
pier jetée *f* [zhetā] 77
pike-perch sandre *f* [säNd(ər)] 104
piles hémorroïdes *f/pl* [āmôrō·ēd] 171
pill pilule *f;* comprimé *m* [pēlē̄l; kôNprēmā] 161
pillar pilier *m* [pēlyā] 125
pillow oreiller *m* [ôrāyā] 87; **~-case**

taie *f* d'oreiller [tā dôrāyā] 90
pilot commandant *m* de bord [kômäNdäN dә bôr] 71
pin épingle *f* [āpeNg'әl] 136; **bobby pins** pinces *f/pl* à cheveux [peNs ä shevā] 140
pin up *(hair)* relever [rәlevā] 155
pincers tenailles *f/pl* [tenä'ē] 57
pinch serrer [serā] 139
pineapple ananas *m* [änänä] 110;
ping-pong: play ~ jouer au ping-pong [zhōō·ā ō pēngpôNg] 180
pink rose [rôz] 194
pinkie auriculaire *m* [ôrēkēlär] 167
pipe tuyau *m* [tē·ēyō] 54
pipe *(tobacco)* pipe *f* [pēp] 140; **~ cleaner** cure-pipe *m* [kēr-pēp] 140
piston piston *m* [pēstôN] 54; **~ ring** segment *m* de piston [segmäN dә pēstôN] 54
pitcher pichet *m* [pēchā] 97; **cream ~** pot *m* à lait [pôtä lā] 97
pity: what a ~ (quel) dommage [(kāl) dômäzh] 22
place place *f* [pläs] 66; **~ of birth** lieu *m* de naissance [lēyā dә nesäNs] 79; **~ of residence** domicile *m* [dômēsēl] 79
plaice plie *f* [plē] 104
plane avion *m;* appareil *m* [ävyôN; äpärā·ē] 68
plate plaque *f* [pläk] 174
plate assiette *f* [äsyet] 97; **bread ~** petite assiette *f* [pәtēt äsyet] 97; **soup ~** assiette *f* à soupe [äsyet ä sōōp] 97
platform quai *m;* voie *f* [kā; vô·ä] 60
play *(verb)* jouer [zhōō·ā] 182
play *(noun)* pièce *f* (de théâtre) [pyās (dә tā·ät(әr))] 178
player joueur *m* [zhōō·ār] 190
playground terrain *m* de jeux [tereN dā zhā] 95
playing cards cartes *f/pl* à jouer [kärt ä zhōō·ā] 144
playroom nurserie *f* [nārsrē] 77
please s'il vous plaît [sēl vōō plā] 20
pleasure: with ~ avec plaisir [ävek plāzēr] 21
plenty assez [äsā] 127
pleurisy pleurésie *f* [plārāzē] 171
pliers pinces *f/pl* [peNs] 57
plug fiche *f;* prise *f* [fēsh; prēz] 92
plum prune *f* [prēn] 110
plumber plombier *m* [plôNbyā] 37
pneumonia pneumonie *f* [pnāmōnē] 171
point point *m* [pô·eN] 188
poisoning empoisonnement *m* [äNpô·äzônmäN] 171
police police *f* [pôlēs] 49; **~ car** voiture *f* de police [vô·ätēr dә pôlēs] 154; **~-man** agent *m* de police [äzhäN dә pôlēs] 122; **~ station** commissariat *m* de police [kômēsärē·ä dә pôlēs] 116
polish *(verb)* faire briller [fār brēyā] 156
political science sciences *f/pl* politiques [sē·äNs pôlētēk] 39
pool hall billard *m* [bēyär] 180
pork porc *m* [pôr] 105
port *(land)* port *m* [pôr] 77
port *(side)* bâbord *m* [bäbôr] 77; **~ fees** taxe *f* portuaire [täks pôrtē·ār] 77
portal portail *m* [pôrtä'ē] 125
porter porteur *m* [pôrtār] 64
portion plat *m* [plä] 115
possible possible [pôsēb'әl] 22
post office bureau *m* de poste [bērō dә pôst] 116; **~ office box** boîte *f* postale [bô·ät pôstäl] 150
postage port *m* [pôr] 150
postal: ~ clerk employé *m* des postes [äNplô·äyā dā pôst] 150; **~ savings book** livret *m* de caisse d'épargne postale [lēvrā dә kes

dāpärn(yə) pôstäl] 150; ~ **transfer** mandat-poste *m* [mäNdä pôst] 146
postcard carte *f* postale [kärt pôstäl] 85; **picture** ~ carte *f* postale illustrée [kärt pôstäl ēlēstrā] 150
postman facteur *m* [fäktār] 150
pot pot *m* [pō] 92; **coffee** ~ cafetière *f* [käfetyār] 97; **tea** ~ théière *f* [tā·ēyār] 97
potatoes pommes *f/pl* de terre [pôm də tār] 108; **baked** ~ pommes *f* de terre rôties au four [~ rôtē ō fōōr] 109; **boiled** ~ pommes *f* nature [pôm nätēr] 109; **fried** ~ pommes *f* sautées [pôm sōtā] 109; **mashed** ~ pommes *f* mousseline [pôm mōōslēn] 109
pound livre *f* [lēv(ər)] 199
pouder poudre *f* [pōōd(ər)] 141; ~ **puff** houppette *f* [ōōpet] 141
power station centrale *f* électrique [säNträl ālektrēk] 122; ~ **steering** direction *f* assistée [dēreksyôN äsēstā] 54
practice entrainement *m* [äNtrānmäN] 188
prawns crevettes *f/pl* [krevet] 104
preach faire le sermon [fār lə sermôN] 123
precipitation chute *f* de pluie [shēt də plē·ē] 27
pregnancy grossesse *f* [grōses] 168
premium super [sēpār] 45
prepaid reply réponse *f* payée [rāpôNs pāyā] 147
prescribed prescrit [preskrē] 159
prescription ordonnnance *f* [ôrdônäNs] 159
present cadeau *m* [kädō] 80
press *(verb)* repasser [rəpäsā] 137
previously avant [äväN] 32
price prix *m* [prē] 92
priest prêtre *m* [prāt(ər)] 123
print *(photo)* épreuve *f* [āprāv] 131
printed matter imprimé *m* [eNprēmā] 145
priority road route *f* à priorité [rōōt ä prē·ôrētā] 58
prison prison *f* [prēzôN] 154
probably probablement [prôbäb'əlmäN] 21
procession procession *f* [prôsesyôN] 125
producer producteur *m* [prôdēktār] 178
production production *f* [prôdēksyôN] 178
program programme *m* [prôgräm] 178
pronounce prononcer [prônôNsā] 24
prophylactics préservatifs *m/pl* [prāzervätēf] 141
Protestant protestant *m* [prôtestäN] 124
psychiatrist psychiatre *m* [psēkyät(ər)] 162
psychologist psychologue *m* [psēkôlôg] 162
psychology psychologie *f* [psēkôlozhē] 39
public: ~ **garden** parc *m* [pärk] 122; ~ **notices** avis *m* au public [ävē ō pēblēk] 191; ~ **rest room** toilettes *f/pl* publiques [tô·älet pēblēk] 122
pull *(tooth)* aracher [äräshā] 173
pulpit chaire *f* [shār] 125
pump room buvette *f* [bēvet] 175
pumpkin courge *f* [kōōrzh] 108
puncture trou *m* [trōō] 47
pupil élève *m* [ālāv] 37
purple pourpre [pōōrp(ər)] 194
purse porte-monnaie *m* [pôrtmônā] 144
purser commissaire *m* [kômēsār] 74
push pousser [pōōsā] 191

Q

quai quai *m* [kā] 77
quail caille *f* [kä'ē] 105
quarter quart *m* [kär] 30
queen *(chess)* reine *f* [rān] 181
question: out of the ~ pas question [pä kestyôN] 21
quickly immédiatement [ēmädē·ätmäN] 48

R

rabbi rabbin *m* [räbeN] 125
rabbit lapin *m* [läpeN] 105
race course *f* [ko͞ors] 187; **~ car driver** coureur *m* automobile [ko͞orār ôtōmōbēl] 187
racing: ~ boat bateau *m* de course [bätō də ko͞ors] 187; **~ car** voiture *f* de course [vô·ätēr də ko͞ors] 187
radiation therapy traitement *m* par les rayons [trātmäN pär lā rāyôN] 175
radiator radiateur *m* [rädē·ätār] 53; **~ grill** volet *m* du radiateur [vôlā dē rädē·ätār] 54
radio radio *f* [rädē·ō] 180; **~ play** pièce *f* radiophonique [pyäs rädē·ōfōnēk] 182; **~ room** cabine *f* radio [käbēn rädē·ō] 74
rag chiffon *m* [shēfôN] 57
rail car automotrice *f* [ôtōmôtrēs] 60
railroad chemin *m* de fer [shəmeN də fār] 67; **~ crossing** passage *m* à niveau [päsäzh ä nēvō] 42; **~ man** cheminot *m* [shəmēnō] 37; **~ station** gare *f* [gär] 67
rain *(noun)* pluie *f* [plē·ē] 25; **it's raining** il pleut [ēl plā] 25
raincoat imperméable *m* [eNpermā·äb'əl] 134
raisins raisins *m/pl* secs [rāzeN sek] 101
ranch wagon voiture *m* familiale [vô·ātēr fämēlyäl] 40
rare *(meat)* saignant [senyäN] 100
rash éruption *f* [ārēpsyôN] 171
raspberries framboises *f/pl* [fräNbô·äz] 110
rather: I'd ~ j'aimerais mieux [zhāmerā myā] 20
raw cru [krē] 100
razor rasoir *m* (mécanique) [räzô·är (mēkänēk)] 141; **safety ~** rasoir *m* de sûreté [räzô·är də sērtā] 141; **~ blades** lames *f/pl* de rasoir [läm də räzô·är] 141; **~ cut** coupe *f* au rasoir [ko͞op ō räzô·är] 157
reading room salle *f* de lecture [säl də lektēr] 74
ready prêt, -e [prā, prāt] 50
real estate agency agence *f* immobilière [äzhäNs ēmôbēlyār] 129
rear: at the ~ à l'arrière [ä läryār] 65; **~ end collision** téléscopage *m* [tāläskôpäzh] 49; **~ lights** feux *m/pl* arrières [fā äryār] 53; **~ motor** moteur *m* à l'arrière [môtār ä l'äryār] 54; **~ view mirror** rétroviseur *m* [rātrōvēzār] 55
receipt quittance *f* [kētäNs] 150
recently l'autre jour [lōt(ər) zho͞or] 32
reception desk réception *f* [rāsepsyôN] 92
recommend recommander [rekômäNdā] 81
record disque *m* [dēsk] 130; **~ player** électrophone *m;* platine *f* [ālektrōfôn; plätēn] 182
recording tape bande *f* magnétique [bäNd mänyātēk] 182
recreation room salle *f* commune [säl kômēn] 95
red rouge [ro͞ozh] 194; **~ cabbage** chou *m* rouge [sho͞o ro͞ozh] 108; **~ currants** groseilles *f/pl* [grô-

zā'ē] 110
reduced réduit [rādē·ē] 62; **~ rate** réduction *f* [rādēksyôN] 83
referee arbitre *m* [ärbēt(ər)] 189
refill remplir [räNplēr] 140
refreshments buvette *f;* bar *m* [bēvet; bär] 191
refrigerator réfrigérateur *m* [rāfrēzhārätār] 92
regards bon souvenir *m* [bôN so͞ovenēr] 16
registered letter lettre *f* recommandée [let(ər) rekômäNdā] 150
registration immatriculation *f* [ēmätrēkēläsyôN] 43; **~ form** fiche *f* d'hôtel [fēsh dôtel] 84
regret *(noun)* regret *m* [rəgrā] 22
regular (essence *f*) ordinaire *f* [(esäNs) ôrdēnār] 45
religion religion *f* [relēzhē·ôN] 125
religious religieux [relēzhē·ā] 125
remedy remède *m* [rəmād] 70
renew renouveler [reno͞ovlā] 79
rent *(noun)* loyer *m* [lô·äyā] 92
rent *(verb)* louer [lo͞o·ā] 41
repair *(verb)* réparer [rāpärā] 46
repair *(noun)* réparation *f* [rāpäräsyôN] 55; **~ shop** atelier *m* de réparation [ätelyā də rāpäräsyôN] 49
replace remplacer [räNpläsā] 138
reply *(noun)* réponse *f* [rāpôNs] 147
report déposer une plainte [dāpôzā ēn pleNt] 153
reservation réservation *f* [rāzerväsyôN] 71
reserve réserver; retenir [rāzervā; retenēr] 62, 82; **~ tank** bidon *m* de réserve [bēdôN də rāzerv] 45; **~ wheel** roue *f* de secours [ro͞o də seko͞or] 47
respiration respiration *f* [respēräsyôN] 168
rest room toilettes *f/pl* [tô·älet] 60
result résultat *m* [rāzēltä] 188
retailer commerçant *m* [kômersäN] 37
retiree retraité *m* [retrātā] 37
retread rechaper [reshäpā] 46
return flight vol *m* de retour [vôl də reto͞or] 71; **~ postage** port *m* de retour [pôr də reto͞or] 150
reverse gear marche *f* arrière [märsh äryār] 53
rheumatism rhumatisme *m* [rēmätēsm] 171
rhubarb rhubarbe *f* [rēbärb] 110
rib côte *f* [kôt] 168
ribbon ruban *m* [rēbäN] 136
rice riz *m* [rē] 109
ride *(verb)* rouler; monter à cheval [ro͞olā; môNtä ä shəväl] 66; 189
rider cavalier *m* [kävälyā] 189
riding équitation *f* [ākētäsyôN] 189; **~ stable** école *f* d'équitation [ākôl dākētäsyôN] 180
rifle range (stand *m* de) tir *m* [(stäNd də) tēr] 188
right! c'est ça! [sā sä] 21
right à droite [ä drô·ät] 40; **~ away** tout de suite [to͞otsē·ēt] 96; **~ of way** priorité *f* [prē·ôrētā] 43
ring bague *f* [bäg] 133; **wedding ~** alliance *f* [älyäNs] 133
rinse rinçage *m* [reNsäzh] 155
rise *(verb)* monter [môNtā] 25
river fleuve *m* [flāv] 70
road route *f* [ro͞ot] 19; **~ conditions** état *m* des routes [ātä dā ro͞ot] 25; **~ sign** panneau *m* de signalisation [pänô də sēnyälēzäsyôN] 43
roast rôti *m* [rôtē] 107; **~ chestnuts** marrons *m/pl* [märôN] 110
role rôle *m* [rôl] 178; **leading ~** premier rôle *m* [premyā rôl] 178
roll petit pain *m* [pətē peN] 98
roll rouleau *m* [ro͞olō] 126
Romanesque roman [rômäN] 125

roof capote *f* [käpôt] 55
room chambre *f*; [shäNb(ər) 82; **single ~** chambre *f* pour une personne [shäNb(ər) po͞or ēn persôn] 82; **double ~** chambre *f* à deux lits [shäNb(ər) ä dā lē] 82; **quiet ~** chambre *f* calme [shäNb(ər) kälm] 82
root racine *f* [räsēn] 174; **~ canal work** traitement *m* de la racine [trātmäN dəlä räsēn] 174
rope cordage *m* [kôrdäzh] 77
rose rose *f* [rōz] 130
rosemary romarin *m* [rōmäreN] 101
rough sea mer *f* agitée [mār äzhētā] 77
round rond [rôN] 156; **~ trip** aller et retour [älā ā reto͞or] 62; **~ trip ticket** billet *m* circulaire [bēyā sērkēlär] 73
route route *f;* ligne *f* [ro͞ot; lēn(yə)] 43; 59
row balcon *m* [bälkôN] 176
rowing aviron *m* [ävērôN] 189
rubber boots bottes *f/pl* de caoutchouc [bôt də kä·ōtsho͞ok] 139
ruby rubis *m* [rēbē] 133
rucksack sac *m* à dos [säk ä dō] 144
rudder rame *f* [räm] 77
ruin ruine *f* [rē·ēn] 122
rum rhum *m* [rôm] 112
run down *(battery)* est vide [ā vēd] 51

S

sacristan sacristain *m* [säkrēsteN] 125
sacristy sacristie *f* [säkrēstē] 125
saddle selle *f* [sel] 107
safety pin épingle *f* de sûreté [āpeNg'əl də sērtā] 136
sail *(noun)* voile *f* [vô·äl] 77
sail *(verb)* faire de la voile [fār dəlä vô·äl] 189; **~-boat** bateau *m* à voiles [bätō ä vô·äl] 75
sailing voile *f;* yachting *m* [vô·äl; yôtēng] 189; **~ school** école *f* de yachting [ākôl də yôtēng] 180
sailor matelot *m* [mätlō] 77
salesperson vendeur *m;* vendeuse *f* [väNdār; väNdāz] 37
saline content teneur *f* en sel [tenār äN sel] 186
salmon saumon *m* [sômôN] 104
salt sel *m* [sel] 97; **~ shaker** salièrè *f* [sälyār] 97
salted, salty salé [sälā] 100
salve pommade *f* [pômäd] 161
sandals sandales *f/pl* [säNdäl] 139
sandpaper papier *m* verré [päpyā verā] 57
sanitary napkins serviettes *f/pl* hygiéniques [servyet ēzhē·ānēk] 141
sapphire saphir *m* [säfēr] 133
Saturday samedi [sämdē] 33
sauce sauce *f;* jus *m* [sôs, zhē] 101
saucer soucoupe *f* [so͞oko͞op] 97
sauerkraut choucroute *f* [sho͞okro͞ot] 108
sauna sauna *m* [sōnä] 175
sausage saucisse *f* [sôsēs] 98
savings book livret *m* d'épargne [lēvrā dāpärn(yə)] 152
say dire [dēr] 24; **~ what?** pardon? [pärdôN] 24
scalp massage massage *m* [mäsäzh] 157
scarf écharpe *f* [āshärp] 134
scarlet fever scarlatine *f* [skärlätēn] 171
scenery décors *m/pl* [dākôr] 178
scheduled flight vol *m* régulier [vôl rāgēlyā] 71
scholar savant *m* [säväN] 37
school école *f* [ākôl] 38
sciatica sciatique *f* [sē·ätēk] 171
scientist savant *m* [säväN] 37

scissors ciseaux *m/pl* [sēzō] 136
screen écran *m* [ākräN] 179; **~ play** scénario *m* [sānärē·ō] 179
screw vis *f* [vēs] 55; **~ -driver** tournevis *m* [tōōrnvēs] 57
scuba diving plongée *f* sous-marine [plôNzhā sōōmärēn] 186; **~ equipment** équipement *m* de plongée sous-marine [ākēpmäN də plôNzhā sōōmärēn] 186
scull rame *f* [räm] 189
sculptur sculpteur *m* [skēltār] 37
sea mer *f* [mār] 77; **~ -sickness** mal *m* de mer [mäl də mār] 75
season saison *f* [sāzôN] 93
seasoned assaisonné [äsāzônē] 100
seasoning épice *f* [āpēs] 101
seat siège *m* [syāzh] 55; **~ belt** ceinture *f* de sécurité [seNtēr də sākērētā] 55; **~ reservation** réservation *f* de place [rāzerväsyôN də pläs] 62; **have a ~** prenez place [prenā pläs] 16
second seconde *f* [segôNd] 32; **~ class** seconde *f* [segôNd] 62
secretary secrétaire *m/f* [sekrātār] 37
security valeur *f* [välār] 152
see voir; visiter [vô·är; vēzētā] 118; **~ you soon!** A bientôt! [ä byeNtō] 17
self-service libre service *m* [lēb(ər) servēs] 129
send envoyer [äNvô·äyā] 147
send *(luggage)* faire enregistrer [fār äNrezhēstrā] 63
sender expéditeur *m* [äkspādētār] 150
separately séparément [sāpärāmäN] 115
September septembre [septäNb(ər)] 33
serious grave [gräv] 165
service charge service *m* [servēs] 93; **~ station** station *f* service [stäsyôN servēs] 48
services service *m* religieux [servēs relēzhē·ā] 123
serving dish plat *m* [plä] 97
set designer décorateur *m* [dākôrätār] 178
setting lotion fixateur *m;* laque *f* [fēksätār; läk] 156
settings décors *m/pl* [dākôr] 178
seven sept [set] 28
sew (re)coudre [(rə)kōōd(ər)] 137
shame: What a ~ quel dommage [kel dômäzh] 22
shampoo shampooing *m* [shäNpô·eN] 141
shape forme *f* [fôrm] 127
shave of stock coupon *m* d'action [kōōpôN däksyôN] 152
sharp *(time)* précis [prāsē] 30
shave raser [räzā] 156
shaving: ~brush blaireau *m* [blārō] 141; **~ cream** crème *f* à raser [krām ä räzā] 142; **~ foam** mousse *f* à raser [mōōs ä räzā] 142; **~ soap** savon *m* à barbe [sävôN ä bärb] 142
shells, shellfish coquillages *m/pl* [kôkēyäzh] 186; 104
shin tibia *m* [tēbē·ä] 168
shining: is ~ brille [brē'ē] 26
ship bateau *m* [bätō] 72; **passenger ~** transatlantique *m* [träNsätläNtēk] 77; **~ -board party** fête *f* à bord [fāt ä bôr] 77
shipping: ~ agency agence *f* maritime [äzhäNs märētēm] 77; **~ company** compagnie *f* de navigation [kôNpänyē də nävēgäsyôN] 77
ship's doctor médecin *m* de bord [mādəseN də bôr] 77
shirt chemise *f* [shemēz] 135
shock choc *m* nerveux [shôk nervā] 171; **~ absorber** amortisseur *m*

[ämôrtēsār] 85
shoe chaussure *f* [shôsār] 139; **~ horn** chausse-pied *m* [shôs-pyā] 139; **~ laces** lacets *m/pl* [läsā] 139; **~-maker** cordonnier *m* [kôrdônyā] 37
shoot tirer [tērā] 188
shop magasin *m* [mägäzeN] 122; **antique ~** magasin *m* d'antiquités [mägäzeN däNtēkētā] 128; **barber ~** coiffeur *m* [kô·äfār] 128; **butcher ~** boucherie *f* [bōōsherē] 128; **china ~** magasin *m* de porcelaine [mägäzeN də pôrsəlen] 128; **cobbler ~** cordonnerie *f* [kôrdônərē] 128; **dressmaker's ~** tailleur *m* pour dames [täyār pōōr däm] 128; **flower ~** magasin *m* de fleurs [mägäzeN də flār] 128; **photo ~** photographe *m* [fōtōgräf] 129; **tailor ~** tailleur *m* [täyār] 129; **watchmaker's ~** horlogerie *f* [ôrlôzhərē] 129; **wine ~** marchand *m* de vin [märshäN də veN] 129
shopping mall centre *m* commercial [säNt(ər) kômersyäl] 122
shore rivage *m* [rēväzh] 77
short court [kōōr] 133; **~ circuit** court-circuit *m* [kōōr-sērkē·ē] 55; **~-sleeved** à manches *f* courtes [ä mäNsh kōōrt] 135; **~ subject** court métrage *m* [kōōr māträzh] 179; **~ wave** onde *f* courte [ôNd kōōrt] 175
shorten raccourcir [räkōōrsēr] 137
shortly *(time)* peu; sous peu [pā; sōō pā] 31
shorts short *m* [shôrt] 135
shoulder épaule *f* [āpôl] 107
show montrer [môNtrā] 83
shower douche *f* [dōōsh] 82
shower *(rain)* averse *f* [ävers] 27
shrimps crevettes *f/pl* [krevet] 102
shuffle battre [bät(ər)] 181
shut fermer [fermā] 88
shutter obturateur *m* [ôbtērätār] 132; **~ release** déclencheur *m* [dākläNshār] 132; **automatic ~** déclencheur *m* automatique [dākläNshār ôtōmätēk] 132
sick malade [mäläd] 12; **I feel ~** j'ai mal au cœur [zhā mäl ō kār] 70
side côté *m* [kôtā] 176; **~ burns** favoris *m/pl* [fävôrē] 158; **~ road** rue *f* secondaire [rē segôNdār] 122; **~ walk** trottoir *m* [trôtô·är] 43; **~ wind** vent *m* latéral [väN lätāräl] 43
sights curiosités *f/pl* [kērē·ôzētā] 117
sightseeing visite *f* [vēzēt] 122
sign *(verb)* signer [sēnyā] 146; **~ up** s'inscrire [seNskrēr] 85
signature signature *f* [sēnyätēr] 79
silk soie *f* naturelle [sô·ä nätērel] 137; **artificial ~** soie *f* artificielle [sô·ä ärtēfēsē·el] 137; **~thread** fil *m* (à coudre) [fēl ä kōōd(ər)] 136
silver argent *m* [ärzhäN] 133
silver *(adj.)* **~ plated** argenté [ärzhäNtā]133, 194; **~-ware** argenterie *f* [ärzhäNtərē] 97
since depuis [depē·ē] 32
sincere sincère [seNsār] 23
sinew tendon *m* [täNdôN] 168
singer chanteur *m;* cantatrice *f* [shäNtār; käNtätrēs] 178
singing chant *m* [shäN] 178
single célibataire [sālēbätār] 79
sink lavabo *m* [läväbō] 93
sir monsieur *m* [məsyā] 13
sister sœur *f* [sār] 35; **~-in-law** belle-sœur *f* [bel-sār] 35
size *(shoes)* pointure *f* [pô·eNtēr] 139
skate patiner [pätēnā] 188
skater patineur *m* [pätēnār] 188

skates patins *m/pl* [päteN] 188
ski *(noun)* ski *m* [skē] 189
ski *(verb)* faire du ski [fār dē skē] 189; **~ binding** fixation *f* [fēksä-syôN] 189; **~ jump** tremplin *m* (de saut) [träNpleN (də sō)] 189; **~ lift** téléski *m* [tālāskē] 189; **~ pants** pantalon *m* de ski [päNtälôN də skē] 135
skiing ski *m* [skē] 189
skin peau *f* [pō] 168; **~ desease** maladie *f* de la peau [mälädē də lä pō] 171; **~ lesion** égratignures *f/pl* [āgrätēnyēr] 171
skirt jupe *f* [zhēp] 135
skull crâne *m* [krän] 168
sky ciel *m* [syel] 26
slack peu serré [pā serā] 51
slacks pantalon *m* [päNtälôN] 135
sled luge *f* [lēzh] 144
sleep dormir [dôrmēr] 12
sleeper wagon-lit *m* [wägôN lē] 60; **~ reservation** réservation *f* de wagon-lit [rāzerväsyôN də wägôN lē] 62
sleeping: ~ bag sac *m* de couchage [säk də kōōshäzh] 95; **~ car** wagon-lit *m* [wägôN lē] 60; **~ pill** somnifère *m* [sômnēfār] 173
slice tranche *f* [träNsh] 98
slide diapositive *f* [dē·äpôzētēv] 132; **~ frame** petit cadre *m* pour diapositives [pətē käd(ər) pōōr dē·äpôzētēv] 132
sliding roof toit *m* ouvrant [tô·ä ōōvräN] 55
slip *(verb)* glisser [glēsā] 53
slippers pantoufles *f/pl* [päNtōōf'əl] 139
slippery road route *f* glissante [rōōt glēsäNt] 43
slow(ly) lentement [läNtəmäN] 24
slow *(clock)* retarder [retärdā] 31; **~ down** ralentir [räläNtēr] 51
small petit [pətē] 127; **~-pox** variole *f* [värē·ôl] 78
smoke (*verb*) fumer [fēmā] 165
smoked fumé [fēmā] 100
smoking: no ~ non-fumeurs [nôN fēmār] 66
smuggling contrebande *f* [kôNtrə-bäNd] 154
snails escargots *m/pl* [eskärgō] 102
snapshot instantané *m* [eNstäNtä-nā] 132
sneakers chaussures *f/pl* de gymnastique [shôsēr də zhēmnästēk] 139
snow *(noun)* neige *f* [nāzh] 27; **~ chains** chaînes *f/pl* antidérapantes [shān äNtedāräpäNt] 52
snowing: it's ~ il neige [ēl nāzh] 27
soap savon *m* [sävôN] 87
soccer football *m;* [fōōtbôl] 189; **~ field** terrain *m* de football [tereN də fōōtbôl] 186; **~ game** match *m* de football [mätsh də fōōtbôl] 187; **play ~** jouer au football [zhōō·ā ō fōōtbôl] 189
sociology sociologie *f* [sôsē·ôlô-zhē] 39
socket prise *f* [prēz] 93; **~ wrench** clé *f* anglaise [klā äNglāz] 57
socks chaussettes *f/pl* [shôset] 135
soft tendre [täNd(ər)] 100; **~ drink** boisson *f* non-alcoolisée [bô·ä-sôN nôn-älkôlēzā] 112
solder souder [sōōdā] 55
sole semelle *f;* plante *f* du pied [semel; pläNt dē pyā] 139, 168; **leather ~** semelle *f* de cuir [semel də kē·ēr] 139; **rubber ~** semelle *f* de caoutchouc [semel də kä·ôtshōō] 139
sole *(fish)* sole *f* [sôl] 104
solid colar uni [ēnē] 137
somebody quelqu'un [kelkeN] 41

something quelque chose [kelkəshōz] 183
sometimes quelquefois [kelkəfô·ä] 32
son fils *m* [fēs] 14
song chanson *f* [shäNsôN] 178; **folk ~** chanson *f* populaire [shäNsôN pôpēlär] 178; **~ recital** récital *m* de chant [rāsētäl də shäN] 178
soon bientôt [byeNtō] 32
sore throat mal *m* de gorge [mäl də gôrzh] 171
sorry: I'm ~ Je regrette [zhə rəgret] 22; **I'm extremely ~** Je regrette infiniment [zhə rəgret eNfēnēmäN] 22
soup potage *m* [pôtäzh] 103
sour aigre [āg(ər)] 115
souvenir souvenir *m* [so͞ovenēr] 80
spa station *f* balnéaire [stäsyôN bälnā·är] 175
space place *f* [pläs] 44
spades pique *m* [pēk] 181
spare: ~ part pièce *f* de rechange [pyās də reshäNzh] 55; **~ wheel** roue *f* de secours [ro͞o də səko͞or] 55
spark plug bougie *f* d'allumage [bo͞ozhē dälēmäzh] 55
speak to parler à [pärlā ä] 15
special spécial [spāsyäl] 46; **~ delivery** exprès [eksprā] 150; **~ issue stamp** timbre *m* d'émission spéciale [teNb(ər) dāmēsyôN spāsyäl] 150
specialist spécialiste *m* [spāsyälēst] 163
spectacles lunettes *f/pl* [lēnet] 138
speed limit limitation *f* de vitesse [lēmētäsyôN də vētes] 43
speedometer tachymètre *m* [täkēmāt(ər)] 55
spell épeler [āpəlā] 24
spice épice *f* [āpēs] 101
spinach épinards *m/pl* [āpēnär] 108
spinal cord moelle *f* épinière [mô·äl āpēnyār] 168
spine colonne *f* vertébrale [kôlôn vertābräl] 168
spleen rate *f* [rät] 168
spoke rayon *m* [rāyôN] 55
sponge éponge *f* [āpôNzh] 142
spoon cuiller *f* [kē·ēyār] 97; **tea-~** petite cuiller *f* [pətēt kē·ēyār] 97
sport shirt chemise *f* de sport [shemēz də spôr] 135
sports sport *m* [spôr] 189; **~ event** manifestation *f* sportive [mänēfestäsyôN spôrtēv] 186; **~ fan** passionné *m* de sport [päsyônā də spôr] 190; **~-wear** vêtements *m/pl* de sport [vātmäN də spôr] 135
spot remover détachant *m* [dātäshäN] 144
sprain se fouler qch. [sə fo͞olā] 164
sprain *(noun)* foulure *f* [fo͞olēr] 171
spring *(techn. noun)* ressort *m* [resôr] 55
spring *(season)* printemps *m* [preNtäN] 33
square place *f;* case *f* [pläs; cäz] 122; 181
square meter mètre *m* carré [māt(ər) kärā] 193
squash courge *f* [ko͞orzh] 108
stadium stade *m* [städ] 122
stage scène *f* [sān] 178; **~ director** metteur *m* en scène [metār äN sān] 178
stain tache *f* [täsh] 137
staircase escalier *m* [eskälyā] 93
stairwell cage *f* d'escalier [käzh deskälyā] 93
stake mise *f* [mēz] 181
stall *(verb)* caler [kälā] 54
stamp *(noun)* timbre-poste *m* [teNb(ər)-pôst] 150

stamp *(verb)* affranchier [äfränshēr] 150; **~ machine** machine *f* à affranchir [mäshēn ä äfräNshēr] 150
standard (oil) normale *f* [nôrmäl] 46
star étoile *f* [ātô·äl] 27; **~-board** tribord *m* [trēbôr] 77
start commencer [kômäNsā] 176
starter démarreur *m* [dāmärär] 55
station gare *f;* arrêt *m* [gär; ärā] 67; 66
station *(broadc.)* station *f* [stäsyôN] 180; **~ master** chef *m* de gare [shef də gär] 67; **~ wagon** voiture *m* familiale [vô·ätēr fämēlyäl] 40
statue statue *f* [stätē] 119
stay rester [restā] 78
steak bifteck *m;* entrecôte *f* [bēftek; äNt(ə)r)kōt] 106
steal, stolen voler, volé [vôlā, vôlā] 153
steamed étuvé [ātēvā] 100
steamer paquebot *m* [päkbō] 77
steep downgrade pente *f* [päNt] 43
steep upgrade côte *f* [kōt] 43
steering conduite *f* [kôNdē·ēt] 56; **~ wheel** volant *m* [vôläN] 56
stern poupe *f* [po͞op] 77
stew pot-au-feu *m* [pôtōfā] 107
steward steward *m* [sto͞o·ärt] 77
stewed braisé [brāzā] 100
still encore [äNkôr] 31
stitch in the side point *m* de côté [pô·eN də kôtā] 171
stock action *f* [äksyôN] 152
stockings bas *m/pl* [bä] 135
stole étole *f* [ātôl] 135
stomach pains maux *m/pl* d'estomac [mō destômä] 171
stop *(noun)* arrêt *m* [ärā] 59
stop *(verb)* s'arrêter [särātā] 66
stopover escale *f* [eskäl] 68
stopped up bouché [bo͞oshā] 88
stopping: no ~ arrêt interdit [ārā eNterdē] 42
store magasin *m* [mägäzeN] 122; **department ~** grand magasin *m* [gräN mägäzeN] 128; **drug ~** droguerie *f;* pharmacie *f* [drôgerē; färmäsē] 128; **grocery ~** épicerie *f* [āpēsərē] 128; **liquor ~** vins et spiritueux *m/pl* [veN ā spērētē·ā] 129; **stationery ~** papeterie *f* [päpātərē] 129; **toy ~** magasin *m* de jouets [mägäzeN də zho͞o·ā] 129; **~ keeper** propriétaire *m* de magasin [prôprē·ātār də mägäzeN] 37
storm tempête *f* [täNpāt] 27
stove fourneau *m* [fo͞ornō] 93
straight ahead tout droit [to͞o drô·ä] 40
straighten out redresser [redresā] 56
strait détroit *m* [dātrô·ä] 77
strand mêche *f* [māsh] 158
strawberries fraises *f/pl* [frāz] 110
street rue *f* [rē] 116
strict sévère [sāvār] 165
string ficelle *f* [fēsel] 57
stroke apoplexie *f* [äpôpleksē] 171
student étudiant *m* [ātēdyäN] 37
study *(verb)* étudier [ātēdyā] 38
stuff marchandise *f* [märshäNdēz] 127
stuffed farci [färsē] 100; **~ animal** animal *m* en peluche [änēmäl äN pelēsh] 144
stuffing farce *f* [färs] 100
styptic pencil bâton *m* hémostatique [bätôN āmôstätēk] 161
subject matière *f* [mätyār] 39
subtitled sous-titré [so͞o-tēträ] 179
suburb banlieue *f* [bäNlēyā] 123
suburban train train *m* de banlieue [treN də bäNlēyā] 123
subway métro *m* [mātrō] 123
suddenly brusquement [brēskəmäN] 54

suède daim *m* [deN] 139; **~ coat** manteau *m* de chamois [mäNtō də shämô·ä] 135; **~ jacket** blouson *m* de chamois [bloo͞zôN də shämô·ä] 135
sugar sucre *m* [sēk(ər)] 114; **cube ~** sucre *m* en morceaux [sēk(ər) äN môrsō] 114; **~ bowl** sucrier *m* [sēkrēyā] 97
suit costume *m;* tailleur *m* [kôstēm; täyär] 135
suitcase valise *f* [välēz] 63
summer été *m* [ātā] 33; **~ dress** robe *f* d'été [rôb dātā] 135
sun soleil *m* [sôlā·ē] 27; **~ tan cream** crème *f* solaire [krām sôlär] 142; **~ tan lotion** lotion *f* solaire [lôsyôN sôlär] 142
sunburn coup *m* de soleil [koo͞ də sôlā·ē] 171
sundae coupe *f* glacée [koo͞p gläsā] 114
Sunday dimanche *m* [dēmäNsh] 33
sunglasses lunettes *f/pl* de soleil [lēnet də sôlā·ē] 138
sunlamp rayons *m/pl* ultraviolets [räyôN ēlträvē·ōlā] 175
sunrise lever *m* du soleil [levā dē sôlā·ē] 27
sunset coucher *m* du soleil [koo͞shā dē sôlā·ē] 27
sunstroke insolation *f* [eNsôläsyôN] 171
super market supermarché *m* [sēpermärshā] 129
supplemental fare supplément *m* [sēplämäN] 62
suppository suppositoire *m* [sēpôzētô·är] 161
suppuration suppuration *f* [sēpēräsyôN] 171
surcharge: seasonal ~ taxe *f* saisonnière [täks säzônyär] 83
surgeon chirurgien *m* [shērērzhē·eN] 163
surgery: plastic ~ chirurgie *f* plastique [shērērzhē plästēk] 163
surroundings environs *m/pl* [äNvērôN] 123
suspenders jarretelles *f/pl* [zhärtel] 135
sweater pull(over) *m* [pēl(ôver)] 135
sweets bonbons *m/pl* [bôNbôN] 114
swelling enflure *f* [äNflēr] 171
swim nager; se baigner [näzhā; sə bānyā] 185
swimmer nageur [näzhär] 186
swimming natation *f* [nätäsyôN] 190; **~ pier** passerelle *f* [päsərel] 186; **~ area, ~ pool** piscine *f* [pēsēn] 122
swimsuit maillot *m* de bain [mäyō də beN] 135
Swiss Francs francs *m/pl* suisses [fräN sē·ēs] 152
switch *(noun)* commutateur *m* [kômētätär] 56
swollen enflé [äNflā] 164
sympathy sympathie *f* [seNpätē] 23
symphony concert concert *m* symphonique [kôNser seNfônēk] 178
synthetic thread fil *m* polyester [fēl pôlyester] 136
system time table indicateur *m;* Chaix *m* [eNdēkätär; shāks] 67

T

table table *f* [täb'əl] 93; **~ tennis** ping-pong *m* [pēng-pôNg] 182
tablecloth nappe *f* [näp] 93
tablet comprimé *m* [kôNprēmā] 161
tailor tailleur *m* [täyär] 37
take prendre [präNd(ər)] 83; **~ out** sortir [sôrtēr] 44; **~ to** accompagner [äkôNpänyā] 17
taken réservé; pris [räzervā; prē] 96

take-off départ *m* [dāpär] 71
talcum powder poudre *f* de talc [po͞od(ər)] də tälk] 161
tampons tampons *m/pl* [täNpôN] 142
tangerine mandarine *f* [mäNdärēn] 110
tape ruban *m* [rēbäN] 136; ~ **measure** centimètre *m* [säNtēmät(ər)] 136; ~ **recorder** magnétophone *m* [mänyātōfôn] 182
target cible *f* [sēb'əl] 189
tart tarte *f* [tärt] 114; **fruit** ~ tarte *f* aux fruits [tärt ō frē·ē] 114
tartar tartre *m* [tärt(ər)] 174
taxi stand station *f* de taxis [stäsyôN də täksē] 116
tea thé *m* [tā] 98; ~ **with lemon** thé *m* au citron [tā ō sētrôN] 98; ~ **with milk** thé *m* au lait [tā ō lā] 98
teacher instituteur *m* [eNstētētär] 37
technical college école *f* supérieure technique [ākôl sēpäryär teknēk] 39
technician technicien *m* [teknēsyeN] 38
telegram télégramme *m* [tālägräm] 147; ~ **form** formule *f* de télégramme [fôrmēl də tālägräm] 147
telegraphic télégraphique [tālägräfēk] 152
telephone téléphone *m* [tāläfôn] 93; **pushbutton** ~ téléphone *m* à touches [tāläfôn ä to͞osh] 150
television télévision *f* [tālävēzyôN] 180; ~ **play** jeu *m* télévisé [zhā tālävēzā] 182
tell dire [dēr] 20
teller caissier *m* [kesyā] 152
temperature température *f* [täNpärātēr] 27; ~ **chart** courbe *f* de température [ko͞orb də täNpärätēr] 172
temple tempe *f;* temple *m* [täNp; täNp'əl] 168; 123
temporarily momentanément [mômäNtänāmäN] 32
temporary provisoire [prôvēzô·är] 173
tender tendre [täNd(ər)] 100
tenderloin filet *m* [fēlā] 106
tendon tendon *m* [täNdôN] 168; **pulled** ~ déchirement *m* des tendons [dāshērmäN dā täNdôN] 171
tennis tennis *m* [tenēs] 190; **play** ~ jouer au tennis [zho͞o·ā ō tenēs] 190; ~ **ball** balle *f* de tennis [bäl də tenēs] 190; ~ **court** court *m* de tennis [ko͞or də tenēs] 190
tent tente *f* [täNt] 95
terrific! extra! [eksträ] 21
tetanus tétanos *m* [tātänōs] 172
thanks, thankyou merci [mersē] 21; ~ **a lot** merci beaucoup [mersē bōko͞o] 21; ~ **very much** merci bien [mersē byeN] 21
thaw dégel *m* [dāzhel] 27; **it's thawing** il dégèle [ēl dāzhel] 27
theatre théâtre *m* [tā·ät(ər)] 178; ~ **schedule** affiche *f* de théâtre [äfēsh də tā·ät(ər)] 178
theft vol *m* [vôl] 153
there là [lä] 40
thermos bottle thermos *f* [termôs] 144
thermostat thermostat *m* [termôstä] 56
thief voleur *m* [vôlār] 154
thigh cuisse *f* [kē·ēs] 167
thimble dé *m* [dā] 136
third troisième [trô·äzyām] 29
thorax thorax *m* [tôräks] 168
thread fil *m* (à coudre) [fēl ä ko͞od(ər)] 136; **screw** ~ filet *m* [fēlā] 56
thriller roman *m* policier [rômäN pôlesyā] 130
throat gorge *f* [gôrzh] 168

through car voiture *f* directe [vô·ä-tēr dērekt] 61
throughway passage *m* [päsäzh] 123
throw up vomir [vōmēr] 163
throw-in touche *f* [tōōsh] 190
thumb pouce *m* [pōōs] 167
thunder tonnerre *m* [tônär] 27
thunderstorm orage *m* [ôräzh] 27
Thursday jeudi *m* [zhădē] 33
thyme thym *m* [teN] 101
ticket ticket *m;* billet *m* [tēkā, bēyā] 59; **one-way ~** billet *m* aller [bēyā älā] 62; **round trip ~** (billet *m)* aller et retour [bēyā älā ā rətōōr] 62; **transfer ~** billet *m* de correspondance [bēyā də kôrespôNdäNs] 117; **~ sales** vente *f* de billets [väNt də bēyā] 178
tie cravate *f* [kräwät] 135
tight serré; étroit [serā; ātrô·ä] 51; 133
tighten serrer [serā] 55
tights collants *m/pl* [kôläN] 135
time temps *m;* heure *f* [täN; ăr] 15; 30; **what ~?** quand? [käN] 15; **any ~** à tout moment [ä tōō mômäN] 32; **on ~** à temps [ä täN] 32; **~ table** horaire *m* [ôrār] 60
tincture teinture *f* [teNtĕr] 161
tint colorer [kôlôrā] 158
tire pneu *m* [pnă] 47; **~ change** changement *m* de pneu [shäNzh·mäN də pnă] 47; **~ pressure** pression *f* des pneus [presyôN dā pnă] 47
tissues mouchoirs *m/pl* en papier [mōōshô·är äN päpyā] 142
to let à louer [ä lōō·ā] 191
toast toast *m* [tōst] 98
tobacco tabac *m* [täbä] 140
toboggan, ~ing luge *f* [lēzh] 190
today aujourd'hui [ōzhōōrdē·ē] 31
toe orteil *m* [ôrtā·ē] 168
toilet W.C. *m* [dōōbləvā-sā] 82; **~ articles** articles *m/pl* de toilette [ärtēk'əl də tô·älet] 142; **~ kit** nécessaire *m* de toilette [nāsesār də tô·älet] 142; **~ paper** papier *m* hygiénique [päpyā ēzhē·änēk] 142
tomato juice jus *m* de tomate [zhē də tômät] 112
tomb tombe *f* [tôNb] 123
tomorrow demain [dəmeN] 17; **the day after ~** après-demain [äprādəmeN] 31; **~ morning** demain matin [dəmeN mäteN] 31
tongue langue *f* [läNg] 168
tonic fortifiant *m* [fôrtēfyäN] 161; **~ water** eau *f* tonique [ō tônēk] 112
tonight cette nuit; ce soir [set nē·ē; sə sô·är] 31; 176
tonsilitis angine *f* [äNzhēn] 172
tonsils amygdales *f/pl* [ämēgdäl] 168
too aussi; trop [ôsē; trō] 47; 51
tool outil *m* [ōōtē] 57; **~ box, ~ kit** coffre *m* à outils [kôfrä ōōtē] 57
tooth dent *f* [däN] 168; **~ brush** brosse *f* à dents [brôs ä däN] 142; **~ paste** dentifrice *m* [däNtēfrēs] 142; **wisdom ~** dent *f* de sagesse [däN də säzhes] 174
toothache mal *m* aux dents [mäl ō däN] 174
toothpick cure-dent *m* [kēr-däN] 97
top *(car)* capote *f* [käpôt] 56
topless sans soutien-gorge *m* [säN sōōtyeN-gôrzh] 185
touch: do not ~ prière de ne pas toucher [prē·ār də nə pä tōōshā] 191
tough coriace [kôryäs] 115
toupé postiche *m* [pôstēsh] 158
tour: guided ~ visite *f* guidée [vēzēt gēdā] 118; **~ guide's office** guide *m* [gēd] 74
tow remorquer [remôrkā] 48; **~ line**

câble *m* de remorquage [käb'əl də remôrkäzh] 49; ~ **truck** dépanneuse *f* [dāpänāz] 49
towel serviette *f* [servyet] 142; **bath** ~ serviette *f* de bain [servyet də beN] 142
tower tour *f* [to͞or] 123
towing service service *m* de dépannage [servēs də dāpänäzh] 49
town ville *f* [vēl] 40; **old** ~ vieille ville *f* [vyā·ē vēl] 121
toy jouet *m* [zho͞o·ā] 144
track voie *f* [vô·ä] 67; ~ **and field** athlétisme *m* [ätlātēsm] 190; ~ **suit** survêtement *m* [sērvātmäN] 135
traffic circulation *f* [sērkēläsyôN] 43; ~ **light** feux *m/pl* [fā] 43; ~ **regulations** code *m* de la route [kôd də lä ro͞ot] 43
tragedy tragédie *f* [träzhādē] 178
trailer remorque *f* [remôrk] 41; caravane *f* [kärävän] 94
train train *m* [treN] 61
trainee apprenti *m* [äpräNtē] 38
tranquilizer calmant *m* [kälmäN] 161
transfer ticket *m* de correspondance [tēkā də kôrespôNdäNs] 59
transfer *(bank)* virement *m* [vērmäN] 152
translate traduire [trädē·ēr] 24
translation traduction *f* [trädēksyôN] 130
translator traducteur [trädēktār] 38
transmission boîte *f* de vitesses [bô·ät də vētes] 56
travel agency agence *f* de voyage [äzhäNs də vô·äyäzh] 82
traveling voyager [vô·äyäzhā] 78; ~ **group** groupe *m* de voyage [gro͞op də vô·äyäzh] 78
tray plateau *m* [plätō] 97
trick levée *f* [levā] 181
trim couper les pointes [ko͞opā lā pô·eNt] 155
trip voyage *m* [vô·äyäzh] 43; **Have a good** ~ ! Bon voyage! [bôN vô·äyäzh] 17
tripes tripes *f/pl* [trēp] 107
tripod pied *m* [pyā] 132
trotting race course *f* de trot attelé [ko͞ors də trō ätlā] 189
troubles efforts *m/pl* [efôr] 21
trousers pantalon *m* [päNtälôN] 135
trout truite *f* [trē·et] 104
truck camion *m* [kämyôN] 41; ~ **driver** camionneur *m* [kämyônār] 38
trump atout *m* [äto͞o] 181
trunk coffre *m* [kôf(ər)] 56
tube chambre *f* à air [shäNbrä ār] 56
tube tube *m* [tēb] 126
tubeless sans chambre *f* (à air); tubeless *m* [säN shäNb(ər) (ä ār); tēbles] 47
tuberculosis tuberculose *f* [tēbärkēlōz] 172
Tuesday mardi *m* [märdē] 33
tug remorqueur *m* [remôrkār] 77
tulip tulipe *f* [tēlēp] 130
tumor tumeur *f* [tēmār] 172
tuna fish thon *m* [tôN] 104
turbot turbot *m* [tērbō] 104
turkey dinde *f* [deNd] 105
turn (re)tourner [(re)to͞ornā] 43
turn *(the car)* faire demi-tour [fār demē to͞or] 43; ~ **off** *(a road)* bifurquer [bēfērkā] 43; ~ **off** *(lights)* éteindre [āteNd(ər)] 182; ~ **on** allumer [älēmā] 182
tweezers pincettes *f/pl* [peNset] 142
two-piece deux-pièces *m* [dā-pyās] 135
two-stroke motor moteur *m* (à) deux temps [môtār (ä) dā täN] 54
typewriter machine *f* à écrire [mäshēn ä ākrēr] 138; ~ **paper** papier *m* machine [päpyā mäshēn] 138

typhoid fever typhus *m* [tēfēs] 172

U

ulcer ulcère *m* [ēlsär] 172
ultrasonics échographie *f* [ākôgräfē] 175
umbrella parapluie *m* [päräplē·ē] 144
umpire arbitre *m* [ärbēt(ər)] 190
uncle oncle *m* [ôNk'əl] 35
under age mineur [mēnār] 34
underpants caleçon *m* [kälsôN] 135
underpass passage *m* souterrain [päsäzh sōōtereN] 65
undershirt *(men's)* gilet *m* du corps [zhēlā dē kôr] 135; *(women's)* chemise *f* [shəmēz] 135
understand comprendre [kôNpräNd(ər)] 185
undertow courant *m* [kōōräN] 185
underwear sous-vêtements *m/pl* [sōō-vātmäN] 135
undisturbed sans être dérangé [säNzāt(ər) däräNzhā] 183
university université *f* [ēnēversētā] 38
unlock ouvrir [ōōvrēr] 92
unstamped non-affranchi [nôN äfräNshē] 150
until jusqu'à [zhēskä] 32
urine urine *f* [ērēn] 168
urinalysis analyse *f* d'urine [änälēz dērēn] 165
urologist urologue *m* [ērōlôg] 163
us nous [nōō] 87
usher ouvreuse *f* [ōōvrāz] 179
uterus utérus *m* [ētārēs] 168

V

vacant libre [lēb(ər)] 66
vaccinate vacciner [väksēnā] 164
vaccination vaccination *f* [väksēnäsyôN] 78
valerian drops gouttes *f/pl* de valériennes [gōōt də välārē·en] 161
valid valable [väläb'əl] 62
valley vallée *f* [välā] 123
valuables objets *m/pl* de valeur [ôbzhā də välār] 84
value declaration valeur *f* déclarée [välār dāklärā] 150
valve soupape *f* [sōōpäp] 47
vanilla vanille *f* [vänē'ē] 101
vase vase *m* [väz] 130
veal veau *m* [vō] 105; **~ stew** blanquette *f* de veau [bläNket də vō] 106
vegetable légumes *m/pl* [lāgēm] 108; **~ market** marchand *m* de légumes [märshäN də lāgēm] 129
vehicle véhicule *m* [vāhēkēl] 41
vein veine *f* [vān] 169
velvet velours *m* [vəlōōr] 137
veneral disease maladie *f* vénérienne [mälädē vānārē·en] 172
venison chevreuil *m* [shevrā'ē] 105
ventilation aération *f* [ä·äräsyôN] 93
verdict jugement *m* [zhēzhmäN] 154
very beaucoup [bōkōō] 21
vest gilet *m* [zhēlā] 135
victory victoire *f* [vēktô·är] 188
video cassette cassette *f* vidéo [käset vēdā·ō] 144
view finder viseur *m* [vēzār] 132
village village *m* [vēläzh] 123
vinegar vinaigre *m* [vēnāg(ər)] 101
violets violettes *f/pl* [vē·ôlet] 130
violin recital récital *m* de violon [rāsētäl də vē·ōlôN] 178
visit visiter [vēzētā] 78
visiting hours heures *f/pl* de visite [ār də vēzēt] 173
vitamin pills comprimés *m/pl* de vitamines [kôNprēmā də vētämēn] 161

vocational school centre *m* de formation professionnelle [säNt(ər) də fôrmäsyôN prôfesyônel] 39
voltage voltage *m* [vôltäzh] 75
volume volume *m* [vôlēm] 130
vomiting vomissement *m* [vômēsmäN] 172
voyage voyage *m* en bateau [vô·äyäzh äN bätō] 77

W

wafers gaufres *f/pl* [gōf(ər)] 114
wait attendre [ätäNd(ər)] 87
waiter serveur *m;* garçon *m* [servār; gärsôN] 38; 96
waiting room salle *f* d'attente [säl dätäNt] 69
waitress serveuse *f* [servāz] 38
wake réveiller [rāvāyā] 86
walking shoes souliers *m/pl* de marche [soolyā də märsh] 139
wall mur *m* [mēr] 93
wallet portefeuille *m* [pôrtfā'ē] 144
want, I ~ je veux [zhə vā] 21
ward service *m* [servēs] 173
warm chaud [shō] 67
warning triangle triangle *m* avertisseur [trē·äNg'əl ävertēsār] 56
warship bâtiment *m* de guerre [bätēmäN də gār] 77
wash nettoyer; laver [netô·äyā; lävā] 47, 95; **~ cloth** gant *m* de toilette [gäN də tô·älet] 142; **~ room** lavabo *m* [läväbō] 94
washing line corde *f* à linge [kôrd ä leNzh] 144
watch montre *f* [môNt(ər)] 142; **pocket ~** montre *f* de poche [môNt(ər) də pôsh]; **wrist ~** montre-bracelet *f* [môNt(ər)-bräslā] 143; **~ band** bracelet *m* (pour montre) [bräslā poor môNt(ər)] 143
watchmaker horloger *m* [ôrlôzhā] 38
water eau *f* [ō] 45; **cooling ~** eau *f* du radiateur *f* [ō dē rädē·ätār] 45; **soda ~** soda *m;* eau *f* de Seltz [sôdä; ō də sels] 112; **mineral ~** eau *f* minérale [ō mēnäräl] 112; **carbonated ~** eau *f* gazeuse [ō gäzāz] 112; **non-carbonated ~** eau *f* non-gazeuse [ō nôN-gäzāz] 112; **~ glass** verre *m* à eau [ver ä ō] 93; **with running ~** avec eau courante [ävek ō kooräNt] 82; **~ skiing** ski *m* nautique [skē nôtēk] 185
waterfall cascade *f* [käskäd] 123
wave vague *f* [väg] 77
way, the right ~ la bonne direction [lä bôn dēreksyôN] 40; **by ~ of** passer par [päsā pär] 61; **no ~!** en aucun cas! [äNôkeN kä] 21
weather temps *m* [täN] 25; **~ prediction** prévisions *f/pl* météorologiques [prāvēzyôN mātā·ôrōlōzhēk] 27; **~report** météo *f* [mātā·ō] 25
wedding mariage *m* [märē·äzh] 123
Wednesday mercredi [märkrədē] 33
week semaine *f* [smen] 31
weekend week-end *m* [oo·ēkend] 32
weekly toutes les semaines [toot lā smen] 32
welcome bienvenu, -e [byeNvenē] 12; **You're ~** Je vous en prie [zhə voozäN prē] 21
well bien [byeN] 12; **Get ~ soon!** Bon rétablissement! [bôN rātäblēs·mäN] 20; **~ done** bien cuit [byeN koo·ē] 100
wet mouillé [mooyā] 155
what? quoi? [kô·ä] 18; **~ for?** pourquoi? [poorkô·ä] 18

wheel roue *f* [ro͞o] 47
when? quand? [käN] 18
where? où? [o͞o] 18; **~ from?** d'où? [do͞o] 18; **~ to?** où? [o͞o] 18; **~ is there...?** où y a-t-il...? [o͞o yätēl] 19
which? quel (-le)? [kel] 18
white blanc, blanche [bläN, bläNsh] 194
who? qui? [kē] 18
wholesaler grossiste *m* [grōsēst] 38
whom? qui? [kē] 18; **to ~?** à qui? [ä kē] 18; **with ~** avec qui? [ävek kē] 18
whose is that? à qui est-ce? [ä kē es] 19
why? pourquoi? [po͞orkô·ä] 18
wide large [lärzh] 127
widowed veuf, veuve [vəf, vəv] 79
wife femme *f* [fäm] 13
wig perruque *f* [perək] 156
win gagner [gänyā] 188
wind vent *m* [väN] 27
windbreaker anorak *m* [änôräk] 135
winding road route *f* en lacets [ro͞ot äN läsā] 43
window fenêtre *f* [fenät(ər)] 65; **~ seat** coin-fenêtre *m* [kô·eN-fenät(ər)] 67
windshield pare-brise *m* [pär-brēz] 47; **~ wiper** essuie-glace *m* [esə·ē-gläs] 55; **~ washer** lave-vitre *m* [läv-vēt(ər)] 56
windy: it's ~ il fait du vent [ēl fā də väN] 25
wine vin *m* [veN] 101; **~ list** carte *f* des vins [kärt dā veN] 96; **red ~** vin *m* rouge [veN ro͞ozh] 111; **white ~** vin *m* blanc [veN bläN] 111
wing aile *f* [āl] 71
winter hiver *m* [ēvār] 33
wire fil *m* métallique [fēl mātälēk] 57
wire télégramme *m* [tālägräm] 147
wish *(verb)* souhaiter [so͞o·etā] 20; **best wishes** félicitations [fālēsētäsyôN] 23
wisp mèche *f* [māsh] 158
withdraw résilier [rāzēlyā] 152
within dans [däN] 32
witness témoin *m* [tāmô·eN] 49
wood carving sculpture *f* en bois [skəltər äN bô·ä] 144
wool laine *f* [len] 136
word mot *m* [mō] 24
work *(verb)* travailler; marcher [trävāyā; märshā] 15; 23
work *(noun)* œuvre *f* [āv(ər)] 178
worker ouvrier [o͞ovrēyā] 38
working: not ~ right pas en bon état [päzäN bôN ātä] 50
worsted laine *f* peignée [len penyā] 137
wound plaie *f* [plā] 172; **~ salve** pommade *f* cicatrisante [pômäd sēkätrēzäNt] 161
wrapping paper papier *m* d'emballage [päpyā däNbäläzh] 138
wrench clé *f* anglaise [klā äNglāz] 57
wrestle lutter [lətā] 190
wrestler lutteur *m* [lətər] 190
wrestling lutte *f* [lət] 190
wrist poignet *m* [pô·änyā] 168
write down écrire [ākrēr] 24
writer écrivain *m* [ākrēveN] 38
writing paper papier *m* à lettre [päpyā ä let(ər)] 138
wrong faux, fausse [fō, fōs] 148

X

x-ray *(noun)* radiographie *f* [rädē·ōgräfē] 173
x-ray *(verb)* radiographier [rädē·ōgräfyā] 173

Y

yard un mètre (0,914 m) [eN māt(ər)] 126
year année *f*; an *m* [änā; äN] 32
yellow jaune [zhōn] 194
yes oui [o͞o·ē] 21
yesterday hier [ē·ār] 31
you vous; tu [vo͞o; tē] 12
young jeune [zhān] 34
younger plus jeune [plē zhān] 34
your votre; vos; ton, ta, tes [vôt(ər), vō; tôN, tä, tā] 12
youth group groupe *m* de jeunes [gro͞op də zhān] 95
youth hostel auberge *f* de jeunesse [ōbārzh də zhānes] 95; **~ card** carte *f* d'A.J. [kärt dä·zhē] 95

Z

zebra crossing passage *m* clouté [päsäzh klo͞otā] 43
zero zéro [zārō] 28
zipper fermeture *f* éclair [fermetēr āklār] 136
zoo zoo *m* [zō] 119
zoology zoologie *f* [zō·ōlōzhē] 39

FRENCH WEIGHTS AND MEASURES

Linear Measures

km	*kilomètre*	=	1 000 m = 0.6214 mi.
m	*mètre*	=	1 m = 3.281 ft.
dm	*décimètre*	=	$^1/_{10}$ m = 3.937 in.
cm	*centimètre*	=	$^1/_{100}$ m = 0.394 in.
mm	*millimètre*	=	$^1/_{1000}$ m = 0.039 in.
	mille marin	=	1 852 m = 6080 ft.

Square Measures

km²	*kilomètre carré*	=	1 000 000 m^2 = 0.3861 sq. mi.
m²	*mètre carré*	=	1 m^2 = 1.196 sq. yd.
dm²	*décimètre carré*	=	$^1/_{100}$ m^2 = 15.5 sq. in.
cm²	*centimètre carré*	=	$^1/_{10000}$ m^2 = 0.155 sq. in.
mm²	*millimètre carré*	=	$^1/_{1000000}$ m^2 = 0.002 sq. in.

Land Measures

ha	*hectare*	=	100 a *or* 10 000 m^2 = 2.471 acres
a	*are*	=	100 m^2 = 119.599 sq. yd.

Cubic Measures

m³	*mètre cube*	=	1 m^3 = 35.32 cu. ft.
dm³	*décimètre cube*	=	$^1/_{1000}$ m^3 = 61.023 cu. in.
cm³	*centimètre cube*	=	$^1/_{1000000}$ m^3 = 0.061 cu. in.
mm³	*millimètre cube*	=	$^1/_{1000000000}$ m^3 = 0.00006 cu. in.

Measures of Capacity

hl	*hectolitre*	=	100 l = 22.01 gals.
l	*litre*	=	1 l = 1.76 pt.
dl	*décilitre*	=	$^1/_{10}$ l = 0.176 pt.
cl	*centilitre*	=	$^1/_{100}$ l = 0.018 pt.
st	*stère*	=	1 m^3 = 35.32 cu. ft. (*of wood*)

Weights

t	*tonne*	=	1 t *or* 1 000 kg = 19.68 cwt.
q	*quintal*	=	$^1/_{10}$ t *or* 100 kg = 1.968 cwt.
kg	*kilogramme*	=	1 000 g = 2.205 lb.
g	*gramme*	=	1 g = 15.432 gr.
mg	*milligramme*	=	$^1/_{1000}$ g = 0.015 gr.